Regions and Regionalism in History

13

THE KEELMEN OF TYNESIDE

LABOUR ORGANISATION AND CONFLICT IN THE NORTH-EAST COAL INDUSTRY, 1600–1830

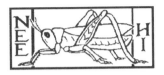

Regions and Regionalism in History

ISSN 1742–8254

This series, published in association with the AHRB Centre for North-East England History (NEEHI), aims to reflect and encourage the increasing academic and popular interest in regions and regionalism in historical perspective. It also seeks to explore the complex historical antecedents of regionalism as it appears in a wide range of international contexts.

Series Editor
Prof. Peter Rushton, Faculty of Education and Society, University of Sunderland

Editorial Board
Dr Joan Allen, School of Historical Studies, Newcastle University
Prof. Don MacRaild, School of Arts and Social Sciences, Northumbria University
Dr Christian Liddy, Department of History, University of Durham
Dr Diana Newton, School of Arts and Media, Teesside University

Proposals for future volumes may be sent to the following address:

Prof. Peter Rushton,
Department of Social Sciences,
Faculty of Education and Society,
University of Sunderland,
Priestman Building,
New Durham Road,
Sunderland,
SR1 3PZ
UK
Tel: 0191–515–2208
Fax: 0191–515–3415
Peter.rushton@sunderland.ac.uk

THE KEELMEN OF TYNESIDE

LABOUR ORGANISATION AND CONFLICT IN THE NORTH-EAST COAL INDUSTRY, 1600–1830

JOSEPH M. FEWSTER

THE BOYDELL PRESS

First published 2011
The Boydell Press, Woodbridge

ISBN 978–1–84383–632–2

The Boydell Press is an imprint of Boydell & Brewer Ltd
PO Box 9, Woodbridge, Suffolk IP12 3DF, UK
and of Boydell & Brewer Inc.
668 Mt Hope Avenue, Rochester, NY 14620, USA
website: www.boydellandbrewer.com

The publisher has no responsibility for the continued existence or accuracy of URLs
for external or third-party internet websites referred to in this book, and does not guar-
antee that any content on such websites is, or will remain, accurate or appropriate.

A CIP record for this book is available
from the British Library

Papers used by Boydell & Brewer Ltd are natural, recyclable products
made from wood grown in sustainable forests

Edited and typeset by
Frances Hackeson Freelance Publishing Services, Brinscall, Lancs
Printed and bound by
the MPG Books Group

Contents

List of Illustrations

Taken by permission of Durham County Record Office from Mackenzie and Dent, *Histories of Northumberland, Durham and Newcastle with several thousand extra Maps, Armorial Bearings, Views, Portraits and other illustrations collected by George Rutland* (Newcastle, 1872).

Acknowledgements

My interest in the keelmen began many years ago when I wrote a dissertation about them for my BA degree. Thereafter, as opportunity offered, I collected additional information, and I am grateful to the archivists and their staffs both past and present who over the years have made their records available to me. The bulk of the material concerning the keelmen is preserved in Tyne and Wear Archives and I owe a special word of thanks to all who have assisted me there. I am likewise thankful for the assistance I received at the Northumberland Record Office (now Northumberland Museum and Archives), Durham County Record Office, Newcastle Central Library, the Library of the North of England Institute of Mining and Mechanical Engineers, the National Archives and the House of Lords Record Office. I am also grateful to Lord Strathmore for permission to quote from the Strathmore papers in Durham County Record Office.

Professor Norman McCord kindly read the draft version and gave expert advice on numerous points. Thanks are also due to my daughter Helen, who read the manuscript at various stages and made useful criticisms, and to my wife Elizabeth for help in the presentation of the text. I am grateful to Mr Peter Sowden for steering the work along the road to publication, and to the North East England History Institute for including the book in their series and providing a subsidy towards publication.

Abbreviations

DNB	*Dictionary of National Biography*
HO	Home Office Papers
NMA	Northumberland Museum and Archives
SP	State Papers
TWA	Tyne and Wear Archives

Glossary

Chaldron	Measure of coal. The Newcastle Chaldron was defined by statute, 6 & 7 William III, at 53 hundredweights. There were between 28 and 29 hundredweights to the London chaldron.
Collier	Ship engaged in transporting coal.
Double coal	Loading the keel so that the Newcastle chaldron was made to equal twice the London measure.
Drop	Device whereby the loaded colliery waggon was lowered and emptied into the ship's hold.
Fittage	The payment received by the fitter for vending the coal.
Fitter	Member of the Hostmen's Company employed by the coal owner to negotiate the sale of his coal to the shipmaster and to provide keels and keelmen to convey it to the ship.
Fit tides	Tides worked by keelmen for a person who had appropriated the owner's keel without permission.
Gift coal	Allowance of extra chaldrons for every twenty purchased.
Keel	As well as being the craft operated by the keelmen, 'keel' was a term used denote the measure of eight Newcastle chaldrons.
Lightermen	Company of London coal dealers.
Lying tides	Tides when before or after loading the ship the keelmen were forced by circumstances beyond their control to remain idle.
Making out	Dividing tens [q.v.] into chaldrons at the staithes. Also the amount made out at London when Newcastle chaldrons were converted into London chaldrons, an amount that might vary considerably especially when overmeasure had been given at Newcastle.
Offputter	Official responsible for supervising the loading of keels at the staithe.
Pan boats	Craft employed at the salt pans, but occasionally, much to the keelmen's resentment, used, or attempted to be used, to transport coal to the colliers.
Premium	Payment by certain coal owners to the London dealers to give preference to their coal. Premiums were paid to the London Lightermen to ensure that the ships concerned were unloaded first. These payments were made illegal in 1711 but the law was frequently broken.

Spouts	Chutes at the staithes down which coal was poured into the keels. At some staithes spouts were eventually adapted to load ships directly, thus supplanting keels.
Staithes	Waterside coal depots at the terminus of colliery waggon-ways with timber structures projecting into the river from which the coal was loaded into keels and in some cases directly into ships.
Staithman	Official employed by the coal owner to take overall charge of the staithe.
Ten	A measure, varying from colliery to colliery, on which costs of working and leading were calculated.
Tide	The keelmen's journey from staithe to ship and return.
Wherry	A river boat, larger and different in structure from the keel, used to transport goods other than coal.

Introduction

The Keelmen and their Masters

As I went up Sandgate
I heard a lassie sing –
Weel may the keel row
that my laddie's in!

He wears a blue bonnet,
a dimple in his chin.
He's foremost 'mong the many
keel lads o' coaly Tyne.

from two versions of 'The Keel Row'

An ancient building, once a hospital, overlooking Newcastle Quay, and a few folk songs such as 'The Keel Row', are now the only mementoes of the keelmen, a group of workers who for hundreds of years played an essential role in the coal industry of Tyneside. Although historians have often shown interest in this colourful, cohesive and often turbulent workforce, this is the first full-scale study of these workers. The saga of their struggles against poverty and grievances connected with their employment adds a new dimension to the history of the north-east coal trade, and provides a particularly good example of embryonic trade unionism.

Rich coal seams lay close to the River Tyne and by the late fourteenth century the export of coal via the river, although as yet small in quantity, had become of major importance to the prosperity of Newcastle.[1] In the course of succeeding centuries coal exports greatly increased and long remained the principal source of the region's wealth. For much of this period the coal destined for London and east-coast ports, or for markets overseas, was brought from the pit-head along waggonways to staithes (elevated timber platforms with adjacent storage facilities), situated at various points on the river banks, the furthest upstream being fourteen miles from the estuary. At the staithes the coal was loaded, by hand or down spouts or chutes, into keels (small barge-like craft with a crew of three men and a boy), and transported to the colliers lying in the lower reaches of the river.

Until systematic dredging was carried out in the 1860s, only small seagoing vessels could proceed up the narrow and dangerous waterway as far as Newcastle, and none of them could pass under the low arches of the bridge

---

[1] J.B. Blake, 'The Medieval Coal Trade of North East England. Some Fourteenth Century Evidence', *Northern History*, II (1967), pp.1–26.

that spanned the river there. The Corporation of Newcastle exercised absolute control over the whole of the navigable river but, although that body gained rich revenues from shipping tolls, it invested little in conserving this valuable asset. In 1774, Constantine Phipps, 'a distinguished sailor' who saw the great potentialities of the river, declared that through 'ignorance, inattention and avarice' it had degenerated into 'a cursed horse-pond'. So bad was its condition that even small ships were apt to run aground or collide with other craft when attempting to pass, and some vessels, when fully laden, were obliged to wait several weeks until a tide sufficiently high enabled them to cross the bar in the harbour.[2]

The Tyne keel was roughly oval in shape, 42 feet long and 19 feet wide, stoutly constructed with flush-fitting planks ('caulker-built'), and capable of carrying up to 26 tons, though the normal load was 8 Newcastle chaldrons (21 tons 4 hundredweights). It had a draught of 4½ feet and was propelled by means of a huge oar, more than 20 feet long, worked by two men and a boy on the port side while the skipper, in unison with the others, managed a shorter oar or swape, which also served as a rudder, at the stern.

> To make a stroke the keelmen bore upon the loom of the great oar until its blade cleared the water. Then, walking in stooping posture in the direction of the stern, they swung the oar on its rowlock and on reaching the summit of their stage, suddenly dipped the wash into the water. All then kicked back their right legs making a strong pull, which they continued as they walked backward in step to the end of the stroke. On reaching this they immediately bore down and swung the oar for another stroke as before.

In shallow water the keel was driven forward by means of long poles worked by a man on each side of the craft 'with the smartness of a drill exercise'.[3] The large hold, which had no cover, left little space for a deck, and, as there were no bulwarks, the crew required 'something akin to sea-legs' to avoid slipping overboard when the craft rocked in rough water. A primitive cabin, known as the 'huddock', was their only means of shelter. The keel was equipped with a large square sail (and eventually, in the course of the nineteenth century, with a more sophisticated fore and aft rig) to be employed when the wind was favourable, and the downward and return journey was generally made with the assistance of the ebb and flood tides respectively.

On reaching the appointed ship and manoeuvring alongside her, an operation requiring great skill in high winds and big swell, the keelmen cast the coal on board, a gruelling task, especially when the vessel had high port holes, but accomplished with remarkable speed and accuracy. Often two keels, one

[2]   R.W. Johnson, *The Making of the Tyne, A Record of Fifty Years' Progress* (Newcastle, 1895), pp.9, 52–4; Sir Lewis B. Namier, *The Structure of Politics at the Accession of George III*, 2nd edn (London, 1957), p.96.
[3]   Quotations from R. Oliver Heslop, 'Keels and Keelmen', manuscript account in the North of England Institute of Mining and Mechanical Engineers, D/71. For an account of how the keel was propelled by poles, see J. Brand, *History and Antiquities of the Town and County of Newcastle upon Tyne* (London, 1789), II, p.261n.

moored on each side of the ship, would be unloaded simultaneously, and, when darkness fell, work continued by light of a brazier. A long or ship tide, as opposed to a bye-tide when only a short distance was travelled, was reckoned as the time taken from leaving and returning to the staithe, usually between fifteen and seventeen hours. All aspects of the work, combining as it did the labours of bargeman and coal-heaver, were physically demanding, and it is not surprising that the keelmen were said to possess 'a combination of nervous and muscular strength not to be found in any other class of men'.[4] Their occupation was not without danger and required an intimate knowledge of the river with its shoals, narrows, undercurrents, submerged wrecks, mooring buoys and other hazards that might be encountered, often in darkness or in dense fogs, on a waterway subject to the vagaries of tide, spates and gales. Accounts of storms in the area often mention the sinking of keels, and in extreme weather there was the ever present risk that these craft, when operating near the mouth of the river, would be swept out to sea.

> Aye, now I've seen your bonny lad,
> Upon the sea I spied him,
> His grave is green but not wi' grass,
> An' you'll never lie aside him

runs a lament concerning a keelman who had suffered what was by no means an uncommon fate. Widows of keelmen were always numerous, and many of their menfolk certainly perished in the course of their work.

The keelmen and their families formed a distinct and close-knit community in and near Newcastle. They generally intermarried and many of their sons followed their fathers' occupation.[5] They spoke 'a singular Tyneside dialect' with a 'strange laughable vocabulary ... entirely their own',[6] and could be easily identified by their dress, especially a blue bonnet, indicative of the high proportion of Scotsmen and their descendants among them, a blue woollen cap once being a common head-dress in Scotland.[7] At the beginning of the eighteenth century there was an extensive seasonal migration of keelmen to and from Scotland. In 1710, the Mayor of Newcastle mentioned the 'many Scotch young fellows who come hither to work att the keels for the sumer only', and two years later the keelmen themselves declared that out of a total of 1,600 men,

---

[4] J. Baillie, *An Impartial History of Newcastle upon Tyne* (Newcastle, 1801), p.142. The description of the keel is based on Johnson, *Making of the Tyne*, pp.298–9. Further information on the keels and the keelmen's work is to be found in the case 'Ex Parte Softly', 16 May 1801, *English Reports*, 102, 1 East, pp.466–74.

[5] R. J. Charlton, *A History of Newcastle-on-Tyne from the Earliest Records to its Formation as a City* (Newcastle, 1885), p.352; Baillie, *Impartial History*, p.142.

[6] Sir Walter Runciman, *Collier Brigs and their Sailors* (London, 1971 edn), pp.80–2. The author knew some of the keelmen in the 1860s. Their language, he observes, had 'barely survived their extinction'.

[7] E. Cobham Brewer, *Dictionary of Phrase and Fable* (New York,1978), p.150. The blue bonnet was eventually replaced by a sou'wester. When not at work, they wore a short blue jacket, slate-coloured trousers, yellow waistcoat and white shirt. Charleton, *History of Newcastle*, p.353 where there is a detailed account of the keelmen's holiday attire. This, the author states, was in the 'good old times' when the keelmen made 'plenty of money', but, as this study will show, that was seldom the case.

400 were in Scotland 'wither they go always in the winter to their families'. Thirty years later this migration still continued, at least in some cases, though many Scottish keelmen appear to have settled in Newcastle.[8]

The majority of the keelmen lived in Sandgate, just outside the City walls, which an observer likened to the Wapping of London.[9] John Wesley, who visited Newcastle in 1742 and was shocked at the 'drunkenness cursing and swearing (even from the mouths of little children)' that he witnessed there, described Sandgate as 'the poorest and most contemptible part of the Town'.[10] Even so he was exceptionally well received by the inhabitants of that quarter. Sixty years later, John Baillie, a presbyterian minister, referred to the 'ferocity and savage roughness' which had characterized the keelmen 'not many years ago', when 'scarcely a day, and chiefly a Sunday, passed but several bloody duels happened, decided by the fists of the fierce and hardy combatants'.[11] Although he reported (perhaps too sanguinely) that the influence of Methodism and the regulations of the keelmen's own benefit societies had recently effected an improvement in their behaviour, Sandgate retained an unsavoury reputation. It was described in 1830 as 'an epitome of low life in its many coloured scenes and gradations where you may wind your way through dark labyrinths of cross passages which lead and twist into all the living sepulchres of the place, comprising an endless mass of rubbish, and exhibiting every variety of vice and misery ... this asylum of bawds, rogues, prostitutes, fortune tellers etc.'[12] Another writer about the same time declared that at night 'the scene was beyond anything Pierce Egan ever depicted in the Black Houses or All Max East'.[13] Some verses, published in 1812 but written earlier, give a similar, if highly coloured, description:

> The airs with glasshouse smoke infected,
> Confusion of all kinds collected,
> Nothing but murmuring noise and swearing,
> Shocks your conscience, grates your hearing,
> Gomorrah ne'er could fuller be
> Than Sandgate with impiety,
> So crammed with immorality is everyone,
> that if there be a place on earth resembling hell,
> That lot on Sandgate surely fell.[14]

---

[8]   Jonathan Roddam to Sir John Delaval, 6 July 1710, State Papers (hereafter SP) 34/12/120; *A farther case relating to the poor Keelmen*, in F.W. Dendy, ed., *Extracts from the Records of the Hostmen's Company of Newcastle upon Tyne*, Surtees Society, CV (1901), p.176; Edward Hughes, *North Country Life in the Eighteenth Century; the North East, 1700–1750* (London, 1952), p.252; TWA 394/10.

[9]   Robert Harley, Earl of Oxford, in 1723, Historical Manuscripts Commission, *Portland*, VI, p.105.

[10] N. Curnock, *Journal of the Reverend John Wesley* (London, 1909), III, pp.13–14.

[11] Baillie, *Impartial History*, p.143.

[12] 'An Afternoon in Sandgate', *Gateshead Intelligencer* (1830), pp.41–9.

[13] Alastair Johnson, *Diary of Thomas Giordani Wright, Newcastle Doctor, 1826–29*, Surtees Society, CCVI (2001), p.78. Pierce Egan (1772–1849) published *Life in London* depicting scenes of high and low life.

[14] John Bell, junior, *Rhymes of the Northern Bards* (Newcastle, 1812), pp.49–52.

In 1849 William Newton, one of the medical officers of Newcastle Poor Law Union, reported some improvements to Sandgate, but considered the bulk of the property belonging to the Corporation on the south side 'totally unfit for human habitation'. When he and a companion visited the area they encountered 'so many of the frail sisterhood that we thought it better to move on'. He graphically described various broken down 'dens' in which the tenants struggled to survive at rents of between eight pence and a shilling per week.[15] By that time the keelmen's occupation was in decline and many of those still in work may have left Sandgate or lived in parts where improvements had been made. R.J. Charleton, writing in 1885, presumably from personal memory, presents an idealized picture of keelmen's houses as 'models of comfort and cleanliness' with plenty of substantial furniture and 'well filled larders'.[16] The nature of the keelmen's labour always demanded a substantial diet – 'they live almost entirely upon flesh-meat and flour, of the best kinds' – declared John Baillie in 1800,[17] but the above description of their dwellings ill accords with earlier evidence.

The keelmen frequently exhibited a remarkable solidarity, reinforced by a strange ritual, an instance of which Robert Harley, Earl of Oxford, described in 1723:

> These people have a particular manner of giving a pledge for their standing by one another upon any occasion, which is by spitting upon a stone, as they lately did upon account of an affront given to one of them by the person who kept a public house on the north side of the Tyne. The keelman that was injured went and spit upon a stone near the house, and renounced any further communication with it, and the rest that were of his mind performed the same ceremony, and they have kept so religiously to their vow that the people are obliged to quit their house for want of business.[18]

As we shall see, the keelmen's concerted action was principally manifested in strikes for better working conditions and in the charity for the support of their own poor and aged which they established at the beginning of the eighteenth century.

A 'hardy and laborious race',[19] the keelmen must have been present from the infancy of the coal trade, before documentary evidence about them is to be found. References to keels in the late fourteenth century indicate that by that time they had long been employed on the river. In 1384 Richard II appointed commissioners to measure all 'keles' and destroy any of greater capacity than 'of old' (whereby tax was evaded) and, five years later, commissioners were

---

[15] *Gateshead Observer*, 7 April 1849.

[16] Charleton, *History of Newcastle*, p.353.

[17] Baillie, *Impartial History*, p.142.

[18] Historical Manuscripts Commission, *Portland*, VI, p.105. Spitting on a stone was a ritual used by other workers in the northern coalfield to 'cement their confederacy'. The Durham pitmen were said in 1738 to regard it as binding 'as the most solemn oath'. David Levine and Keith Wrightson, *The Making of an Industrial Society – Whickham 1560–1765* (Oxford, 1991), pp.392–3.

[19] Baillie, *Impartial History*, p.142; Brand describes them as a 'thoughtless and hardy race', *History of Newcastle*, I, pp.450–1.

1 Scene on the Quay: keelmen playing at cards. Tough customers in a different context

ordered to ensure that the measure of these craft was 'according to ancient custom'.[20] That such action was taken to preserve the revenues of the crown suggests that there was then a substantial number of keels on the Tyne. Somewhat earlier, a large consignment of coal for Windsor Castle was conveyed to the ships in thirty-three keels manned by 165 men,[21] but it is not known what proportion of the total number of keels and keelmen this represents. By 1516 the keelmen were sufficiently numerous and important to be included among twenty-six trade crafts in Newcastle. The 'Craft of Keelmen' was again mentioned in 1538, and nearly twenty years later as an independent society,[22] but this body evidently became defunct, probably as a result of changes accompanying the rapid expansion of the coal trade in the latter part of the sixteenth century. The keelmen were not among the guilds listed in the City's charter of 1604, but at some point the municipal authorities found it necessary to organize the masters and skippers of keels into a company to exercise discipline over their men, especially to stop them throwing ballast into the river, 'which they

---

[20] *Calendar of Patent Rolls, Richard II, 1381–85*, p.449; *1388–92*, p.30. In 1421 the portage of the keel was stated to be 20 chaldrons on which customs duties were assessed but some keels had been made to carry 22 or 23 chaldrons in order to defraud the revenue, *Calendar of Patent Rolls, Henry V, 1416–22*, p.394.

[21] Blake, 'The Medieval Coal Trade', p.4.

[22] Brand, *History of Newcastle*, II, p.361 and I, p.450, citing *inspeximus* of a decree in Star Chamber, 28 May 30 Henry VIII, i.e. 1538, not, as the author states, 1539. They appear as an independent society in the *inspeximus* of another decree of 23 June 3 & 4 Philip and Mary, 1557.

usually doe for their ease'.[23] This was probably the 'Company of Kelemen' which in 1607 presented Ralph Shotton for selling his master's coal,[24] but within the next decade this body, too, had ceased to exist. Thus in 1617 the Privy Council, hearing that as a result of the keelmen's misbehaviour the Tyne was 'like to be wracked and dorred up' by ballast, ordered that the former company should be reconstituted:

> Whereas there are about 160 masters and skeepers of keeles who in tymes past had a commission in a kinde of brotherhoode from the Maior and aldermen of Newcastle, by vertue whereof they did impose fynes upon such keelemen as did hurte to the river, and caused them to pay the said fynes, by meanes whereof muche hurte was prevented, and since the same was dissolved, grete dammage hath ben done to the river by many of the said keelemen and their servantes; that therefore the said company of keelemen may have the said warrant and power renewed and confirmed unto them as formerly.[25]

It seems unlikely that an independent organization resulted from the Privy Council's order, since the keelmen were by this time being governed by the Company of Hostmen, the most powerful body of merchants in Newcastle. In the 1580s the Hostmen had acquired possession of the main sources of coal supply, especially the collieries of Whickham and Gateshead, 'potentially the most productive and lucrative in Britain',[26] and claimed, and to a large extent successfully exercised, a monopoly of the trade. They were incorporated in 1600 by royal charter, whereby in return for consenting to a levy by the crown of a shilling per chaldron on coal shipped coastwise from the river they received the exclusive right to vend coal on Tyneside. Moreover, they gained a virtual monopoly of the municipal offices in Newcastle, and thenceforth most of those who attained high office in the City, including the Mayor and aldermen, were members of the Hostmen's Company.[27] The Mayor was elected annually from the ten aldermen who in effect held office for life, and the Mayor and aldermen were justices of the peace for the City.

The Hostmen quickly exploited their power. In 1603 complaints were made that they had engrossed all the coal mines and keels and abridged the wages of the keelmen and other workers 'to their extreme impoverishment and excessive charge of the Town'.[28] The Hostmen denied the charge, at least so far as the mine workers were concerned,[29] but they kept a tight grip over the keelmen, and made every effort to prevent members of their own Company profiting

---

[23] *Acts of the Privy Council of England, 1616–1617*, pp.147–8; S. Middlebrook, *Newcastle upon Tyne, its Growth and Achievement* (Newcastle, 1950), p.62.

[24] Dendy, *Records of the Hostmen's Company*, p.57.

[25] *Acts of the Privy Council, 1616–1617*, pp.145–6, 147–8, 149; 'Conservatorship of the River Tyne' in M.A. Richardson, ed., *Reprints of Rare Tracts and Imprints of Ancient Manuscripts* (Newcastle, 1849), III, p.16; Brand, *History of Newcastle*, II, p.584.

[26] John Hatcher, *The History of the British Coal Industry, Before 1700: Towards the Age of Coal* (Oxford, 1993), p.513.

[27] Middlebrook, *Newcastle upon Tyne*, pp.65–6.

[28] Dendy, *Records of the Hostmen's Company*, p.20.

[29] *Ibid.*, p.22.

by irregularities committed by this often unruly workforce. In 1601 some Hostmen were accused of daily purchasing large quantities of coal from keelmen thus encouraging them in 'their theevishe course in stealinge of coles'.[30] Any Hostman found guilty of this 'grievous abuse' was to be expelled from the Company and the offending keelman excluded from employment by a Hostman for a year, but frequent repetition of complaints of such delinquency indicates that attempts to stamp it out failed.[31] When keelmen were found guilty of any offence, those who employed them were obliged to impose the penalties prescribed by the Hostmen's Company on pain of incurring fines themselves. The Hostmen thus exercised, or at least attempted to exercise, over the keelmen the sort of discipline that would formerly have been exerted by their own guild. In future bids to gain independence, the keelmen never claimed rights as members of an ancient organization which suggests that no trace of such a body had survived.[32]

About the beginning of the seventeenth century, some members of the Hostmen's Company began to specialize in negotiating the sale of coal to the shipmasters and providing keels and keelmen for its transport to the ships.[33] These men, known as 'fitters' or 'trading brethren', eventually predominated in the Hostmen's Company, and though some coal owners could always be found among its members, the term 'Hostman' and 'fitter' became synonymous. J.U. Nef, the historian of the coal industry, might be right in stating that the skippers of the keels originally performed the functions assumed by the fitters, and that 'as long as the skipper retained some initiative in dealing with the ship-masters for the disposal of the merchants' coal, he had a chance to set aside substantial savings, and to live in comfort and good social standing among the Newcastle citizens'.[34] Certainly from the few keelmen's wills that have survived from the late sixteenth and early seventeenth centuries it appears that some of them had acquired a modest degree of wealth and property and could call on various tradesmen, and in one case an alderman, to be witnesses or supervisors of their bequests.[35] With the advent of the fitters any opportunity that the skippers might once have had for substantial gain disappeared. In most respects the skippers differed little from the rest of the keelmen, except that they received slightly more pay, but as captains of the keels with associated responsibilities they possessed a certain status, recognized even in official documents such as Acts of Parliament, which always referred to 'Skippers and Keelmen'. Eventually both became bound to the fitters from year to year. In some circumstances, such as when there was a scarcity of labour, the annual binding-time offered workers an

---

[30] *Ibid.*, p.41.

[31] *Ibid.*, pp.42, 57, 61, 97.

[32] J.U. Nef, *The Rise of the British Coal Industry*, 2nd edn (London, 1966), I, p.441.

[33] *Ibid.*, I, p.440.

[34] *Ibid.*

[35] Durham Probate Records, University of Durham, Archives and Special Collections, wills of George Kytchyn, 1565/6, Register I, fol.23v; William Herrysonn, 1582/3, Register IV, fol.185v; Christopher Hynde, 1583, Register VI, fols 43–43v; Henry Lawson, 1609; John Warryner, 1619.

opportunity to negotiate more favourable terms,[36] but the bond gave employers a legal hold over their men which they could exploit when, as frequently happened, strikes occurred.

Occasionally the Newcastle keelmen combined with those who transported coal down the neighbouring River Wear, but, apart from these rare instances of co-operation, the two bodies tended to go their separate ways. There were a number of differences in the circumstances of the two workforces. There was no Hostmen's Company in Sunderland, nor was there any equivalent to the charity which featured so prominently in the history of the Newcastle keelmen; indeed, the men on the Wear refused to contribute when an attempt was made to establish a charity for them on the Newcastle model. The keels, longer and lighter than those on the Tyne to suit the shallower River Wear, were navigated by only one man and a boy, assisted, in adverse weather conditions, by a team of men, women and children on the tow-path who would haul along several keels roped together.[37] Although some mention of the Wearside men will be made, this study is mainly concerned with the keelmen of the Tyne and their part in the often turbulent industrial history of the area.

That the industrial population of Tyneside in general, and the keelmen in particular, were liable to become volatile on the slightest pretext was a sentiment oft repeated by the magistrates of Newcastle. Between 1700 and 1830, not a decade passed without one or more major strikes or riots by keelmen, pitmen or seamen, the three groups of workers on which the coal trade depended. The City militia was ill-disciplined and unreliable, and when strikes or other disturbances occurred the magistrates were usually quick to call on central government for troops, but most strikes were eventually settled by negotiation and without bloodshed. As the prosperity of the City and neighbourhood depended so much on the coal trade, the magistrates, many of whom were themselves directly or indirectly involved in it, had every incentive to settle disputes peaceably.

Much of the industrial discontent throughout this period concerned wages, the imposition of hardships, and threats to employment, but in 1740, as in other parts of the country, there were several food-related riots in the north-east, culminating in a serious outburst in Newcastle. In years of scarcity later in the century there were again disturbances in the City and elsewhere in the region. Historians disagree in their interpretations of such uprisings. E.P. Thompson attacked 'crass economic reductionism' that viewed them as mere rebellions of the belly – the 'instinctive reaction of virility to hunger', or of poverty to rising prices – so obscuring what lay behind 'a highly complex form of direct action, disciplined and with clear objectives'. While recognizing that riots might be

---

[36] The pitmen were on occasions able to secure better terms at binding-time, but there is no evidence that the keelmen succeeded in doing so. After 1810, the pitmen were given an allowance per day when they were prevented from working through no fault of their own, but this did not apply to the keelmen except in the case of lying tides. P.E.H. Hair, 'The Binding of the Pitmen in the North-East, 1800–1809', *Durham University Journal*, LVIII, n.s. XXVII (1965–66), pp. 1–13.

[37] Heslop, 'Keels and Keelmen'. On their refusal to contribute to the charity, see below, Chapter 4, n.22.

triggered by a sharp price increase or by hunger, he argued that the insurgents nearly always acted in the belief that they were defending traditional rights and customs – an 'identifiable bundle of beliefs, usages and forms associated with the marketing of food in times of dearth' – against malpractices by dealers. This 'legitimizing notion' was grounded on a popular consensus of the proper economic functions of the several parties within the community derived at least in part from a paternalistic model of marketing existing in law and custom dating largely from Tudor times. The totality of such ideas, combined with the 'deep emotions stirred up by dearth', Thompson termed 'the moral economy of the poor', and contended that outrage at its violation by what the crowd regarded as illicit manipulation of the market by profiteers, just as much as actual deprivation, provoked direct action, which often took the form of forced sale at a low price rather than outright plunder.[38]

While most modern historians agree that food-related insurgency arose from a rational rather than an instinctive response to dearth, some question the validity of Thompson's analysis. John Bohstedt, for example, argues that the moral economy concept does not fit every situation, and that Thompson exaggerated the food rioters' traditionalism and misconstrued their actions. It is better, he suggests, to think in terms of 'a pragmatic economy'. Riots were 'community politics', in which both the insurgents and the authorities responded to the events of the moment 'with an eye to political calculation' of the possible outcomes on the basis of their existing relationships and the traditions of earlier conflicts. By the end of the eighteenth century, a 'complex politics of provision' had evolved, in which riots, repression and measures for relief interacted to produce a 'protocol of riot' whereby all concerned restrained the use of force.[39]

Thompson coined the term 'moral economy' in respect of food riots, but, as he showed in a subsequent essay defending his original thesis, other historians had applied the concept to a variety of contexts, including industrial disputes.[40] Some have regarded this as especially appropriate when workers were defending existing rights and customs rather than striving for new advantages. It will be useful to keep these ideas in mind when we examine the numerous

---

[38] E.P. Thompson, 'The Moral Economy of the English Crowd in the Eighteenth Century', *Past & Present*, 50 (1971), pp.76–136, reprinted in his *Customs in Common* (London, 1991), pp.185–258; and 'The Moral Economy Reviewed', *ibid.*, pp.259–351.

[39] John Bohstedt, 'The Pragmatic Economy, the Politics of Provision and the "Invention" of the Food Riot Tradition in 1740', in Adrian Randall and Andrew Charlesworth, eds, *Moral Economy and Popular Protest: Crowds, Conflict and Authority* (London, 2000), pp.55–92; and Bohstedt, *Riots and Community Politics in England and Wales, 1790–1810* (Cambridge, Massachusetts, and London, 1983), pp.5, 10–11, 20, 26, 202–3.

[40] Thompson, *Customs in Common*, pp.338–51. Thompson mentions with approval Adrian Randall's 'Industrial Moral Economy of the Gloucestershire Weavers', and another view that 'something like a moral economy is bound to surface anywhere that industrial capitalism spreads', which severs the concept from a traditional viewpoint and allows it continuously to regenerate as an 'anti-capitalist critique' (pp.340–1). It has also been applied to peasants' conceptions of social justice in respect of access to land, customs of land use and entitlement to its produce, though this view has been challenged (p.341).

strikes and other disturbances in which the keelmen were involved, but it will become evident that these complex events do not completely conform to any single model.[41]

---

[41] See John Rule, 'Industrial Disputes, Wage Bargaining and the Moral Economy' in Randall and Charlesworth, *Moral Economy*, pp.166–86. Rule considers that the moral economy cannot completely explain 'the complex forms and episodes of eighteenth century industrial conflict'; these 'complex phenomena' were neither entirely within or without the reach of the moral economy (pp.166, 181).

1

Early Troubles, 1633–99

In the latter part of the sixteenth century, as supplies of wood diminished and demands for coal as an alternative fuel increased, the rapidly expanding industry brought an influx of workers into Tyneside. The population of Newcastle, estimated at 10,000 in the mid-sixteenth century had doubled by about 1760 and the growth continued with increasing rapidity thereafter. In the early part of the period, many of these workmen hailed from areas notorious for lawlessness, and, as a report to the central government in or about 1638 pointed out, their presence in or near Newcastle was a source of anxiety for the municipal authorities, especially when the coal trade was interrupted:[1]

> There is in Newcastle upon Tyne of keelmen, watermen, and other labourers, above 1800 able men, the most of them being Scottish men and Borderers which came out of the Tynedale and Reddesdale. By reason of the stop of trade occasioned by cross winds this year, they have wanted employment and are thereby in great necessity, having most of them great charge of wives and children. And unless they have employment they must be relieved by the charity of others, the inhabitants of the town, many of whom are so poor that they are scarce able to maintain themselves, or else we doubt, that in regard of their great necessity and rude condition, they will be in danger to assemble themselves and make an uproar in the town, as they did of late.

The late tumult was probably that of 1633 which, started by some apprentices, soon involved the whole working population, ever apt 'to turn every pretence and colour of greivance into uproare and seditious mutinye'.[2] The keelmen were a particularly formidable group. In 1653, a customs official, George Dawson, suggested that in the prevailing scarcity of seamen one or two hundred keelmen might be impressed into the navy, but their poverty and uncouth condition soon caused him to doubt the wisdom of the measure. 'We find they have nothing but what they have on their backs and no means of procuring clothes', he reported, 'and such nasty creatures on board would do more harm

---

[1] National Archives, SP 16/408 fol. 96; Middlebrook, *Newcastle upon Tyne, its Growth and Achievement*, pp.63, 116, 150, 175. William Gray writing in 1649 noted the large labour-force involved in the Newcastle coal trade, which 'began not past forescore yeares since…Woods in the South parts of England decaying, and the City of London, and other Cities and Towns growing populous, made the trade for Coale increase yearely, and many great ships of burthen built, so that there was more Coales vented in one yeare then was in seven yeares, forty years by-past; this great trade hath made this part to flourish in all trades', *Chorographia, or a Survey of Newcastle upon Tyne* (reprinted, Newcastle, 1818), pp.34, 37.
[2] Report of Council of the North, quoted Roger Howell jr., *Newcastle upon Tyne and the Puritan Revolution* (Oxford,1967), p.57. For further details of the disturbance, see below, Chapter 16.

than good'.[3] Nevertheless more than one hundred keelmen were impressed. 'It falls heavy upon married men having families and who are very poor', declared Dawson, who still had misgivings, and a captain who had seized fifty keelmen was forced to discharge them because of the 'mighty clamour of their wives'. Probably even more compelling than the protests of these redoubtable women was the fact that the coal trade had been brought to a standstill. Many 'nimble' keelmen had escaped into the surrounding countryside and the rest would not work while the risk of impressment remained.[4]

The increasing need for keels and keelmen in the first third of the seventeenth century was governed not only by the growing demand for coal but by the advent of large ships which, although purpose-built for the trade, could not proceed far up the Tyne in its un-dredged state. The Hostmen did not welcome this development. In 1634 they complained that ships that took their whole load at Shields caused them greatly increased expense

> In sending and imploying of more keeles then otherwais would be needfull and many times a losse & hazard of the keeles comminge so farr and a great hindrance to the makeinge of the more voyages, for that the keeles cannot so often loade the shipps as when they come farther upp to the said Towne of Newcastle.[5]

The Hostmen therefore ordered that no ship should be loaded in the lower reaches of the river unless it had taken half its cargo at or near Newcastle, but by 1656 they had to accept that most ships frequenting the Tyne were large and took the greater part of their coal in or near the estuary. This demanded double the number of keels, a corresponding increase in the costs of repair, and treble the risk of their loss. Formerly, keels which plied further up the river could continue in service for fifty or sixty years, but now through damage from stress of weather near the sea they lasted 'not above a fourth part' of that time. As many keels were being 'spoyled, sunk, driven into the sea and lost', the Hostmen imposed a charge of one shilling per chaldron on coal loaded near the mouth of the river to offset this 'extraordinary losse and damage', but the shipowners appealed to the Lord Protector and Council and this levy for 'lighter hire' had to be suspended.[6] There are varying estimates of the number of keels on the Tyne in the seventeenth and early eighteenth centuries. In 1626 there were said to be 300, but, a few years later, another estimate put the number at only 200.[7] Ralph Gardiner, who attacked the monopoly over the river and its trade exercised by the Corporation of Newcastle and the Hostmen, stated that there

---

[3]   Dawson to Admiralty Committee, 12 and 14 May 1653, *Calendar of State Papers Domestic, Commonwealth* ,vol. 5, 1652–3, pp.324, 330.
[4]   Dawson to Admiralty, 23 May 1653; Captain Bart. Yale to Robert Blackborne, 26 May, *ibid.*, pp.348, 353.
[5]   17 March 1633/4, Dendy, *Records of the Hostmen's Company*, pp.74–5. William Gray mentioned the 'many great ships of burthen' built for the coal trade, *Chorographia*, p.37.
[6]   17 March 1655/6, Dendy, *Records of the Hostmen's Company*, pp.107–8; petition of Hostmen to the Lord Protector and Council, c. April 1656, *ibid.*, pp.110–11, and order, 24 April 1656, *ibid.*, p.112.
[7]   J.U.Nef, *Rise of the British Coal Industry* (2nd edition, London, 1966) I, p.389.

were 320 keels in 1655. Fifty years later it was estimated that there were 400 keels and between 1,500 and 1,600 keelmen, the latter figure emanating from the keelmen themselves.[8]

While the Hostmen were unhappy at the increased risk to their keels, the keelmen who now had to venture frequently to the mouth of the river were obviously more concerned about the hazard to their lives and the additional labour involved. As Dawson, the Customs official quoted above, pointed out, many keelmen were extremely poor, and their poverty was certainly increased when coal shipments were disrupted between 1652 and 1654 by war against the Dutch. Although mining continued lest the pits should become flooded, little coal was vended. The shipmasters seized the opportunity created by the resulting stockpile and called for seven chaldrons of coal free of charge with every twenty they purchased, and 'for a long time' the Hostmen 'to their great losse and allmost utter ruin' were forced to comply with this demand.[9] It is highly probable, as later practice suggests, that the keelmen had to load, navigate and unload this free coal without additional pay, and the overloading of the keels, the inevitable concomitant of this largess, increased the danger of accidents, especially during storms. In August 1654 the keelmen enforced a strike, the first that has been recorded.

> We have had a great stop of Trade by our Keel-mens pretence of too small wages from their Masters [it was reported on 21 August]; they all as one man stood together, and would neither worke themselves, nor suffer others, though our Major used all possible means to satisfie them; whereupon he made a Proclamation, but all was to no purpose. And now though a Company of foot, and a Troop of Horse be drawn into Town, yet they continue in their obstinacie, notwithstanding that some of their Leading men have been apprehended. The Justices intend to meet, and try if they can compaese the busines.[10]

The magistrates met the following day and recognized that the keelmen had to endure 'much more hard labour & hazard of their lives by carrying their loadened keeles much oftner to Shields than formerly', and that they did not receive sufficient recompense to support themselves and their families as the labour and risk merited. Therefore, 'lest some obstruccon might happen in the coletrade, and for avoiding further inconveniences likely thereupon to ensue', they decreed that the men should receive from the shipmaster three shillings per keel over and above the existing 10s 4d 'for their wages, dues, me[a]te, drinking money, and loaders'. If, however, a ship took in as much of its load as possible above part of the river known as 'The Pace' (about four miles above Shields) and the remainder below that point, it was exempted from the additional charge. For every lying tide (when for circumstances beyond their control

8   Gardiner, *England's Grievance Discovered* (1655, reprint, Newcastle 1796), p.105; Brand, *History of Newcastle*, II, p.303; Dendy, *Records of the Hostmen's Company*, p.176.
9   Petition to the Lord Protector, Dendy, *Records of the Hostmen's Company*, pp.110–11..
10 *Mercurius Politicus*, 22–31 August 1654, pp.3722–3; see also Bulstrode Whitelocke, *Memorials of the English Affairs* (London, 1682), p.581; Howell, *Newcastle and the Puritan Revolution*, p.292.

the keelmen were obliged to remain idle before or after loading a ship) they were to have 1s or 2s 6d per keel depending upon its position above or below the Pace. The magistrates concluded the settlement with sanctions against keelmen who stole coal or disobeyed orders.[11] To have gained an advance in wages without a prolonged strike represents a considerable victory for the keelmen, and 13s 4d remained the basic rate for a journey to Shields until 1809; but, though they might then 'gett more for one tides work than usually …for three', this did not always compensate for the risk and other disadvantages. When Sir Henry Vane argued that a staithe situated at South Shields would greatly benefit poor keelmen and other workers, an opponent of the scheme replied that the keelmen often suffered loss when they went near the mouth of the river, 'for often by frosts & westerly winds they are kept there till they spend more than they gett, and they have as little incouragement for all their great wages that the owners have much ado to gett them to Shields att any time in regard of the hazard to the keeles & keelmen'.[12] It was later said that constant experience showed that in a given time twice as much coal could be cast aboard ships upriver than at Shields where work was liable to be impeded by storms and the heavy swell of the incoming tide.[13]

As the Hostmen's records show, illegal and surreptitious practices continued in the coal trade despite efforts to suppress them. Some of these must have affected the keelmen: the loading of ships by bulk instead of by the measured keel-load, the 'underhand dealing' of Hostmen who 'to the utter undoing of the Company' gave away large quantities of coal, and those who 'fitted' (made use of) other men's keels without permission.[14] Keelmen employed by those guilty of this practice and who worked clandestine 'fit tides' probably received less than the normal rate, and the misappropriation of keels may have deprived other men of their legitimate employment. There were plenty of opportunities for grievances to arise in the coal trade and it is not surprising that the keelmen did not long remain content after their victory of 1654. In March 1660, protesting at 'some new orders lately made by the coal owners', they assembled tumultuously and blocked navigation by mooring their keels across the river above the bridge at Newcastle. They then petitioned the magistrates. After receiving a full answer they promised to remove the keels, but failed to do so. The magistrates believed that the strike had been instigated by some of the shipmasters who were 'tamperinge with the skippers & kelemen to stand

---

[11]   22 August 1654. University of Durham, Archives and Special Collections, volume containing copies of various local documents, Earl Grey Papers, V, Miscellaneous Book 6, fols 255–7.

[12]   Sir Henry Vane's reasons for the conveniency of a staithe at South Shields, c.1646, and answer to Vane's reasons, *ibid.*, fol.112.

[13]   Defence and Answer of the Mayor and Burgesses of Newcastle, 1653, M.A. Richardson, ed., *Reprints of Rare Tracts and Imprints of Ancient Manuscripts*, III (Newcastle, 1847–49), p.52.

[14]   Loading by bulk and secret and disorderly practices, Dendy, *Records of the Hostmen's Company*, p.67; fitting other men's keels, *ibid.*, pp.51,76; gift coal, *ibid.*, pp.84, 94–5; underhand dealing, *ibid.*,pp.93–4.

upon some other termes'.[15] This suggests that the 'new orders' (which are not recorded in the Hostmen's minute book) were disadvantageous to the ship-masters as well as to the keelmen. The shipmasters must have been upset a year earlier by the Hostmen's order that every brother of the Company was to have his keels measured so that the correct load was indicated by nails 'wet in the water without any allowance'. Formerly, on account of the 'uncertainty of measure by reason of the stokage of the keels', the shipmasters were granted an extra chaldron of coal per keel-load, but once the 'uncertainty' was removed, the allowance could be withdrawn.[16] The shipmasters regarded an 'accustomed overmeasure' as their 'very livelihood',[17] and its withdrawal may have led them to incite the keelmen in hope of gaining some advantage for themselves. The magistrates issued a proclamation commanding the men to resume work on pain of imprisonment, but this had no effect, nor did a further attempt to give them satisfaction. The keelmen, about five hundred in number, merely moved the keels higher up the river and blocked it again. 'Feareinge least some greate prejudice might happene to trade and not knowing what other inconvenience might ensue', and anxious lest 'some misinformation or causless complainte' may have been made to the Council of State against them in this matter, the magistrates called in the military to break the strike.[18] The supply of coal to London was now a matter of national importance and a strike by the keelmen, especially if prolonged, had more than local repercussions. Indeed, if the coal trade was interrupted for any reason as in 1605, 1638 and 1656, the central government was ready to intervene.[19]

In 1666, the keelmen and pitmen were reduced to the verge of starvation when the Hostmen ordered all pits to stop production, because great quanti-ties of coal already wrought could not be vended on account of renewed war against Holland. The order, originally for three months, was later extended, and, although the Hostmen attempted to relieve the necessities of the workforce, many of the unemployed were reduced to begging.[20] Hundreds of the inhabit-ants of Sandgate had no bread, and for weeks 'lived only on oatmeal, water and cudbush boiled together'. ('Cudbush' may have been the plant known as cud-weed, but in any case the name suggests that its normal use was for cattle

---

[15]　Copy letter from Robert Shafto and other magistrates to an unnamed person, 24 March 1659/60, Tyne and Wear Archives (hereafter TWA), Papers concerning the Keelmen, 394/1; Robert Ellison to General Monk, 19 March 1659/60, *Calendar of State Papers, Domestic 1659–60*, p.397.

[16]　18 March 1658/9, Hostmen's minutes and order book, 1654–1742, TWA, GU/HO/1/2,f. 104; Dendy, *Records of the Hostmen's Company*, p.117.

[17]　Petition of owners and masters of ships trading to Newcastle for coals c.1638, *Calendar of State Papers Domestic, Charles I*, vol. 13, 1638–9, p.250.

[18]　Copy letter from Robert Shafto and others, 24 March 1659/60.

[19]　27 July 1605, regulation dissolved, Dendy, *Records of the Hostmen's Company*, p.56; 14 April 1638, order of King in Council on great scarcity of Newcastle coals, *Calendar of State Papers, Domestic, Charles I*, vol.12, p.347; 24 April 1656, lighter hire suspended, Dendy, *Records of the Hostmen's Company*, p.112.

[20]　Orders, 8 May and 14 August 1666, Dendy, *Records of the Hostmen's Company*, pp.131–2; Richard Forster to Joseph Williamson, 7 December 1666, *Calendar of State Papers, Domestic, Charles II*, vol. 6, 1666–67, p.327.

rather than for humans.) When collectors of the hearth tax ventured into the area 'the ruder people stoned them away' and on making a second attempt they were repelled 'with violence'. The Mayor, Sir William Blackett, sent assistance, but there were 'none but women, the keelmen's wives, to be seen'. The Mayor and other magistrates eventually managed to subdue the tumult by making it clear that the tax would be levied only on those willing to pay.[21] The coal trade had continued in stagnation because the laden colliers in the harbour could not go to sea without an escort of warships. This, as well as unfavourable weather, involved delays as shown by the following extracts from a series of reports from Newcastle by one Richard Forster:[22]

> 3 August 1666, two or three hundred colliers 'long awaiting a convoy'.
> 10 August, coal fleet still in harbour. 'Dutch and French capers on coast prevent the light ships [that had delivered their cargo] coming in'.
> 14 August, light colliers arrived with three frigates as convoy.
> 17 August, coal fleet still in harbour; the light ships have been loaded.
> 24 August, most of the laden coal fleet has started to sail with five men-of war as convoy.
> 7 December 1666, some ships that sailed on Friday [30 November] arrived safely but the rest are said to have met 14 Dutch men-of-war which captured some and drove the others ashore. 'Some of the laden colliers would have sailed this morning but the men-of war hindered them'.
> 21 December, some colliers did not sail with the others on 30 November because this was post day and 'the man-of-war expecting letters refused to sail'. All sailed the next day but were driven back [by the wind] and have continued in harbour ever since. A fair wind today but the fleet might not sail because the man-of-war is receiving provisions. Need for 'a convoy that understood the trade of the place: the life of it is in quick dispatch'.
> 22 December, the convoys are now 'sensible of their mistake and will neglect no opportunity to sail'.
> 25 December, wind too high for sailing.
> 28 December, the fleet has sailed.

The coal trade was always subject to disruption by bad weather, but the numerous and prolonged wars in which England was involved between the late seventeenth century and the early nineteenth century could have a similar effect, not only by delays arising out of the need for escorts, but on account of the threat to seamen, and sometimes to keelmen, of impressment into the navy.

In June 1671, news of a 'tumultuous assembling' of keelmen came to the notice of the central government. The men complained of being 'ill dealt with by the masters of ships following the coal trade in the matter of their hire and wages'. Nothing further concerning their grievances has come to light, but they must have involved a breach of the 1654 settlement. 'Considering the dangerous

---

[21] Forster to Williamson, 7 and 8 December 1666, *ibid.*, pp.327,330,336; R. Welford, *Men of Mark 'Twixt Tyne and Tweed* (Newcastle, 1895), I, p.299.
[22] Forster to Williamson, *Calendar of State Papers, Domestic, Charles II*, vol. 6, 1666–67, pp.7, 10,25, 39,47, 63, 327, 364, 365, 369, 375.

consequences of such riots if not speedily dispersed', the King ordered the Earl of Ogle, Lord Lieutenant of Northumberland and Newcastle, to instruct the magistrates to proceed 'with all possible vigour' to suppress the tumult. Lord Widdrington, a deputy lieutenant, was ordered to conduct the operation by the town militia, aided by that of Northumberland, with 'the utmost force & vigour' if necessary. The disturbance was quickly ended, and the Privy Council ordered that the leading men should be imprisoned and tried at the next Assizes.[23] An entry in Gateshead Parish Register, 'paide for powder and match when the keelmen mutinied, 2s 0d', indicates the alarm felt in the area.[24]

It seems unlikely that the keelmen's grievances were redressed on this occasion, for in September 1676 they again expressed discontent about their wages. The Hostmen set up a committee to consider the matter and report to the magistrates before the next quarter sessions.[25] In the following February, the keelmen petitioned the magistrates, and stated that the existing dues payable to them at various points below Newcastle were as follows:[26]

> Every keel of coales cast aboard of any vessell above the Bournes mouth, 6s 4d.
> Betwixt the Bournes mouth and lower end of Byker Shoare, 7s 4d.
> In Dent's Hole, 7s 10d.
> From thence to the lower end of the Bill Ratch, 8s 4d.
> For every keel laid aboard of any ship casting ballast at any of the shoares below the Pace 13s 4d., and onely for ships casting their ballast on any of the shores above the Pace 10s 4d.

The last point was in substance what had been fixed in 1654 – the other rates were probably in force before that date – but, since any ship that took on board as much coal as 'with conveniency and safety' it could above the Pace was exempt from the additional charge of 3s when it completed its load lower down the river, the shipmasters took advantage of this loophole in the settlement and paid the keelmen only 10s 4d, although their ships received the greater part of the coal at Shields. The keelmen complained that their dues were 'soe little as that your petitioners and their families are not able to subsist thereon', while for 'diverse years last past' their employment had been much abated by slackness of trade. They therefore begged that they might have 10s 4d (instead of 8s 4d) for loading a ship at the Bill Ratch, and 13s 4d for every keel-load cast aboard any ship below the Pace, no matter where she had deposited her ballast and irrespective of her size, as the labour involved was the same. They also called for the usual allowances for lying tides as the shipmasters had lately refused to make these payments.

The keelmen may have gained this last point, but not increased wages. In 1680 they again petitioned the magistrates on that account, though without

[23] SP 44/31 fol.72; Historical Manuscripts Commission, *12th Report part VII, Le Fleming Mss,* 5 and 9 June 1671, p.79.
[24] M.A. Richardson, *The Local Historian's Table Book*, Historical Division (Newcastle, 1841), I, p.301.
[25] 15 September 1676, Dendy, *Records of the Hostmen's Company*, p.137.
[26] February 1677/8, TWA, 394/57.

mention of lying tides.[27] They set forth that they were 'poor workemen who take great pains and earne their liveings by hard labour' and repeated that their dues were 'soe small that they and their families cannot subsist therewith'. Their reluctance to load ships near the mouth of the river is evident in both petitions. If their request was granted, they argued, more ships would go higher up-river (to avoid the greater keel-dues), 'which would not tend onely to your petitioners' advantage but to the benefitt of the inhabitants and tradesmen of Newcastle, whereas now many shipps are furnished with provisions and necessaries at Sheils'. The magistrates ordered a copy of the petition to be delivered to the Hostmen and decreed that 'if they return noe answer and that speedily the request is to be granted'.[28] There is no evidence of objection by the Hostmen, or of further complaint on these matters by the keelmen, which suggests that the outcome was to their satisfaction. Indeed the settlement that was evidently then made endured in substance for thirty years.[29] The keelmen had to face other problems, however, as an undated petition to the magistrates, possibly made near the end of the seventeenth century, shows:[30]

> Wee presume to inform yo[r] Worships what our Demands is which wee hoope is reasonable and legall which wee hoope you will grant yo[r] Answer in this our pettion … Wee desire that every hostman shall pay ore cause to be payed to each skipper of his imployment good and sufficient moneys that is passible in this kingdom either large old moneys ore new, and that every weeks worke our moneys may be payed on fryday wth out delay. And also that every hostman shall nott cause any pann boasts ore lighters to lay any coalls aboard of any ship ore ships within this harbour.
>
> Lykewise wee desire, which is as great a hindreance as anything, that caire may be taken of our marketts, for wee have althings att double raits because theire is such liberty given to the forstallers of our marketts by littleness of bread and hooksters bying other commoditys, theirefor wee humbly beegg that some speedy course may be taken, that all things may be quallyfyed.

The Hostmen had evidently been paying in tokens or goods instead of coin of the realm, but this is the only instance of an explicit complaint of this kind being made by the Newcastle keelmen.[31] As we shall see when we discuss the riot of 1740 and its aftermath, the practice whereby profiteers forestalled the market by buying up what was available to sell at a high price was all too common. The use of pan boats, normally employed in the salt trade, to transport coal to the ships was a threat to the keelmen which from time to time they

---

[27] January 1679/80, TWA 394/1.

[28] *Ibid.*, with endorsement made at a General Quarter Sessions, 14 January 1679/80.

[29] In 1710 the Mayor declared that the keelmen were demanding an increase in wages 'beyond what has been paid them these thirty years', SP 34/12 fol.126

[30] TWA 394/1. The petition is undated. The reference to old and new money may relate to the great re-coinage of 1695–96 when £6,750,000 worth of silver coinage was called in, melted down and re-coined. C.H.V. Sutherland, *English Coinage 600–1900* (London,1982), p.177. 'Hookster' (Huckster) was a retailer, hawker or trickster.

[31] In 1719 it was said that the Sunderland keelmen were paid in truck at the beginning of the season, John Hedworth to Delafaye, 23 June 1719, SP 35/16/139, but the Newcastle magistrates stated that the keelmen there were paid weekly in 'ready money' SP, Regencies, 43/61.

sought to prevent. The petitioners once again called for recompense for lying tides, a payment which was evidently frequently evaded.

Certain characteristics of the keelmen, already evident in this early period, became more manifest in the course of time. The great physical strength that their occupation demanded could easily express itself in violence when grievances arose, and it behoved both their employers and the local authorities to exercise caution in dealing with them. Charles Montague, a prominent coal owner, recognized this during a dispute with his former partner, Rawlins, in 1696. If Rawlins persuaded the keelmen to remove the coal at issue, 'I know no remedy against such rabble', Montague declared. If ten keels and forty men were sent by Rawlins, an equal force would have to be mustered against them, 'and at this time these ruffians being like[?] to starve, I know not but some publique disturbance might be occationed & laid to my charge in discourse which I would not have for all the coales on the staith'.[32] In 1746 when it was rumoured that disaffected persons were plotting to seize Newcastle, 'where they expect many of the keelmen to be ready to assist', the Mayor reported that the magistrates had refrained from arresting two keelmen named in an information, 'not thinking it prudent to do so, as that might probably put the keelmen in motion who are too ready to rise and become tumultuous upon the least pretence'.[33] Despite their disposition to turbulence, the keelmen were not an indisciplined rabble. They could exhibit strong solidarity and devise coherent petitions to the magistrates and Hostmen, but before examining further the relations of the keelmen with their employers, we must consider their attempt to combat the poverty that was such a constant feature of their lives, though this too led to conflicts closely associated with those in the industrial sphere.

---

[32] Montague to George Baker, 7 July 1696, Montague family letter book, microfilm in the Central Library, Newcastle.

[33] Sir Edward Blackett to Cuthbert Smith, Mayor, 11 April 1746; Smith to the Duke of Newcastle, 21 April, SP Domestic, George II, 83.

2

The Keelmen's Charity, 1699–1712: Success, Conflict and Collapse

At the best of times the keelmen lived at subsistence level and variations in trade or even a prolonged spell of unfavourable weather could plunge them into distress. There were always many among them stricken by old age, accident or sickness, as well as widows and orphans, and as neither the parish nor private charity rendered adequate assistance, the keelmen determined to provide for their poor themselves. In 1699, representatives of the keelmen declared in a petition to the Hostmen's Company, that on account of the 'pinching want and extremities' from which they often suffered, they were willing that four pence per tide should be deducted from the wages of crews of keels carrying 6 to 8 chaldrons, and three pence from those of keels bearing a lesser load, to create a fund for relief of the needy. They begged the Hostmen to make rules for the government of this charity.[1] The petition was reported in the Hostmen's books with a gloss to obviate the implication that the keelmen's wages were insufficient:[2]

> Whereas the skippers and keelmen have for many years by sad experience found that their great miseries and wants suffered and endured by them and their poor families have been occasioned by their improvidence in not laying up and making provision out of what they earn and get by their labours in summer time to subsist themselves in winter and to enable them to bind their children apprentices to trades and callings and to help such skippers and keelmen as are aged and past their work …

therefore, 'deeply sensible of their own misgovernment', they had resolved that a fund should be established under the Hostmen's control to assist those in need. Accordingly, the Hostmen ordered that the stewards of their Company should collect the money to be deducted by the fitters and distribute it each quarter as the Company directed. Six months later they ordered a clause concerning the charity money to be inserted into the keelmen's bonds, and the sum already collected to be distributed after a list of the 'poorest sort' had been examined by the Company.[3]

Soon the major part of the fund was devoted to building a hospital to accommodate sick and aged keelmen and keelmen's widows. Whether the idea of a hospital originated from the keelmen or the Hostmen is not clear, but on 4 October 1700, following a petition from the keelmen, the Mayor and

[1] TWA 394/43.
[2] F.W. Dendy, ed., *Extracts from the Records of the Hostmen's Company of Newcastle upon Tyne*, Surtees Society, CV, pp.154–5.
[3] 10 November 1699, *ibid.*, p.155.

Corporation leased a plot of land on the outskirts of Newcastle to the Hostmen for ninety-nine years at a nominal rent for use of the keelmen.[4] Within a year a building, two storeys high, constructed in a square around a small court 'in the form of colleges and monasteries', and containing sixty dwelling rooms, an office and a club room, had been erected at a cost of more than £2,000.[5] The author of *An Account of the Hospital*, published in 1829, considered that the charges for the building, which had greatly exceeded the keelmen's expectations, were 'perhaps as far above what was necessary to answer the purposes intended':

> Had several expensive particulars been omitted, and the house itself made a storey higher, it would have answered a much better purpose than it can possibly do, and the charge of unnecessary ornaments that were at first about it would have either extended the necessary parts, by making a larger square, or raised it higher.

Even so, the hospital provided a refuge for the destitute and, at least at the outset, the very existence of the building must have served as a source of hope for keelmen who were approaching the end of their working lives or who were stricken by illness or misfortune. The Hostmen deserve credit for their assistance without which the project could not have succeeded, but almost immediately problems arose which boded ill for the future. Early in 1700, the keelmen complained of 'diverse abuses' and called for more careful management of the money, and towards the end of the year the Hostmen made an order imposing penalties on those who neglected to hand over what they had collected from the keelmen.[6] Some months later, the Company ordered two of their brethren, William Emmerson and Thomas Forster, to pay what they owed to the fund under penalty of a fine of £5 and, when Emmerson failed to comply, the Company decreed that the arrears and the fine should be levied by distress and that he should not receive the money in future.[7]

While the Hostmen endeavoured to prevent such abuses, they strove to keep a tight grip over the charity and the keelmen themselves. Every year (at least from 1700) they appointed twenty keelmen to be stewards or overseers of their fellows, especially with regard to the hospital, but with some wider responsibilities.[8] In December 1700 the twenty men were rewarded by the City's Common Council for preventing tippling on the Lord's day and for keeping Sandgate free of inmates, and in 1704 the Council again rewarded them for preventing tippling in ale houses or rowing on the river on the sabbath.[9] At first

4   *Ibid.*, p.156.
5   E. Mackenzie, *A Descriptive and Historical Account of the Town and County of Newcastle upon Tyne* (Newcastle, 1827), II, pp.550–3; *Articles of the Keelman's Hospital and Society with Rules for the Hospital, to which is added an Account of the Hospital and Society* (Newcastle, 1829).
6   4 January 1699/1700; 13 November 1700, Dendy, *Records of the Hostmen's Company*, pp.156–7.
7   Hostmen's minute book, 1654–1742, TWA, GU/HO/1/2, fol.441; Dendy, *Records of the Hostmen's Company*, p.158.
8   *Ibid.*, fol.440.
9   TWA, Calendar of books of the Common Council, 1699–1718.

2   Keelmen's Hospital and Procession. The Hospital was a focal point for the keelmen. Wesley often preached in its precincts.

the Hostmen appointed the twenty men in response to the keelmen's petition, but soon they tried to impose their own choice of officers on them. However, according to a later account, the keelmen, aided by Sir William Blackett, their 'constant benefactor and friend', turned out the 'pretended governors and stewards', and had ever since chosen their own officials, though much against the Hostmen's will.[10] Blackett, an extensive coal owner, magistrate, and MP for the City, died in December 1705, and soon the Hostmen regained control of the charity. Thus on 4 February 1706/7, following several petitions from the keelmen, the Hostmen appointed a committee to 'settle matters about the Twenty men and what and how many of the Keelmen may be thought proper to be concerned in the affairs of the Keelmen in relacon to the Hospitall and the Managemt thereof'. It was further ordered 'that noe more of the Keelmen be appointed Constables'. Again, on 4 January 1708/9, every fitter was ordered to nominate one of his skippers out of which number the Governor and stewards of the Company were to select twenty men 'usually chosen every year for the better ordering and governing the keelmen'.[11] These officials did not necessarily have a say in the government of the charity. When a new collector of the money was needed, the Hostmen decided that their Governor and

---

[10]   'The Case of the poor Skippers and Keelmen' [1711], in Dendy, *Records of the Hostmen's Company*, pp.172–4.
[11]   *Ibid.,* pp.171, 178.

the Mayor should make the appointment without consulting the twenty men.[12] The most serious contention between the Hostmen and keelmen arose over the dispensing of the fund. At first, the accounts of Edward Grey, the Hostman manager of the fund, virtually tallied with those kept by the keelmen, but for the period 1702–4 his accounts of expenditure exceeded the keelmen's by £955.[13] A committee of Hostmen concluded that the keelmen were 'mightily mistaken': Grey's accounts were fair and exact, and he should receive £50 out of the keelmen's stock as a reward for his careful management. The Company unanimously endorsed the committee's report, but the keelmen could hardly fail to resent that, without consulting them, £50 of their fund had been granted to a person whom they had ceased to trust. However, there was a delay of five years before Grey received the £50, and the payment may then have been made from the Hostmen's own fund, though this is not certain.[14]

Sir William Blackett had intended that the charity should be established by Act of Parliament, and almost immediately after his death, William Carr, the other MP for Newcastle, took up the scheme. In a letter to Lyonel Moor, the collector of the charity money, he urgently sought the necessary authority from the keelmen:

> Sir William Blackett's continued weakness before his death and the hopes of his being better put a stop to the dispatch of the poor Keelmen's affair would have had, but as it was his constant desire, and almost his last, that such a work might go forward, I send you their petition which you gave me, that it may be signed by a convenient number of them and that it may be returned forthwith, because I would have no time lost in promoting so good a work.[15]

Some weeks later a petition for leave to bring in a bill to confirm the charity and to constitute the Mayor of Newcastle and his successors governors of the hospital was presented to the Commons. Carr, and two other MPs with local connections, Sir Robert Eden and Sir William Bowes, were appointed to prepare the measure, but the session ended before it was brought before the House.[16] About a year later, a petition from some of the keelmen begged the Mayor and the Governor of the Hostmen's Company to endeavour to obtain an Act to perpetuate the charity, and empowered them to act 'as fully to all intents and purposes as though we were personally present declaring our consent thereunto'.[17] Such phraseology indicates that the petition was not composed by the signatories themselves. Moreover it was not acceptable to all the keelmen. In July 1707, the Hostmen complained that an 'instrument' drawn up by a

---

12   Hostmen's minute book, 4 January 1706/7, TWA, GU/HO/1/2, fol.531.
13   *Ibid.*, fol.504; Dendy, *Records of the Hostmen's Company*, pp.166–7.
14   Hostmen's minute book, TWA, GU/HO/1/2, fol.503; Dendy, *Records of the Hostmen's Company*, pp.166, 253.
15   11 December 1705, TWA, Cotesworth Papers, CJ/3/1.
16   16 January 1705/6, *Journals of the House of Commons*, 15, p.90; *The Case of the poor Skippers and Keelmen...Truly Stated*, British Library 8223 E9 (32).
17   Petition to Nicholas Ridley and Sir Ralph Carr, c.1707, TWA 394/2.

scrivener on the order of several skippers and keelmen contradicted the petition and tended 'to create tumults and disorders'. The Company ordered that no fitter should employ any of the troublemakers under penalty of £5, but this did not curb the disorder. Three weeks later, the Hostmen noted that the skippers and keelmen had 'privately combined together and entered into a writing or obligation under a penalty', refused to work, contrary to their bonds, and demanded increased wages. The Company again passed orders to deprive the offenders of employment.[18] Trouble erupted once more the following year. 'Trade now seems to have a promising aspect if our New-castle magistrates do not interfere & will take effectual measures to suppress publick ryotts in ye bud for ye future', James Clavering observed, 11 May 1708, adding that there had been 'a notable one lately among ye keelmen'.[19] The following March, the Mayor, Robert Fenwick, referred to a 'dangerous riot' by the keelmen that had stopped the coal trade in the midst of the previous summer. He believed that their 'misapplied charity' had contributed to the strike. The Hostmen prosecuted some of those involved in the 'mutany'.[20] Nothing more has come to light about the disturbances in this period, but there was clearly a close connexion between the charity and industrial action. Early in 1708, the Hostmen had been alarmed by a report that attempts were being made to seek an Act to establish the charity without consulting them.[21] A committee appointed to inquire and stop anything prejudicial to their Company issued a warning that there must be

> no decisive vote relating to that affair without the consent of the Governor and the two stewards of the Hostmen's Company ... and we the rather urge this as very reasonable because the keelmen who raise this charity are our bond servants and the money cannot be collected but by us or those employed by us.[22]

It was the Hostmen's constant fear that the keelmen might gain independent control of the charity, an apprehension that the magistrates shared, though in other respects there was sometimes dissension between the two bodies over government of the fund and hospital.

In 1709, a new initiative, designed to remove any friction between the Hostmen and the magistracy on this matter, began under the Mayor, Robert Fenwick, who was also Governor of the Hostmen's Company. A petition was drawn up in the name of the keelmen, begging in a particularly deferential manner that the charity might be placed under the control of the Mayor, five senior Aldermen, and the Governor and stewards of the Hostmen's Company. About two hundred keelmen signed this document which referred to the former

---

[18] Dendy, *Records of the Hostmen's Company*, pp.172, 177, 253.
[19] To Lady Cowper, 11 May 1708, Edward Hughes, ed., 'Some Clavering Correspondence', *Archaeologia Aeliana*, 4th series, XXXIV, pp.14–26.
[20] Durham Cathedral Library, Additional Ms 97; Dendy, *Records of the Hostmen's Company*, accounts, 19 March 1708/9, p.253.
[21] 12 February 1707/8, Dendy, *Records of the Hostmen's Company*, pp.178–9.
[22] 17 February 1707/8, TWA 394/2.

representation giving the Mayor and Governor full power to act for them.[23]
A petition to the Commons praying for leave to introduce a bill to settle the
charity as the keelmen requested was then framed and signed by Fenwick
in his dual role.[24] Fenwick, however, had angered some of the coal owners
by his dealings with the keelmen. In time of war, the keelmen were liable to
impressment into the navy, though protections against this conscription were
usually obtained from the Admiralty and issued by the Mayor. On this occasion Fenwick withheld the protections from keelmen involved in the previous
year's disturbances.

> I thought it convenient [he declared] (to prevent the like for ye future) to
> demand security for their good behaviour; this with a design of stoping a
> misapply'd charity, which the keelmen some years ago agreed to give for
> releif of their own poor, was the only reason of their not haveing protections
> for some days; by this nothing else was intended but ye preserveing the pub-
> lick peace.[25]

Without protections, however, the keelmen refused to work. Anne Clavering,
whose family's business suffered, was extremely angry at the Mayor's conduct
and busied herself in organizing measures to prevent any repetition of it. She
believed that in the process she had curbed Fenwick's power. ''Tis plain', she
declared, with obvious satisfaction, 'what has already been done has putt a
stop to the act for the making the mayor governour of the Keelmen's hospital'.[26] Unfortunately she did not elucidate this statement, but a member of the
family later alleged that Fenwick had withheld the protections to force the
keelmen to sign a petition supporting his intended application to Parliament,[27]
and Fenwick's own statement that he was seeking to stop a 'misapplied charity' lends credibility to the allegation. The aggrieved coal owners obtained the
protections directly from the Admiralty thus freeing the keelmen from any pressure that Fenwick was attempting to exert. His petition was not presented to
the Commons, which indicates the truth of Anne Clavering's somewhat cryptic
statement. The whole episode shows how the charity could become embroiled
in local magnates' jealousies and squabbles, rooted to a large extent in divisions over politics. After a controversial election in 1708, James Clavering
declared that the Tory magistrates had behaved

> after their usual arbitrary way, which gave a Lord, not a Peer, occasion to say
> he thought himself in another kingdom on ye other side of ye sea & not in a
> nation govern'd by good laws or where liberty and property ruled.

Clavering wished that additional JPs, 'whose affection and zeal for the present
government is void of suspicion', might be appointed to Newcastle, as the

23 10 February 1708/9, TWA 394/2.
24 *Ibid.*
25 Durham Cathedral Library, Additional. Ms 97.
26 29 March 1709, H.T. Dickinson, ed., *The Correspondence of James Clavering* (Surtees Society,
    CLXXVIII 1967), pp.28–9.
27 Nevile Ridley to [? M. White], 24 January 1711/12, TWA 394/4.

town would be lost 'unless some method be found to curb the insolence of these present magistrates who are as arbitrary within their dominions as the King of France'.[28]

Meanwhile, the charity was falling into disorder. Lionel Moor, appointed collector of the money by the Hostmen in 1705,[29] served for only one year, and his successor, Timothy Tully, was evidently chosen by the keelmen themselves, or (as a polemical account written several years later put it) by some 'ill-designing men among them, who cou'd not be satisfy'd unless they had the fingering of the money, in order to dispose of it at their pleasure.'[30] The Hostmen, obviously unhappy at this appointment, demanded that Tully should give security, and, when he delayed, ordered that no money be paid to him until he complied.[31] Eight months later, the Company ordered the fitters to detain the keelmen's money until the Governor and the Mayor appointed a steward.[32] Despite this attempt to displace him, Tully remained in office for four years. Towards the end of that period, complaints alleging misapplication of the funds began to be made. In November 1709, the twenty keelmen supervisors and others declared in a petition to the Hostmen that their money in Tully's hands was extravagantly wasted, and, a few weeks later, similar allegations were made in another petition subscribed by more than a hundred keelmen. They wished to have no further concern with Tully, nor to pay such a vast salary for collection of the contributions, a task that could be done by two men from each fitter's work.[33] A committee of Hostmen found that almost £47 had been 'extravagantly waisted' in public houses, all of which Tully declared to have been disbursed by order of the twenty men who had forced him to pay 'whether he would or noe'.[34] He later claimed that during his term of office more than £180 had been 'waistfully spent by the skippers and keelmen in drink in several alehouses', about £120 of which had been disbursed out of the hospital funds. The rest, he believed, remained unpaid.[35] The Hostmen ordered that in future the charity money should be collected by their own stewards, but, if Tully gave security, he might continue to receive the cash until further orders.[36]

The keelmen remained dissatisfied. They alleged that some items in Tully's accounts were false, and between March and May 1710 they persistently called on the Hostmen and magistrates for redress. On 5 May, a 'vast number' of keelmen petitioned the Hostmen to set about procuring an Act of Parliament for the charity. They also asked that John Kerr (or Carr) should be appointed to

---

[28]　*Ibid.*; James Clavering to Lady Cowper, 11 June and 9 July 1708, 'Clavering Correspondence', *Archaeologia Aeliana*, 4th series, XXXIV, pp.14–26; E. Cruickshanks, S. Handley and D.W. Hayton, *History of Parliament, The Commons 1690–1715*, II, *The Constituencies* (Cambridge, 2002), pp.455–6.

[29]　Dendy, *Records of the Hostmen's Company*, p.167.

[30]　*Case of the poor Skippers and Keelmen*, British Library 8223 E9(32).

[31]　Hostmen's minute book, 7 June 1706, TWA, GU/HO/1/2 f.517.

[32]　4 Feb. 1706/7, Dendy, *Records of the Hostmen's Company*, p.171.

[33]　*Ibid.*, pp.178–9.

[34]　*Ibid.*, pp.178–9.

[35]　Copy affidavit, 10 November 1711, TWA 394/5.

[36]　Dendy, *Records of the Hostmen's Company*, pp.178–9.

receive their money in place of Tully, and, as they 'conceived that Mr Tully and the workmen contrived false bills to wrong them', demanded that only those tradesmen who supported by oath their claims for work on the hospital should be paid.[37] The Hostmen appointed a committee to examine all claims concerning the hospital, but this body proceeded to pay a large sum to workmen who had not testified as the keelmen demanded.[38] On hearing of this, the keelmen

> in a rage and disorderly manner drew together and went to the committee and discharged them from paying the rest of their money except the persons demanding gave such satisfaction as they had required, offering that upon such satisfaction being given they would raise as much money as would clear them of debt, and required that the money left should be given up to Mr Carr for their use. But the committee left that money at the Coffee House untill the 1[st] or 2[nd] Monday following on which the Oastmen's Company met when it was expected by the K'men that it would be ordered that who had a demand should be swore before authority, and Mr Carr established ... But contrarywise the money was privately paid by ye s[ai]d committee, and the K'men given to understand that Mr Tully should continue receiving and paying until they the K'men were out of debt which the K'men doubted would be endless. For they perceived that Mr Tully was contracting new debts &c. Also the committee deny'd them Mr Tully's accounts, which strengthened their jealousy of being cheated in the latter accounts.[39]

The committee, however, reported that they found Tully's accounts to be just, and it was accordingly ordered that the remaining debts should be discharged out of the next money from the keelmen which, however, should be paid only to a collector appointed by the Hostmen's Company.[40]

Tension was mounting among the keelmen, and, evidently before the committee reported, an angry mob assembled on the Garthheads near Sandgate. The author of the above account, whose identy is unknown, was informed that the 'better or more reasonable sort' could not restrain the rest, and that the lives of Edward Grey and Charles Atkinson, the Hostmen's stewards, would be in danger if the 'mischievous party' encountered them that day.[41] Despite the threat of an imminent outburst, calmer counsels prevailed for a time. On 4 June a petition, said to be signed by 813 keelmen, to the same effect as that of 5 May, was presented to the Mayor and Aldermen.[42] It was drafted to form the basis for an application to the Commons and was certainly not composed by the keelmen themselves. The petitioners claimed that they were

> very sensible of the great loss and damage which we have sustained for several years past by the late receivers appointed for the collecting of our charity

---

[37] *Ibid.*, p.179; TWA, Cotesworth Papers, CJ/3/6.
[38] Cotesworth Papers, CJ/3/6.
[39] *Ibid.*
[40] 26 May 1710, Dendy, *Records of the Hostmen's Company*, p.180; Hostmen's minute book, TWA, GU/HO/1/2 fol.582.
[41] Cotesworth Papers, CJ/3/6.
[42] Copy with endorsement stating the number of signatories, TWA 394/5.

money by the misapplication thereof by the said receivers and by a party of turbulent and factious skippers and keelmen who have waisted and spent the same and not applied the said moneys as was intended for the relief and support of the poor decayed keelmen, their widdowes and children which are in the hospitall that was built by the said keelmen at their own charge.

Therefore, 'and for the preventing of any tumults, riotts or troubles for the future which may arise by such ill persons', they desired that an Act might be obtained to place the hospital under the Mayor and five Aldermen. They also requested that these governors should choose as steward 'such a person that can give good security', and that the twenty men might present candidates for places in the hospital.

A few days later, however, the keelmen enforced a strike accompanied by much disorder and threats of even more violence. Although the dispute over the charity had embittered relations between masters and men, it was not the principal cause of the prolonged stoppage that ensued. (The men's numerous grievances will be examined in Chapter 5.) Even so, the strikers repeated demands that Kerr be appointed steward and be given possession of Tully's receipts and those of others who had handled the funds, and that tradesmen who had worked on the hospital should substantiate their claims by oath. Nothing was to be allowed for 'idle drinking'.[43] The strike lasted several weeks and a combination of shipmasters, who shared some of the keelmen's grievances, had also disrupted the coal trade. The Queen and Privy Council ordered an enquiry into 'the present combinations and complaints'.[44] The 'poor keelmen' and others presented petitions, and a committee of the Privy Council met several times in an effort to remove the difficulties that had caused 'so great an obstruction' to the trade. The shipmasters were 'made easy', and the keelmen who appeared before the Council to voice their complaints were said to be satisfied.[45] Although many of their grievances related to their employment, they took the opportunity to make complaints about the charity. The Lord President ordered the Attorney General to file a bill in the Exchequer to oblige the fitters to exhibit their receipts and payments, but William Carr, who had sponsored the previous abortive attempt in parliament, promised that a bill would be brought forward to do the keelmen justice and prevailed upon the Council to countermand the order. Carr regarded himself 'obliged to see it done', even after his defeat in the Newcastle election a few months later.[46]

The keelmen, however, were now determined to cast off all dependence on the Hostmen and magistrates and to seek a charter of incorporation in order to govern the charity themselves. They were probably persuaded to adopt this course by Daniel Defoe, who had become acquainted with them while in Newcastle and embraced their cause, the more so because he believed that an independent

[43] Petition to George Whinefield, Mayor, and Aldermen, TWA 394/3; 394/57.
[44] Quoted E.R. Turner, 'The English Coal Industry in the Seventeenth and Eighteenth Centuries', *American Historical Review*, XXVII (1921–22), pp.1–23, citation p.15.
[45] J C. Boyle to the Mayor, 1 August 1710, SP 44/109.
[46] Carr to M. White, 23 February 1711/12; N. Ridley to M. Fetherstonhaugh, same date, TWA 394/4.

body of keelmen would curb illegal practices by their employers that raised the price of coal in London. It was alleged that he promised the keelmen that he would procure an Act of Parliament to make them freemen and that he received more than £100 belonging to the hospital for that purpose.[47] Money had been 'shamefully squeez'd out of these poor deluded people, towards obtaining a Charter of Incorporation', declared another opponent,[48] but Defoe claimed that he received only £40 from the keelmen and that he was greatly out of pocket through his attempts to serve them.[49] He championed the keelmen in several publications and vehemently attacked the Hostmen and magistrates. 'What sort of spiritt possesses that man?', asked Henry Liddell, one of the coal owners. He seemed 'by the print of which he is suspected to be the author to encourage modestly speaking a refractoriness among that sort of people'.[50]

More than one thousand keelmen signed a petition to the Queen in which they alleged that they had suffered great loss

> by the persons entrusted with the said money, by mis-application, embez-zelments, insolvencies, and other disasters by which your petitioners have been greatly injured, their poor miserably starved, their hospital ... entirely neglected, and the charitable design of their said contribution in danger of being ruined and destroyed.

They therefore begged the Queen to take into consideration their 'sad and deplorable condition' and incorporate them as 'The Governor and Society of the Skippers and Keelmen of the River of Tyne', with power to choose their own officers, collect the charity money, and apply it to the purposes for which it was contributed.[51] The petition was read to the Queen in Council on 10 April 1711 and referred to the Attorney General, but the magistrates entered a caveat against it on the grounds that the keelmen had now agreed to petition parliament to have the charity placed under the magistrates' control.[52] In pursuance of this measure the magistrates evidently orchestrated several petitions from the keelmen. One from forty-five skippers and keelmen employed by Charles Atkinson requested that an Act should be procured to place the charity under the magistrates 'according to our former petition', presumably that of 4 June 1710.[53] A petition to be presented to the Commons was drawn up and signed by about two hundred keelmen, but it is not recorded in the *Journals* of the House. According to Defoe, many of the signatories later sought to retract. They alleged that they had been persuaded by promises of favour if they signed and threats of dismissal if they refused. They therefore reaffirmed their desire for

---

[47]   Draft affidavit of David Gibson and Walter Ormston, 11 November 1711, TWA 394/3.
[48]   *Case of the poor Skippers and Keelmen*, as in n.16.
[49]   N. Ridley to M. Fetherstonhaugh, 27 March 1712, TWA 394/4.
[50]   J.M. Ellis,ed., *Letters of Henry Liddell to William Cotesworth* (Surtees Society, CXCVII 1987), p.13.
[51]   TWA 394/6; Cotesworth Papers CJ/3/13; *The Review*, 16 February 1712.
[52]   *The Review*, 16 February 1712; 'Further Case of the poor Keelmen', in Dendy, *Records of the Hostmen's Company*, pp.175–7.
[53]   TWA 394/5.

a charter of incorporation. Their masters, they declared, wanted to control the charity 'with a design to oppress, influence and rule the whole body of skippers and keelmen with respect to their rates and preference in their labour', thus illustrating, once again, the perceived connexion between the charity and the keelmen's conditions of employment.[54] The same point was made in another publication (evidently by Defoe, as articles similar in content and language later appeared in his *Review*), arguing that the magistrates, often the men's employers, should not be given control of the charity, as they would then have power

> to awe and over-rule the poor keelmen, either in their work or in their charity, as they please, excluding them from the charity if they refuse to be imposed upon in their labour, or refusing them employment if they do not submit to be imposed upon in their charity.

The men ought not to be compelled to pay this voluntary contribution to persons of whom they disapproved. There was no reason why they should not have power to dispose of their own money for which they worked hard and could ill afford to spare. They were the only rightful judges as to the persons needing assistance, and many poor families might starve if the magistrates did not see fit to relieve them out of the charitable fund. If, as a result of the magistrates' opposition, their bid to obtain incorporation failed, they were unanimously resolved to cease their contributions and leave themselves and their poor dependent on provision from the parish. As for the 'vain and frivolous pretence' that a majority of them wanted the magistrates to control the charity, more than one thousand keelmen had signed the petition to the Queen and the rest of them were willing to do so if required.[55]

To counter allegations of intimidation, the magistrates obtained affidavits declaring that the signatures in support of their scheme had been given 'freely and voluntarily'.[56] They also procured an affidavit alleging that John Kerr, the keelmen's steward, and others, had threatened residents in the hospital with expulsion if they did not sign a paper 'for the getting an Act ... for the making them freemen', and that many signatories of that instrument were not keelmen.[57] The Mayor, Matthew Fetherstonhaugh, sent these affidavits and other documents to his friend Nevile Ridley, who was collaborating with William Carr to prepare a bill to regulate the charity. One item, 'Reasons to be offered against the keelmen's having any grant for incorporation unless under the government of the mayor and aldermen of Newcastle only', set forth that formerly a good foundation had been laid for the charity under the magistrates' direction and care of the Hostmen's Company, but 'some turbulent skippers and keelmen, designing ... to get the charity moneys into their hands', had for some years past obstructed collection of the contributions by anyone appointed by

---

[54] Petition printed in *The Review*, 16 February 1712.
[55] Cotesworth Papers, CJ/3/13.
[56] Draft affidavit of John Rotherford, William Mathews and others, 31 October 1711, TWA 394/3.
[57] Draft affidavit of David Gibson and Walter Ormston, 11 November 1711, TWA 394/3.

the magistrates, and had ever since misapplied the money, much of it being dissipated on drink at their meetings. Moreover, during the mutiny of 1710, a large sum that should have been employed in relief of the poor was 'spent extravagantly' to support imprisoned rioters. Most of the keelmen were without religion or manners, and, if they were made into an independent corporation with money at their disposal, it was greatly to be feared that they would embark on frequent mutinies and tumults. The whole trade of the Tyne would be in their power.[58] 'Communicate all to Mr Carr', Fetherstonhaugh urged Ridley, 'and let nothing be wanting for the best of councill'.[59] When Ridley requested evidence of the keelmen's 'good management' of their charity money, Fetherstonhaugh sent Tully's declaration that during his stewardship they had spent more than £180 on drink.[60] Fetherstonhaugh was anxious that the Attorney General's report on the petition for incorporation might be obtained as soon as possible, 'for there can be no expectation of the keelmen's consent to a Bill in Parliament till they be disappointed in this'.[61]

The magistrates' petition was presented to the Commons on 18 January 1711/12. They claimed that the skippers and keelmen had begged them to procure an Act to perpetuate the charity because recently a great part of the contributions had either not been duly collected or the money had been misapplied. They therefore prayed that a bill might be introduced to place the charity under good and orderly government.[62] Leave was granted, and the House appointed William Wrightson and Sir William Blackett, MPs for Newcastle, and Sir Robert Eden, MP for County Durham, to prepare the measure. The bill had in fact been drafted more than two months earlier, and the next day it was presented to the House and read for the first time.[63] By its terms, the Mayor, five senior Aldermen and the Governor of the Hostmen's Company for the time being, together with Wrightson and Blackett, were to be incorporated as governors of the charity with power to examine on oath anyone who had retained money from the men's wages, and, in case of a deficiency, to levy double the sum by distress. Every year the skippers and keelmen were to elect twenty men to present to the governors those most deserving of benefit and to report any misdemeanour committed by those concerned with the fund.[64]

The bill appeared to address many of the keelmen's concerns, but, as Fetherstonhaugh had predicted, while they continued to hope for a charter of incorporation they were unlikely to submit to an alternative scheme. Soon a petition against the bill was signed by 981 keelmen.[65] Defoe strenuously backed their protest by articles in *The Review*, and two other publications, *The Case*

---

[58] TWA 394/3.
[59] Fetherstonhaugh to N. Ridley, 2 November 1711, TWA 394/3.
[60] Ridley to Fetherstonhaugh, 6 November 1711, TWA 394/3; copy of Tully's affidavit, 10 November, TWA 394/5.
[61] Fetherstonhaugh to Ridley, 10 November 1711, TWA 394/5.
[62] 21 December 1711, TWA 394/3.
[63] *Journals of the House of Commons*, 17 (1711–14), pp.31–2.
[64] Copy bill, House of Lords Record Office.
[65] TWA 394/57; *Journals of the House of Commons*, 17, p.141.

of the poor Skippers and Keelmen of Newcastle, and *A farther Case relating to the poor Keelmen*, both evidently designed to be presented to the Commons, in which he fiercely attacked the Hostmen and magistrates and asserted the keelmen's right to govern their charity themselves.[66] It would be a very great hardship, he argued, if its government were placed in the hands of the very persons whose 'unjust encroachments, evil practices, wrongs and injuries' were the grounds for the keelmen's petition for incorporation, whereby they hoped to call to account many of the Hostmen for embezzling and wasting great sums to the 'miserable starving of the poor'. He repeated that threats, promises and other corrupt practices had been employed to obtain signatures in favour of the magistrates' 'specious scheme, ... the most unjust and most wicked design that has been known for these many years'. Rather than consent to government by those who had 'enriched themselves with the poor's bread', the keelmen would let the hospital sink, though it had already cost them above £3,000. If the keelmen were

> subjected to the Hoastmen who are magistrates on the one hand, and coal-owners on the other, all the laws lately made by this present Parliament against combinations, contracts, and engrossing of coals, will be rendred ineffectual; for that the said coal-owners having the poor keelmen thus at their command, will be able to put what price they please upon the coals, load and refuse to load what ships they please, and by the same undue preferences, both at Newcastle and at the markets, which they formerly practiced, bring the coal trade to the same degree of a monopoly which it was in before.

He did not explain exactly how the keelmen could prevent illegal practices by their employers, but this idea seems to a large extent to have motivated his concern with the keelmen's affairs. It was, of course, a good ploy to attract support from the public.

The promoters of the bill responded to Defoe's broadsides with *The Case of the Poor Skippers and Keel-men of New-Castle, Truly Stated: with some Remarks on a Printed Paper, call'd and pretended to be their Case*.[67] This 'pretended case', full of falsehoods, was the work of 'a mercinary writer well acquainted with some instances of the wasting and misapplying [the keelmen's] money collected for better ends'. The keelmen and their families had always received 'great benevolence' from the Corporation of Newcastle: their children were taught without charge by masters 'very liberally rewarded by the Town', their poor of all ages were clothed yearly and received other relief, and the hospital was built on ground granted by the Corporation. The 'greatest part' of the keelmen had petitioned the magistrates to obtain an Act of Parliament, and the present bill would cure most of the mischiefs described by Defoe. It would also 'prevent many such tumultuous riots as have frequently been raised and continued by the misapplication of that charity', particularly the money 'squander'd away' in 1710 to support those who were now opposing the bill.

---

66 Dendy, *Records of the Hostmen's Company*, pp.174–7.
67 *Case of the poor Skippers and Keelmen*, British Library 8223 E9(32).

Undeterred, Defoe continued his attack on the Hostmen and magistrates in *The Review*. He had 'no gain to make, nor any other end, but meet charity to the poor, sense of liberty and detecting a horrid plot upon near two thousand innocent families as well as upon trade'. The 'plot' was not only to rob but to enslave the keelmen, and so once again to make the coal trade an absolute monopoly, 'under a secret unheard of conspiracy against law, against reason, against English liberty, against right and against charity'. The Hostmen and fitters, 'famous for their late combinations with the Lightermen of London for engrossing the coal trade', found it necessary to have absolute command of the keelmen, 'and thereby of the whole coal trade', to resume their former practices. Having failed to gain control of the charity by 'infinite frauds and corrupt dealings', and fearing that some of them would be brought to account for embezzling and frauduently detaining its funds, the Hostmen and fitters, together with the magistrates, many of whom were themselves Hostmen, had entered a caveat against the keelmen's petition for incorporation, and by 'horrid and barbarous methods' set about obtaining support for the present bill. He printed in full a petition of the keelmen who had been prevailed upon to sign in favour of that measure but who now withdrew their consent, and reiterated that if the Hostmen and fitters succeeded in getting the keelmen at their mercy they would be able to 'put what price upon their coals they please'.[68]

Meanwhile opposition to the bill had arisen from other sources. In a private conversation, Richard Ferrier, a merchant and MP for Yarmouth, argued that the measure would raise the price of coal by establishing a rate of $2\frac{1}{2}\%$ on the keelmen's labour. William Carr replied that the contribution had been levied for several years without having that effect. The contribution would continue, even if Parliament failed to settle the charity, but the money would then be 'squandered away' and used when the keelmen saw fit to raise tumults and stop all trade on the river. This would affect Yarmouth as much as any other place.[69] Ferrier, however, persisted 'with much zeal' in his opinion, raised new objections, and warned MPs of constituencies which imported coal that the measure would have ill consequences. Nevile Ridley and his friends countered these assertions by arguing that the prevention of interruptions and riots would greatly benefit the coal trade. Ridley advised that this should be pointed out to the Duke of Richmond, who during the strike of 1710 had been deprived of his duty of one shilling per chaldron, and might therefore use his interest in both houses of Parliament in favour of the bill.[70] Carr won the support of another magnate, Lord Scarborough, who began to lobby for the measure.[71]

Carr expected a debate on the second reading, but, although the bill passed that stage unchallenged, opposition to it had not subsided and indeed gained

---

[68] *The Review*, 12, 14, 16 and 19 February 1712.
[69] Carr to Fetherstonhaugh, 19 January 1711/12, TWA 394/4. Richard Ferrier, c.1671–1728, was described as 'a very sensible understanding merchant', E. Cruickshanks, S. Handley and D.W. Hayton, *History of Parliament, The Commons, 1690–1715*, III, pp.1,026–7.
[70] N. Ridley to Fetherstonhaugh, 22 January 1711/12, TWA 394/4.
[71] Carr to M. White, 24 January 1711/12, *ibid.*

strength. Ferrier 'gave all the air he could' to the allegation that the former Mayor, Robert Fenwick, had attempted to force some keelmen to sign a petition concerning the charity by witholding their protections against impressment. Carr responded that Fenwick had merely required security for good behaviour from some mutineers and had not granted the protections because they were demanded when he was going to church on a state holy day.[72] Ferrier, still 'inveterately against the bill', strove to obstruct it in committee, but his efforts proved counter-productive. 'I found none there that gave it better assistance than he did', Carr declared,[73] and, if its opponents proved no more effective, the bill would easily pass the Commons. Almost immediately, however, a new problem threatened to wreck it.

The fitters announced that they intended to petition against some of its clauses and Fetherstonhaugh instructed Wrightson to halt proceedings until their case could be heard. Ridley, in alarm, immediately warned Fetherstonhaugh of the consequences: 'Your directions to Wrightson have at present put a stop to your bill (which was to have been reported this day) and if he pursue them will certainly loose it'. The fitters' proposal was so unreasonable that no one would move such an amendment. 'The paragraph they complain of', he continued, 'is so essentially a part of the bill that it will pass neither house without it, and it seems your fitters are conscious of what the *Review* complains on, or they never would be desirous to be exempted from doing the keelmen justice so'. They could be answerable only for the amount they deducted from the keelmen's wages, which 'in reason and conscience they ought to pay', and they could not be injured by the proposed penalty (double the amount in their hands) unless they detained the poor men's money. He believed that if the bill had been presented without these clauses they would have been inserted by order of the House. A nobleman who was 'most concerned for the bill' declared that it would be 'lame and ineffectual' without them. Ridley pressed Wrightson to proceed, 'but he looks upon your commands an injunction upon him and waits your further orders'. Thus, Ridley gloomily concluded, 'Mr Review hath a fair opportunity to clogg the bill with petitions'.[74] Carr was equally astonished at the fitters' stance. It was 'unaccountable' that they had not been made easy long ago, and he could not understand their objections. 'Had they not better account with their neighbours and friends', he asked, 'than be called to do it before the Barons in the Exchequer ?' – as they would have been obliged to do a year ago had he not intervened. Like Ridley, he believed that few members would consider it reasonable to omit the section concerned, even if it could be done 'without confounding the whole bill'.[75] Ridley reiterated these points: it was a pity that 'so good a bill should be lost in screening the fitters'; it was impossible that it could pass in the form that they wished.[76]Fetherstonhaugh,

---

[72] *Ibid.*; Ridley to [? White], 24 January 1711/12, *ibid.*
[73] Carr to Fetherstonhaugh, 21 February 1711/12, *ibid.*
[74] Ridley to Fetherstonhaugh, 21 February 1711/12, *ibid.*
[75] Carr to White, 23 February 1711/12, *ibid.*
[76] Ridley to Fetherstonhaugh, 23 February 1711/12, *ibid.*

who arrived in London a few days later, was now anxious that the bill should proceed, 'lett the fitters do what they will on their petition'.[77]

The petition of twenty-five fitters was presented to the Commons on 18 March. They complained that although they had applied the charity money by direction of the governing part of the keelmen during the past twelve years, the bill would make them liable to examination on oath to account 'not only for the sums they shall receive or retain, but also for the sums they have received or retained' out of the men's wages. It was unreasonable that they should be subjected to such an account 'for so longtime past as for the time to come', and made liable to the summary penalties appointed by the bill. In some cases, they might be obliged to pay the contribution out of their own money. All this was inconsistent with the ordinary usage in cases concerning wages owed by masters to servants and would be a considerable disadvantage to them in their business.[78] The Commons ordered that their counsel should be heard at the bar of the House on the third reading, when a petition of John Kerr and 981 keelmen would also be considered.[79]

The keelmen's petition was couched in terms very similar to those of Defoe's publications. They repeated the allegation that a great part of the charitable contributions had been embezzled or detained by their employers and others who knew that the keelmen could not sue unless each one brought writs against them. The bill not only established the magistrates and their successors as perpetual governors of the hospital and charity but turned a voluntary contribution into a compulsory tax upon the keelmen's labour, though, unlike the parishes, they were not obliged by law to maintain their own poor. They denied that eight hundred keelmen had signed in favour of the bill, though by threats and corrupt practices the magistrates had obtained about two hundred signatories, most of whom had now revoked their support and voluntarily signed the present petition against the bill.[80]

'Wee much question whether ever this petition was sent to be signed', one of the promoters of the bill commented. 'I wish it could be detected, which pray endeviour'. Many of the names appeared to be from several old lists, but Ferrier was proud of the keelmen's petition and was Kerr's 'humble servant'. 'Had not the fitters occasioned delay we had had none of this trouble', the writer concluded.[81] Ridley thought that both the fitters' and the keelmen's petitions were 'frivolous', but feared that 'time may make them considerable'. Another delay arose because Wrightson was unwilling to move for the third reading without Sir William Blackett whose friends might not support the measure in his absence. Ridley urgently pressed Blackett to attend, but feared that he would go to the races at Newmarket instead. 'Young gentlemen

[77] Fetherstonhaugh to White, 1 March 1711/12, *ibid.*
[78] *Journals of the House of Commons*, 17, p.141; *The Case of Charles Atkinson, John Johnson* [and others], Lincolns Inn Tracts, M.P., 102, fol. 86.
[79] *Journals of the House of Commons*, 17, p.141.
[80] Copy petition, TWA 394/57.
[81] Notes concerning the petition, *ibid.*

will mind their pleasures', he remarked, clearly annoyed at Blackett's conduct. Still, 'tho Daniell Defoe spairs no pains', he was confident of success.[82] His optimism proved to be justified. On 29 March, after the petitions against the bill had been read and counsel on both sides heard, the bill was read a third time and passed to the House of Lords.[83]

Defoe had anticipated defeat in the Commons and sought to enlist the support of his patron, Lord Harley, Earl of Oxford, to whom he had previously related the 'oppressions' of the keelmen. They were

> now like to have the government and management of their own charity subjected to the fitters and magistrates by which a new foundation also will be lay'd to influence and enslave the poor men and thereby again make a monopoly of the coal trade.

There was 'so much justice and charity in the case' that he believed Harley would gladly take up their cause.[84] The magistrates, too, canvassed for support from the peers. In reply to a letter from Fetherstonhaugh, the Earl of Sussex, mindful of 'the civility you all shew'd me when I was in Newcastle', promised to use every endeavour to forward the bill.[85]

After the second reading in the Lords, the bill together with petitions from the fitters and keelmen was referred to a committee chaired by the Earl of Clarendon. The fitters' petition, with twenty-eight signatures, was identical with that presented to the Commons except for the significant addition that it seemed unreasonable that they should be compelled against their wills and at their own cost to receive, pay over and keep accounts of the contributions.[86] Obviously, if they refused to collect the contributions the bill would be wrecked. Although it was rumoured that some of the fitters were prepared to drop their objections,[87] the main argument presented by their counsel was that they considered it 'hard to be made Trustees against our wills'.[88]

The keelmen's petition was signed by John Kerr and two keelmen on behalf of the whole body of about 1,600, who, it was claimed, if time were given, would all sign it. Besides repeating the main points of their representation to the Commons they raised the new objection that the magistrates were seeking to turn the voluntary contribution into a tax

> by means whereof about five hundred of our number who live in Scotland and other distant places must (how distrest soever they be in their own families) pay towards the support of the poor of Newcastle (which the parishes there are now by law bound to keep and maintain) exclusive to other poor keelmen in other places, which will not only be an invasion on your poor peticoners

---

[82] Ridley to Fetherstonhaugh, 13 March 1711/12, 27 March 1712, TWA 394/4.

[83] *Journals of the House of Commons*, 17, p.160.

[84] George Harris Healey,ed., *The Letters of Daniel Defoe* (Oxford, 1955), pp.332, 369.

[85] 22 January 1711/12, TWA 394/6.

[86] House of Lords Record Office, 202/31, 2891(b).

[87] Henry Liddell to George Liddell, 10 April 1712, Ellison Mss, TWA, A35/57.

[88] Historical Manuscripts Commission, series 17, *The Manuscripts of the House of Lords*, n.s., IX, pp.230–1.

peculiar right and interest, but must destroy the very end for which this charitable contribution was at first designed.[89]

There was nothing in the bill to justify the allegation that the charity was to be
applied to the poor of Newcastle who were not keelmen, nor was it intended to
limit it to keelmen who resided in the town. In fact it was stipulated that when a
vacancy in the hospital arose 'one other poor aged or disabled skipper or keelman or the widow of such deceased skipper or keelman as was usually imployed
upon the said River Tyne' should be chosen from those presented to the governors by the twenty men. The objection probably arose because the governors
were to be incorporated under the title 'the Governours and Directors of the
Hospistall Lands possessions and Charity of the Skippers and Keelmen inhabiting within the Town and County of Newcastle upon Tyne', which certainly
appeared to curtail its scope. This may have been careless drafting, without
sinister intent, but it gave the opponents of the bill opportunity to score points.
Ferrier had raised a similar objection in the Commons.[90] The petitioners' argument about Scottish keelmen was an entirely new departure, as there had never
been any question about their contributing to the fund. It is not known how
much weight the keelmen's counsel gave to these arguments. That they desired
to be 'under a governance agreeable to them' is all that is recorded of the submission made on their behalf.[91] Counsel for the bill argued that 'these sorts
of people ought to have good government and governors' and that this was a
necessary and reasonable charity.[92]

The committee made only one amendment to the bill by omitting the two
sitting MPs for Newcastle from the board of governors. The reason is not
clear, but this was likely to strengthen the magistrates' hold over the charity by
removing two persons who did not belong to their body. The Earl of Clarendon
reported that the committee thought the bill fit to pass without further amendment, but, after a debate, the motion for the third reading was defeated.[93] The
details of the debate have not been recorded, nor is it known how great was
the majority against the bill, but in view of the opposition of both keelmen and
fitters it would have proved unworkable had it passed into law.

The rejection of the bill might have appeared to be a triumph for the keelmen,
but it was a hollow victory. Their bid for incorporation, essential if they were
to manage the charity themselves, proved fruitless, and it appears that Defoe
had no further involvement with them. Although the magistrates were pursuing
their own agenda, their bill safeguarded the keelmen to such an extent that the
fitters were alarmed and opposed the measure. 'Tis a design of the magistrates
to bring them [the fitters] under a lash which has occasioned their petitioning',

---

[89]   House of Lords Record Office, 202/32, 2891(c).
[90]   Ridley to Fetherstonhaugh, 22 January 1711/12, TWA 394/4.
[91]   *Manuscripts of the House of Lords*, n.s. IX, pp.230–1.
[92]   *Ibid.*
[93]   *Ibid.; Journals of the House of Lords*, XIX, p.426.

Henry Liddell remarked.[94] Although most of the magistrates as well as the fitters were members of the Hostmen's Company, and some magistrates were actively involved in the coal trade, there was clearly tension between the two groups over the charity. A compromise between the keelmen and magistrates on the basis of the bill might eventually have been reached, but Defoe's intervention made this impossible. Moreover the accusations he levelled indiscriminately against Hostmen and magistrates naturally alienated all concerned and it is not surprising that the fitters determined to disassociate themselves entirely from the charity. Accordingly, in the course of the following year the Hostmen repealed the order under which the fitters deducted the contributions from the keelmen's wages. The stock was divided among those who had contributed to the last, but there was not enough to give every man a shilling. The scheme so successfully begun thus came to an ignominious end.[95]

---

[94] 28 February 1711/12, J.M. Ellis,ed.,*Letters of Henry Liddell to William Cotesworth*, Surtees Society, CXCVII, p.13. Liddell was here quoting an unnamed correspondent.

[95] 22 January 1712/13 and 5 May 1713, Hostmen's minute book, TWA, GU/HO/1/2, fols 604, 606; *Account of the Keelmen's Hospital* (Newcastle, 1829), TWA 1160/1.

3

The Keelmen's Charity: Attempts at Revival, 1717–70

If the keelmen attempted to carry on the charity without the Hostmen or magistrates, it soon became clear that they had no hope of success. By about 1717, some skippers and keelmen, fearing that the hospital was 'in all probability agoeing to decay without some immediate repair', petitioned the magistrates to request that a society, supported by a subscription from those keelmen who wished to benefit, be established under the governorship of the Mayor and settled by Act of Parliament.[1] The petitioners clearly did not expect all the keelmen to participate. The magistrates took no action and the matter dropped for the time being. Soon the keelmen had to endure the 'hard and tedious winter' of 1717–18 during which many of their families were 'almost starved for want of necessarys'.[2] Moreover they had many grievances against their employers and were on the verge of mutiny.[3] It is not surprising that these circumstances revived their desire for independence. Early in March 1718/19, the Hostmen were alarmed by a report that endeavours were on foot to procure an Act of Parliament to incorporate the keelmen or establish their former charity, and hastened to appoint a committee to investigate, since 'such an incorporacon or establishment, without being under a due regulacon or the government thereof in proper hands with sufficient power rightly to manage and apply the same, would be an entire ruin not only to this Company but the Corporation and trade in generall'.[4] Unfortunately the committee's report has not been preserved, but the Hostmen's alarm illustrates the connexion they perceived between the charity and industrial action.

A few years later the Hostmen were informed that the keelmen had petitioned the magistrates and Governor of the Company to manage the charity.[5] Some of the wording of what appears to be a draft of this petition (the original has not been found) is identical with one presented to the Mayor, William Ellison, in 1710, which suggests that Ellison, who again held that office, may have orchestrated this new initiative. The petitioners admitted that (presumably under Defoe's influence) they had later opposed the former representation,

> being induc'd and perswaded thereto by some keelmen and othrs who waisted and spent the said charity and did not aplie the same as was intended, whereby the said hospitall is not yett finished but that part already built will

1. Petition to Ralph Reed, Mayor 1716–17, and Aldermen, TWA 394/6.
2. Petition to Francis Rudston, Mayor, and Aldermen, presented in April 1718, TWA 394/7.
3. George Liddell to William Cotesworth, 4 May 1718, Cotesworth Papers, CP/1/45.
4. Hostmen's minute book, 1654–1742, TWA, GU/HO/1/2 fol. 664; Dendy, *Records of the Hostmen's Company*, p.186.
5. 18 February 1722/3, Dendy, *Records of the Hostmen's Company*, p.188.

go to decay without immediate repair and the people placed therein are in very great want.[6]

Most of the fitters reported that their skippers were willing that the charity should be re-established, and the Hostmen, having unanimously resolved to forward 'so good a work', appointed a committee to meet the magistrates and bring it 'to perfection'.[7] At the subsequent meeting elaborate articles were drawn up for its governance. The Mayor, Recorder, Aldermen and Sheriff, together with the Governor and stewards of the Hostmen's Company, were to be trustees of the fund. No disbursements were to be made without a written order from three trustees, one of whom was to be the Mayor or the Governor. Seven keelmen, chosen annually as overseers by keelmen electors, were to present 'objects' for charity to the trustees, and inspectors appointed by the men of each work were to keep the overseers informed of anyone in need. The keelmen electors were to appoint a clerk to keep account of the treasurer's receipts and payments. No fitter was to bind a skipper who did not consent in writing to allow fourpence per tide to the charity.[8]

The Hostmen's committee reported that agreement had been reached with the magistrates on all points except those concerning the trustees, and recommended the addition of a further five members of their Company.[9] The question had already occasioned much debate in the Company and was complicated by the fact that the Governor, Richard Ridley, who ruled in a high-handed manner and was capable of 'prodigious passion' when crossed, was himself a magistrate. George Liddell, a fellow coal owner, believed that Ridley would 'in spight of them make the comm[itt]ee and be as absolute as is possible'.[10] When Ridley predictably asserted that the keelmen wanted the magistrates to be their trustees, Liddell sensed a scheme to make the men 'entyrely dependant upon them, that for the future they will not dare to complaine of them be the cause never so great, and in case of measure, and other matters, he [Ridley] will have them at his beck'. Worse still, Liddell feared, 'in case of another rebellion they [the keelmen] may become very troublesome to the whole neighbourhood, not to say the Government'.[11] Liddell was not alone in fearing that the keelmen might become politically motivated, but such apprehensions were never realised. His notion that the magistrates aimed to curb industrial action by the keelmen through control of the charity (a view similar to that earlier propounded by Defoe) was the antithesis of the oft expressed fears of both

---

[6] Draft endorsed '1722 Peticon of the keelmen about their charity in order to have it under the management of the magistrates, Wm Ellison Esq. Mayor', TWA 394/10. The 1710 petition to Ellison is in TWA 394/5.

[7] Hostmen's minute book, TWA, GU/HO/1/2 fols 695–6; Dendy, *Records of the Hostmen's Company*, p.188.

[8] *Ibid.*, fol.696.

[9] *Ibid.*

[10] Liddell to Cotesworth, 9 September 1722 (2 letters), and 17 March 1722/3, Cotesworth Papers CP/1/56, 57, 88.

[11] Liddell to Cotesworth, 17 March 1722/3, quoting from a letter to him from [George] Iley, a fitter, Cotesworth Papers CP/1/88.

Hostmen and magistrates that under the men's own control the charity would become the source of continual mutinies. From both viewpoints the charity was perceived to be inextricably linked to the industrial sphere.

The question of trustees continued to cause 'a good deale of battleing' in the Hostmen's Company, between those who favoured the Tory magistrates and those who supported the government. Ridley insisted that the Mayor, Aldermen and Governor should be appointed, while others, especially two fitters who 'bore briskly up to him', argued for a body composed of the Governor, stewards and nine trading brethren of the Company. Eventually the Company resolved that the charity should be 'solely under the management and direction of this fraternity'. 'I think it will come to little', Liddell observed, 'for I fancy as the magistrates have not carryed it they will not push it forward; tho the Governm[en]t will have a majority among the trustees'.[12] The charity had been drawn into the political arena, but control by the Hostmen was unacceptable to the keelmen. Adam Craggs, one of the twenty men who had once helped to govern the hospital, declared in a representation to the Mayor that, contrary to the Hostmen's decision,

> the keelmen in generall (as he this supplicant dare say) would have your Worshipp and your successors to governe the same. That he and the rest of your supplicants his brethren, in conjuncon with him, prays that your Worshipp will please to aid them herein, as may seem best in your Worshipp's great and singular wisdom.[13]

Liddell's prognosis was correct: nothing came of the proposals which left both magistrates and keelmen dissatisfied.

In December 1728 another attempt was made to revive the charity. A petition to the Hostmen by about eighty keelmen on behalf of the whole body begged that no man who refused to contribute a penny per working tide to the charity should be employed, that a clause to enforce this payment should be inserted in the bonds, and that the fitters should be obliged to pay all contributions to the treasurer on specified days.[14] The Hostmen made an order complying with the request, but on 16 May 1729, 'by common consent' the order was rescinded. According to a report of nearly thirty years later, the reason was 'so well known [that it] need not now be mentioned'.[15] In the absence of more explicit evidence we can only speculate that once again allegations of misapplication of the funds had been made by one, if not by both, of the parties concerned.

In 1730 about two hundred keelmen formed a benefit society to which they agreed to pay an equal sum every six weeks, thus avoiding a potential source of discontent inherent in the former scheme whereby those who worked the

---

[12] Liddell to Cotesworth, 22 March 1722/3, Cotesworth Papers CP/1/90; meeting of the Hostmen, 20 March, Dendy, *Records of the Hostmen's Company*, p.189.

[13] 26 March 1723, TWA 394/57.

[14] Hostmen's minute book, TWA, GU/HO/1/2, fol.724; Dendy, *Records of the Hostmen's Company*, p.191.

[15] 15 December 1758, Dendy, *Records of the Hostmen's Company*, p.205.

greatest number of tides contributed most to the fund. Since the majority of the keelmen failed to join this new venture, the organizers admitted other workers, but even in this form the society did not flourish. About fifty years later, its secretary, Alexander Murray, a schoolmaster, stated that the 'honesty and care which are necessary to the thriving of such societies were wanting in this new one; so that very little was given to the distressed members and yet hardly so much could be spared as to keep the Hospital in due repair'. By 1770 'the stock was almost nothing, the building in need of every repair, not a hundred members … and of those a great number of old men, fitter to be supplied themselves, than to support others'. During the next decade, however, there were great improvements: membership rose to 240, over £200 was spent on repairs, benefits to distressed members were doubled, legacies and funeral charges were advanced, and several hundred pounds remained in stock.[16] Even if most of the members were keelmen, this represented only a small proportion of the whole body, and for many non-members overcome by sickness or old age the stark alternatives, as Murray depicted them, were to beg or starve. The 'deplorable situation of the aged and starving keelmen' who had neglected to join the society during their health and youth was, he declared, sufficient warning to others to take a wiser course.[17]

From time to time other measures had been proposed to tackle the ever present problem of poverty among the keelmen. In November 1758, the Governor of the Hostmen's Company drew attention to a big increase in the poor rate in All Saints' Parish 'occasioned as said by the great number of poor from the people in Sandgate imployed as keelmen'.[18] A committee appointed to investigate was unable to discover that the problem was due 'chiefly to the increase of poor … by keelmen', many of whose widows and poor were said to be supported by collections made in their 'societyes or box meetings'.[19] Evidently there were other groups, besides the society described above, that made provision for members' future needs, but neither these schemes nor parochial relief (in so far as it was available) provided a sufficient remedy. The committee concluded that if the former charity were revived, with the Hostmen as its 'special trustees', it would make a 'decent, constant and handsome provision' for the keelmen on every occasion. The Company ordered the trading brethren to recommend to their keelmen measures for the better support of their own poor who had become 'very numerous and necessitous'.[20] After the fitters reported that most of their men would agree to a charge of a halfpenny on every chaldron carried per tide, and that they would accept the Hostmen as trustees, the Company appointed a committee to consider heads for an Act of

---

[16] *Articles of the Keelmen's Hospital & Society* (1781), copy in the North of England Institute of Mining Engineers, Bell Collection for a History of Coal Mining, XIII, fols 532–8.

[17] A. Murray, *An Address to Young Keelmen* (1781), Bell Collection, XIII, fols 538–40.

[18] Hostmen's minute book, 7 November 1758, TWA , GU/HO/1/5.

[19] *Ibid.*, 15 December 1758 (not 7 November as stated by Dendy, *Records of the Hostmen's Company*, p.205).

[20] 19 December 1758, Dendy, *Records of the Hostmen's Company*, p.206.

Parliament, but nothing further was done.[21] Several years later, the Company ordered that counsel be instructed to devise a plan for the hospital, but this initiative likewise came to nought.[22]

Although the Hostmen lacked the ability or will to overcome the obstacles that evidently frustrated these plans, they were clearly concerned about the extent of poverty among the keelmen. A principal cause was that the many keelmen who were natives of Scotland were not eligible for regular poor relief. Even if they laboured as 'indented servants from year to year for forty or fifty years together', they could not obtain a parochial settlement in Newcastle, as their bonds did not entitle them to a settlement by hiring or service.[23] In 1770, Edward Mosley, a magistrate and fitter, stated in evidence to a House of Commons committee that it was 'the custom to pass *Scotch* keelmen and their families to their own country upon their becoming indigent'. He understood, however, that they always had relief as 'occasional poor' until their settlements were discovered.[24] This partly explains the apparent contradiction between the Hostmen's statements in 1758 that they were unable to find that keelmen were responsible for the increased poor rate, but that their poor had become very numerous and necessitous. The forced return of indigent keelmen to their place of settlement, under the Act of 1662, was given an impetus in 1740 by a serious food riot in which keelmen took a prominent part. Soon afterwards the magistrates requested the fitters to return an exact list of their keelmen with particulars of the time each had been in Newcastle and his place of birth or settlement.[25] The purpose is obvious.

In 1768 the keelmen began a new attempt at self-help. During a strike against the overloading of the keels, they obtained the services of an attorney, Thomas Harvey, who undertook to organize them into a society to fulfil the objects of the former charity and to regulate their conditions of work, particularly with regard to the keel-load. To raise funds for an application to parliament for these ends, the keelmen imposed a levy on each crew, and when some declined to pay the others enforced another strike to make them comply. The stoppage was not prolonged,[26] and Harvey, who distanced himself from these proceedings, drew up a deed of settlement to found the society.[27] The magistrates, most of whom were then actively involved in the coal trade, and the rest of the fitters, were alarmed at Harvey's influence over the keelmen, the more so because an air of secrecy surrounded his activities. Mosley noted:

---

[21] 8 February 1859, *ibid.*, p.206.

[22] 16 February 1765, *ibid.*, p.209.

[23] Murray, *Address to Young Keelmen*; evidence of Thomas Harvey, *Journals of the House of Commons*, 32, 1770, p.777. The yearly bond did not constitute proof of continuous service for a complete year. In 1822 the Court of King's Bench found that because of certain holidays allowed to the pitmen of Gateshead, and 'other exceptions by which the hiring for a year is declared incomplete', their bonds were insufficient in law to entitle them to a settlement, Bell Collection, XIII, fol. 555.

[24] *Journals of the House of Commons*, 32, p.778.

[25] 16 July 1740, TWA 394/10.

[26] TWA 394/29, and see below Chapter 8.

[27] *Ibid.*; *Newcastle Courant*, 7 May 1768.

Harvey has now such an assendance over the whole body of keelmen wch are very considerable, and apprehend w[it]h the least intimation can make them do what he please, think it too much power to be trusted with him and as the tendency of their several meetings to sign parchments the public knows not the contents of, apprehend it may be attended w[it]h dangerous consequences hearafter – as such may not Harvey be compelled to produce them. If any good meant why are not the magistrates consulted who are acknowledged even by themselves to be always ready to redress their grievances?[28]

'I have used my endeavours to come at the contents of the contract Harvey has drawn 'mongst the keelmen', William Cramlington, one of the fitters, reported to the Mayor, 3 August 1768, 'but he has enjoin'd them so strongly to secrecy that I can come at few particulars'.[29] Another correspondent likewise remarked on keelmen's secretiveness.[30] The fitters, who had heard various rumours, wished to know

if any and what deed, agreement or covenant is entered into by the several keelmen on the Tyne to compel payment of a certain sum, and how much to him [Harvey] for every new keelman that enters into the service of any fitter in Newcastle, and in case such new keelman refuses to pay, if the keelmen now employed on the said river are not bound by such deed not to allow such person or persons to work in their respective keels. If any such deed in whose hands, and to compel same to be produced.[31]

They regarded such instruments as 'highly injurious to the coal trade' and considered that if the keelmen had signed any such deeds they should, if possible, be released from them. The keelmen were 'very artfull and must be watch[e]d', Mosley later remarked. He had heard that, when 'in their cupps', they would shout 'Harvey and Liberty', and utter other 'unwarrantable expressions'.[32]

The magistrates and fitters resolved on pre-emptive action over the charity, and the Mayor therefore advised Harvey that they intended to prepare heads of a bill for that purpose. Harvey informed representatives of the keelmen of this unexpected development, but in conveying their thanks he pointed out that they were determined to proceed with their own plan to raise money, not to frustrate their masters' good intentions, but to make a necessary provision 'previous to a parliamentary sanction being obtained'. They had unanimously resolved that two covenants should be inserted into the yearly bond, one to empower the fitters to deduct from their men's wages a halfpenny for every chaldron of coal they carried, and the other to oblige payment of the resulting cash to persons appointed by the keelmen. Any keelmen who bound themselves without these covenants would incur a considerable fine. They presumed that these measures

[28] Part of Mr Mosley's evidence drawn up in preparation for appearance before a House of Commons committee in 1770, TWA 394/29.
[29] Cramlington to Edward Mosley, 3 August 1768, TWA 394/29.
[30] 28 August 1768, 394/29.
[31] 'Memorandums for Mr Moseley', TWA 394/30.
[32] Mosley to Mr Ridley, 4 January [1769], TWA 394/29.

would be acceptable to their masters.[33] 'Contrary to all expectation', however, the fitters proved unwilling to collect any money before an Act of Parliament was obtained. If there were a strike, the keelmen might demand the cash for a 'bad purpose', and it would be difficult to refuse to deliver what had been detained without such a sanction.[34] Harvey's scheme suffered a further set-back when many keelmen bound themselves without the two covenants, and realizing that it would be impossible to enforce compliance, and fearing that some men might be dismissed and a tumult ensue, he conceded that every keel-man might bind himself 'in such manner as he pleases'. He angrily castigated 'undeserving men as have no understanding nor integrity to know and act for the good of themselves and families'. He called for a list of all who intended to become members of the charity, a poor substitute for the power to oblige every keelman to contribute to it.[35] Even so, Mosley repeated his concern at Harvey's ascendancy over the keelmen: 'So much power in such a hand may be attended w[i]th difficulty to the trade, and some time or other very bad consequences'. He had taken a strong line with his own keelmen when they 'beg[ge]d and pray[e]d to be bound and taken into fav[ou]r again', telling them that he would never consent to any propositions that came from Harvey, who, from his present 'unfortunate circumstances', might be tempted to make them believe that he could do great things for them when he could not. Rather than trusting a 'stranger', they ought to have confidence in their masters, who, at their 'earnest request', were willing to make a proper application to parliament.[36] Mosley did not explain what he meant by Harvey's 'unfortunate circumstances'. Perhaps he was in financial difficulties.

A committee of fitters, aided by counsel, drew up heads of a bill to establish the charity, but the keelmen unanimously resolved that

> having agreed to a Deed of Settlement (which they intend to have estab-lished by an Act of Parliament) for a future provision &c more agreeable to themselves and better calculated for the speedy and impartial relief of their brethren and under all circumstances than the proposed heads, they do there-fore decline giving any assent to the proposed heads being made a public Act.[37]

They complained that they had not been consulted at the outset of their mas-ters' scheme, and, when the proposals were submitted to them, they were given only twenty-four hours to reply on 'so weighty a matter'. They were not being treated 'w[it]h that respect and attention due to such useful and laborious men as the nature of their case deserves'. The proposed measure committed 'the absolute superintendancy, conduct and management' of their contributions to the Hostmen, and they recalled that formerly under that management the

---

[33] Thomas Harvey to John Baker (Mayor), 23 November 1768, TWA 394/29.
[34] Harvey to the keelmen, 27 December 1768; Mosley to Ridley [4 January 1769], TWA 394/29.
[35] Harvey to the keelmen, 27 December 1768, TWA 394/29.
[36] Mosley to Ridley, 4 January [1769], TWA 394/29.
[37] Mosley to Ridley as above; 'Unanimous resolution' of the keelmen, 23 January 1769, TWA 394/29.

contributions had been misapplied, causing 'numberless instances of distress' among the keelmen and their families who did not receive 'the same pub-lick relief … in their necessities as they were intitled to by the laws of the poor'. Their masters had 'slighted or rejected' their many humble requests for re-establishment of the charity, and had now disapproved of the deed of settle-ment without specifying their objections, thus leaving no room for negotiation. Some fitters had threatened to dismiss keelmen who collected contributions to their new society.[38]

Early in January 1770, Harvey gave the Hostmen a copy of the keelmen's proposed petition to the House of Commons. The first part concerned the over-loading of the keels (see below, Chapter 8), and the remainder set forth that in cases of distress the keelmen had been 'truly miserable for want of parochial or public relief … especially as to such of them as were natives of Scotland'. They had lately established a relief fund to be raised by stoppages from members' wages, but this could not be made effectual unless the fitters were 'armed with a proper authority'.[39] A committee of Hostmen resolved that, though an Act for the relief of distressed keelmen was desirable, confirmation of the keelmen's deed of settlement 'w[oul]d be very inconvenient to the trading brethren and of dangerous consequence to the public'. Thus they determined to press forward with their own plan, despite the keelmen's many objections to it.[40] Mosley agreed to represent the fitters when the keelmen's petition came before the Commons and to oppose it, if a 'proper bill' could not be obtained.[41]

Mosley and another fitter, Thomas Waters, attended the committee appointed to consider the keelmen's petition. Mosley soon complained of Harvey's 'extraordinary windings', and feared that a long stay in London, 'with our lodgings and the good company we must consequently keep', would prove very expensive.[42] One obstacle to Harvey's plan seems to have arisen more by accident than by his opponents' design. The petition associated the Wearside keelmen with those of Newcastle against the overloading of the keels, but from the way it was summarized in the *Journals of the House of Commons* it appeared that they were to contribute to the Newcastle charity.[43] Soon a counter petition was presented from the Wearside men, denying that they had any knowledge of the Newcastle petition until it appeared in the *Votes* of the House, and stating that their employment differed greatly from that of the Tyne keelmen: they earned a 'competent maintenance' and in case of necessity they could obtain relief from their respective parishes. The proposed scheme would load them with an unnecessary charge for the relief of others with whom they neither had, nor desired to have, any connexion.[44] This representation, clearly

[38] Keelmen's resolutions, 5 January 1770, TWA 394/29.
[39] Copy of keelmen's intended petition, 5 January 1770, TWA 394/29.
[40] Harvey to J. Hedley, 8 January 1770, TWA 394/29.
[41] Resolutions 'for Mr Mosley to transact', 6 February 1770, TWA 394/29.
[42] Mosley to the Hostmen's committee, 16 February 1770, TWA 394/30.
[43] 2 February 1770, *Journals of the House of Commons*, 32, p.664.
[44] 19 February 1770, *ibid.*, p.709.

orchestrated by the Wearside men's employers, besides disassociating them from the charity, destroyed any conjunction they had with the Newcastle men against their mutual grievance of overmeasure.

Most of the evidence given to the committee concerned that matter, but Harvey stated that the charity was necessary because 'great numbers of the keelmen employed at Newcastle are natives of Scotland and from the mode of binding, hiring and service are not ... allowed to gain settlements in the Parish of All Saints where most of them reside'. Mosley admitted that Scottish keelmen and their families were sent back to their own country when they became indigent. The fitters had no objection to the establishment of a charity for the keelmen, provided it was governed by local gentlemen of rank and fortune; but they did not think that it should be left to the keelmen themselves, as proposed by the deed of settlement, to which they had other objections, and 'if it should be insisted on to have that deed ... established by Act of Parliament they must beg to offer their reasons against it'.[45]

The committee resolved that the Act regulating the measurement of keels was ineffectual and ought to be amended and that it was expedient that a bill should be brought in for the relief of the keelmen and their families residing in and about Newcastle.[46] Harvey drafted a bill to deal with both matters but, evidently on advice, altered his original plan. The deed of settlement and rules of the society already founded were to be declared void, and the money already raised transferred into a new fund to which the keelmen were to contribute 2s 6d each per year, plus a halfpenny for every chaldron of coal (king's measure) they transported. Removal of the oppression of overmeasure would enable them to afford the contributions. The fitters were to deduct the halfpenny per chaldron from their men's wages and were to keep a muster roll showing the numbers of keels, keelmen and tides worked. The fitters and collectors were to be liable to examination on oath before the Mayor and two aldermen; refusal would incur a fine of £10. Any sums that appeared to have been concealed, embezzled or misapplied were to be levied by distress. The governors of the Society were to be chosen annually from its membership and might sue or be sued. Only claims from 'proper objects' were to be considered: the ablebodied who refused to work were specifically excluded. A number of trustees (of unspecified status) were to be appointed with power to invest the funds in government or other securities.[47]

Mosley sent a copy of the bill to the fitters for their comments. Meanwhile, he would 'certainly oppose it in all its circumstances'.[48] The fitters unanimously approved his conduct. The bill invested 'a power in the hands of a sett of people who ought not by any means to be trusted' and was to be resisted 'in every particular'.[49] Mosley was confident that Harvey's 'designs' would

---

[45] *Ibid.*, pp.777–8.
[46] *Ibid.*, p.779.
[47] Copy of Harvey's bill, TWA 394/29.
[48] Mosley to the Hostmen's committee, 6 March 1770, TWA 394/29.
[49] J. French to Mosley, 9 March 1770, TWA 394/30.

be defeated, and, after receiving other letters to that effect, the fitters informed their keelmen that it was impossible that the existing bill would be passed, but, if they chose to have the charity placed under gentlemen who would see it properly administered, every effort would be made to promote it. The keelmen, however, remained determined to abide by Harvey's plan, and the fitters therefore reiterated their resolve that 'every possible opposition' should be made to it.[50] Harvey soon realized that he had no chance of success, and, to the fitters' relief, abandoned his bill.[51] As for their own proposal, the fitters concluded that 'no bill [was] much better than one disagreeable to the keelmen'.[52] Thus, once again an attempt to establish the charity on a firm basis came to nought.

[50] J. French to Lord Ravensworth, 12 March 1770, TWA 394/30.
[51] Endorsement on copy of Harvey's bill; J. Airey to Mosley, 24 March 1770, TWA 394/29. For Rose Fuller and the overmeasure question see below, Chapter 8.
[52] Airey to Mosley, 24 March 1770, TWA 394/29.

4

The Charity Established

In or about 1786, an 'acting committee' of keelmen, led by John Day and Henry Straughan, assisted by William Tinwell, a schoolmaster who had succeeded Alexander Murray as secretary of the Hospital Society in 1785, began to consider a new plan.[1] It was calculated that a halfpenny per chaldron from the crews of 355 keels each carrying eight chaldrons of coal and working on average 160 tides per year would yield £946 13s 4d, and an additional sum from keels loaded with materials such as ballast, stones and lead would bring the total to approximately £1,000 per annum.[2] Judging by the average outgoings of the Hospital Society with two hundred members over the past ten years, it was estimated that the annual disbursements from a fund with a membership of 1,000 would amount to £400 for the sick, a like sum for the aged, and £200 for widows. The number of aged in the first few years was likely to be small, and, if the £400 earmarked for their relief was invested, the proceeds could be applied to the building of a hospital with eighty rooms to house the widows and the permanently disabled.[3] The committee drew up a number of articles for government of the proposed association. The fund would remain closed for the first three years; benefits to the sick and disabled would thereafter be 5 shillings per week for a maximum of twenty weeks in a year; the permanently disabled would receive 4 shillings per week, widows £5 per annum, and both would have free accommodation in the proposed hospital. Thus a keelman overtaken by age or infirmity could look forward to 'a comfortable maintenance for life', instead of being 'forsaken by his former friends and left destitute'. As the keelmen would be under self-imposed rules, it was optimistically asserted that 'every irregularity amongst them will be cured, disturbances avoided, and peace and good order established'. Moreover, these ideals would extend into the industrial sphere:

> As it sometimes happens that causes of complaint are given to the keelmen, and they being separated from one another have not an opportunity of knowing each others' sentiments, by which means matters are often carried too far to the manifest disadvantage of all concerned; but by this Association all these disagreeable circumstances will be avoided, as the opinion of the whole body of keelmen will be easily got, laid before the Magistrates, and immediately decided.[4]

[1]   Draft plan of keelmen's institution c.1786, TWA 394/30.
[2]   Calculations, TWA 394/57.
[3]   *Ibid.*
[4]   Abstract of rules of keelmen's proposed association, TWA 394/57.

Various suggestions were made to deal with the frequent overloading of the keels, which besides being a major grievance to the keelmen would deprive the charity of revenue, as it would receive nothing from the excess coal carried. The most comprehensive proposal was that those who forced any crew to carry more than statute measure were to be fined, and that crews who accepted over-measure were to forfeit 13s 4d to the use of the hospital.[5] Probably to placate the employers, it was proposed that the crew of an under-loaded keel should also be fined, but the employers were unlikely to accept another suggestion that if the makings-out at London showed that overmeasure had been given to any ships the fitters concerned should pay one shilling for each excess chaldron.[6] Furthermore, if the keelmen did not get 'wholesome beer' when they loaded a ship they should receive 1s 4d, and they should be paid in cash for all work at the staithes.[7] It was clearly expected that besides its charitable purpose the association would regulate the keelmen's conditions of employment, a notion that had wrecked previous schemes.

The committee gave 'immediate concurrence' to a proposal by Nathaniel Clayton, the Town Clerk, that the Mayor should be governor of the society and four gentlemen of Newcastle should be included among the trustees.[8] As the scheme evolved, Clayton's influence became paramount. The draft which he eventually produced for submission to Parliament placed the government of the charity under the Mayor, certain Aldermen, the two MPs for the City, and the Governor, stewards and other members of the Hostmen's Company. The keelmen's role was considerably reduced from what they had originally envisaged, and specific proposals against the overloading of keels were replaced with the bland formula 'that some mode which shall be deemed most effectual shall be adopted by the Bill to prevent all overmeasure and any grievance or oppression arising therefrom'. Even this was controversial. Johnathan Airey, one of the fitters, contended that 'no mode whatever should be introduced in this bill in regard to Measure'.[9]

The involvement of the magistrates and Hostmen greatly increased the chance of success. Again, contrary to what had so often been the case, the project probably gained impetus as a result of industrial trouble. In February 1787, a slump in the market led many ship owners to order that, until conditions improved, their vessels should lie idle for three weeks before taking in any coal. Many keelmen, pitmen and others whose employment was thereby disrupted became 'very tumultuous' and brought trade to a standstill.[10] On 5

5   *Ibid.*
6   Draft 'plan of Keelmen's Institution', TWA 394/30.
7   Abstract of rules, TWA 394/57.
8   William Tinwell, clerk of the Keelmen's Society, to the Governor and gentlemen of the Hostmen's Company, 11 December 1786, TWA 394/31.
9   'The scheme of the bill for the relief and support of indigent keelmen, their widows and children to be brought in this present session of parliament', addressed to J.E. Blackett, Governor of the Hostmen's Company; 'Mr Clayton called with this letter'. TWA 394/29. Nathaniel Clayton (1754–1822) was Town Clerk of Newcastle 1785–1822, R. Welford, *Men of Mark 'Twixt Tyne and Tweed*, I, p.576.
10 *Newcastle Courant*, 24 February, 3 and 10 March 1787.

March, the coal owners, magistrates and fitters agreed to support unemployed keelmen, provided that all behaved peaceably and that those who had work returned to it immediately. A committee distributed money to the men and their families according to their necessities. This 'laudable conduct' ended the stoppage, but the episode highlighted the extent of poverty among the keelmen which even a temporary interruption to their employment could aggravate to a dangerous extent.[11] The need to remedy a situation that had always existed, but which was evidently growing worse, was made patently obvious.

A petition from the keelmen was presented to the Commons in February 1788. It set forth that from the nature of their work they were obliged to reside in the same parish which, when they needed relief, was either grievously burdened or could only provide inadequate assistance. As a permanent fund for their own support could not be achieved without the aid of Parliament, they prayed that a bill might be introduced for that purpose. After Clayton confirmed the facts stated in the petition, the House granted leave, and Sir Matthew White Ridley and Charles Brandling, MPs for Newcastle, and Charles Grey, MP for Northumberland, were ordered to prepare the measure. The bill was read a first and second time on 5 May, and after several unspecified amendments in committee, was passed on 23 May. A few days later it passed the Lords without further amendment, and on 11 June received the Royal assent.[12]

From 1 July 1788, 'The Society of Keelmen on the River Tyne' was constituted under twenty-one Guardians – the two MPs for Newcastle, the Mayor, Recorder, Sheriff, four senior Aldermen, and the Governor and stewards of the Hostmen's Company always being included in that number. The remaining nine Guardians were to be fitters, chosen annually by the keelmen's stewards, themselves elected by their fellows. The Guardians were incorporated and empowered to make bye-laws, provide a hospital for the destitute, give allowances for funeral expenses and grant pensions to widows. The amount of the contribution to be deducted from the wages of each crew was not to exceed a penny per chaldron of coal or other material carried. The fitters were to enter all necessary particulars on a muster roll, a duplicate of which was to be supplied to the collectors. Both fitters and collectors were liable to examination on oath, under a penalty of £10 for refusal, and in case of embezzlement or misapplication of the funds the deficit was to be levied by distress. No keelman or his dependants would receive relief without being certified as proper objects of charity by the stewards, nor would benefit be paid if the applicant had not contributed his quota for a complete year without wilful interruption. The cost of obtaining the Act (over £200) was to be a first charge on the fund and, to allow it to accumulate, no charitable disbursements were to be made before 2 July 1790. Surplus cash amounting to £100 was to be invested in public funds. Finally, the off-putters at each staithe were required to swear that to the best of their skill and judgement they would cause the keels to be 'fairly and justly

---

[11]   North of England Institute of Mining Engineers D/70; *Newcastle Courant*, 10 March 1787.
[12]   *Journals of the House of Commons*, 43 (1788), pp.201, 440, 444, 498, 545.

loaded after the due and accustomed rate of eight chaldrons to each keel'. A copy of the oath was to be filed in the Town Clerk's office and to be open to inspection by the keelmen.[13]

Although the Act gave the keelmen certain safeguards against misapplication or embezzlement of the funds, the government of the Society was placed very much under their masters' control. Besides the nine elected fitters, some of the other twelve Guardians were likely to be directly or indirectly concerned in the coal trade. Moreover, instead of being made liable to a fine for overloading the keels, the off-putters were merely to swear to load them fairly to the best of their ability. This vague formula which left plenty of room for dispute was hardly 'the most effectual mode' of preventing overmeasure. Although the off-putters could be charged with perjury if they deliberately exceeded the eight chaldron limit, the keelmen themselves could not sue, and, as those Guardians who were involved in the trade might profit from the practice, it was unlikely that they would be willing to do so. However, no time was lost in carrying out the provisions of the Act. Arrangements were made for the election of the keelmen stewards, the oath was administered to the off-putters, and William Tinwell, the schoolmaster mentioned above, was appointed to collect the contributions which were fixed at a halfpenny per chaldron.[14]

The stewards proceeded to consult the men in their respective works on several articles to be laid before the Guardians. Some of these articles concerned administration of the fund, but, as at the outset, others related to the keelmen's employment, especially the overloading of the keels and payment for certain tasks in liquor instead of in cash. The articles received general approval, though there was much opposition to a proposal that those who were employed at glasshouses, or who worked 'short tides', should pay a reduced subscription to the fund.[15] The substance of the articles was incorporated into a petition, signed by 229 keelmen, thanking the Guardians for procuring the Act, and informing them of the 'real state of the people'.[16] As there were 'constant broils' about the beer provided by the shipmasters, the petitioners called for payment of 1s 4d per keel instead, 4d of which would be applied to the fund and the rest spent as the men pleased; they were not to be 'compelled to drink it upon any account'. Likewise the petitioners requested payment in coin for work done at the staithes. As some keels were still being overloaded, they called for the appointment of an inspector 'to bring any offputter who does not fulfil his duty to justice to be punished for perjury'. They clearly expected their new Society to serve an industrial as well as a charitable purpose. The same expectation is evident in another representation to the Guardians drawn up 'in

[13] The text of the Act is printed in Brand, *History of Newcastle*, I, p.655.
[14] Draft of letter [N. Clayton(?)] to the fitters, 28 June 1788; copies of off-putters' oaths, 1–7 July 1788; notice from committee of the Guardians, 4 July 1788, TWA 394/32. Tinwell was paid 10 guineas for his services as clerk up to July 1790, £30 for 1791, the same for 1792 and £40 per annum thereafter. Guardians' minute book, TWA 394/54.
[15] Articles and keelmen's replies, TWA 394/32.
[16] Petition c.25 August 1788, TWA 394/29.

the name of the people at large' by 'the Committee of the Keelmen' (probably the body that had originated the scheme):

> We beg leave to advise from our knowledge of the people's sentiments since the passing of the Act, our own regard to justice, and a desire of preserving the public peace, that you will be pleased to order the stewards to inspect the offputters at the several staiths to see that justice be done to all parties. And that the offputter may be enabled to fulfil his oath in the execution of his office, and for the preservation of the trade in general, we hope that you, Gentlemen, whose business it is to see all concerned have their rights, will empower the offputter not to load a keel unless she swims fair.

This was not entirely straightforward. The petitioners acknowledged 'from long experience' that, according to the 'strength or weakness of the water' in some parts of the river, an additional third of a chaldron was required to put a keel down to her marks. They called on the Guardians to petition Parliament to have the keels weighed and measured either at their respective staithes or at places judged suitable to give justice to all. They also suggested that the off-putters at Sunderland should be required to take the same oath as those at Newcastle. The people would then be 'freed from a great oppression', justice would be done to everyone concerned, and the public revenue would be greatly increased. Failure to adopt such a measure immediately would 'hurt our trade, ruin the Corporation and bring the curses of the people upon us instead of their blessings'.[17] The petitioners further requested that, as the stewards were not allowed to be present at the auditing of the accounts, a clerk should be appointed to oversee all receipts and disbursements, thus enabling them to 'give the people at all times a just account of their affairs'. Finally, they raised the question of the hospital. The Guardians had discretion under the Act to build a new hospital or add to the existing one, but it was feared that, as in that building and several others elsewhere, too much attention would be paid to ornament and too little to utility.

The high hopes that effective action would result from this representation were soon disappointed. The Guardians made no attempt to prevent grants of overmeasure, or to prosecute those who overloaded the keels – complaints about this practice were still being made thirty years later. Nor did they act concerning payments in liquor, even though the fund was to benefit if they were commuted into cash. (This was agreed to be done in 1791 as a result of a strike, not through representations by the Guardians.) No action was taken about the hospital. The Guardians neither commissioned a new one nor improved the existing building which remained, without assistance from the new fund, in the care of the Society founded in 1730.

Not all the keelmen were grateful for the Act. Thirty men from several employments above Newcastle Bridge, who described themselves as 'worse than the slaves in foreign countries', their wives 'poor to a proverb', and their children 'beggars or burthensome to the contiguous parishes', resented

---

[17]   Petition, n.d., TWA 394/29.

contributing to the cost of obtaining the Act from their 'small endeavours… now too little to support our families above that…given to the weekly poor'. They did not see why they should 'crouch down under another burthen without knowing the least lawful reason for so doing'.[18] They were equally unhappy that the Guardians had power to deposit the money in the London banks and appropriate it to what use they pleased, 'as if our own corporation was not competent to be intrusted therewith'. If the beer allowance were commuted into cash, they were willing to contribute four pence per keel to the fund, but they were strongly opposed to a proposal, widely canvassed and approved by many keelmen, that this should be additional to the four pence per tide already deducted from their wages. It is not known why these keelmen were evidently more impoverished than their fellows nor whether the resentments they expressed were confined to themselves alone.

Benefits became payable under the Act in July 1790. The Guardians decreed a weekly allowance of 5 shillings to those disabled by temporary lameness or sickness, 3 shillings to those superannuated or disabled by age, 1s 6d to widows without children, 2 shillings to widows with two children and 2s 6d to those with a greater number. Funeral allowances were fixed at £2 for a keel-man, his wife or widow, and 10 shillings for a child under fourteen years of age, if the father was dead. (The Hospital Society, which continued to func-tion independently, paid out £2 for a funeral and £8 as a legacy in respect of a deceased member; the usual allowance to those in need was 2s 6d per week which compared favourably with the generally meagre relief given to paupers by the overseers of the poor in the Parish of All Saints in which most of the keelmen lived.) A further bye-law of the new Society permitted the superannu-ated and those unable to work in the keels to take other employment, but their allowances from the fund would be reduced if they earned between 4 shillings and 6 shillings per week. Those who earned 7 shillings would receive no ben-efit, and any whose wages were 8 shillings or more were to contribute sixpence per week to the fund. In July 1794 the Guardians ordered that contributions should also be made by keelmen who worked bye-tides, i.e. where the distance travelled was less than a long or 'ship tide'. A reward of a guinea was offered for the discovery of anyone who neglected to account for these tides. Offenders would be deprived of benefit for one year for a first offence, two years for a sec-ond, and totally excluded for a third.[19] The keelmen's employment in the lower reaches of the river was increasingly threatened by colliers loading directly from the staithes by means of spouts. As the revenues of the charity were con-sequently reduced, the Guardians recommended that for the benefit of the fund a charge of three farthings per chaldron should be imposed on coal loaded by spout, but, contrary to expectations expressed in the press, the coal owners declined to make this concession.[20] Heavy demands were being made on the

[18] TWA 394/29.
[19] Guardians' minute book, 1788–95, TWA 394/54; records of the Hospital Society, TWA 1160/6; Overseers' accounts, Parish of All Saints, 1777–92, TWA microfilm 349.
[20] TWA 394/54, 22 November 1794.

fund. In July 1795, besides those being assisted during temporary illness, 102 superannuated keelmen, 53 widows and 7 orphans were receiving support, and it was anticipated that the number needing relief would increase.[21] Despite these difficulties, and fears that the fund would prove inadequate to meet the demand, the scheme continued to function, unlike one on a similar plan for the keelmen on the River Wear. An Act for their relief and support was passed in 1792, but, as the men refused to make any contribution, it remained inoperative.[22] According to a letter from a keelman which appeared in the *Newcastle Courant* of 23 May 1815, other bodies of workers did not form societies similar to that of the Newcastle keelmen chiefly because if members of such bodies applied for parochial relief, the amount due from the society was deducted from what they would have received from the parish, thus leaving them no better off than the other poor. The keelmen regarded this as a great hardship. Their charity, they contended, was not established to diminish parochial relief to those eligible to receive it.[23] This, however, was open to question. The preamble to the 1788 Act stated that a fund for relief of the keelmen would effect 'a reduction in the poor rates in the parishes or townships where they are settled'; and, once the charity began to function, the authorities regarded it as the keelmen's sole source of assistance. 'Parochial relief as to keelmen is done away', the Mayor of Newcastle declared in 1803, after three stewards of the fund had been impressed for naval service and so were unable to grant certificates to infirm keelmen from their respective works. No relief was available to them until new stewards were elected later that year.[24] However, in 1822, when the fund could not meet all claims upon it, the magistrates ruled that until an allowance from it was restored, 'each parish or township in which the keelmen deprived of relief is legally settled must provide for the keelmen ... in the same manner as for other persons'.[25]

Pressure on the fund had meanwhile steadily increased. In 1815 payments to claimants amounted to £2,235 and remained at that level for the next three years while the balance against the fund rose from £47 to almost £162. By 1819 it was supporting 138 superannuated members, 182 widows, 6 orphans and 22 sick.[26] It appeared that benefits would have to be reduced unless additional income could be obtained, but, while local industries had made 'very liberal' donations to other charities, the keelmen's fund had received only £5 from that source. The keelmen concluded that they were considered of 'very

---

[21]   *Ibid.*, enclosure, 2 September 1795.

[22]   32 George III cap. 29. 'With the terms of this Act...the keelmen refused to comply or pay one farthing towards the fund; and the expences of the Act were only discharged very lately under a mandamus from the Court of King's Bench', George Garbutt, *Historical and Descriptive View of the Parishes of Monkwearmouth and Bishopwearmouth and the Port and Borough of Sunderland* (Sunderland, 1819), p. 354.

[23]   *Newcastle Courant*, 23 May 1815.

[24]   Thomas Clennell to captain Adam Mackenzie, 23 May 1803, National Archives, ADM 1/2141.

[25]   Nathaniel Clayton to Richard Nicholson and James Potts, 28 December 1822, TWA 394/46.

[26]   Abstract account of the state of the funds of the Keelmen's Society, National Archives, HO 42/196/430, and printed in A. Aspinall, *The Early English Trade Unions* (London, 1949), p.333.

little importance in the community', but for this they had themselves to blame, the above-mentioned correspondent to the *Newcastle Courant* declared, since, like others 'bred to great exertions and hardships', they were 'not so courteous nor polished as those whose business lies behind the counter and obliging customers'. He suggested that the fund might be augmented by a charge levied on coal loaded by spout, as proposed in 1794.[27]

Since that date, loading by spout had greatly increased and the consequent erosion of the keelmen's employment combined with other grievances (including overmeasure) led to a strike in 1819. As a part of the settlement eventually reached, the coal owners agreed to donate £300 to the fund immediately, and to supplement it further by a grant of one farthing on each chaldron of coal exported from the Tyne (whether transported by keel or loaded by spout). This avoided the delicate issue of a specific tax on what was loaded by the spouts. The grant was confirmed by Act of Parliament which received the Royal Assent on 8 July 1820.[28] This greatly augmented the fund, and, as coal exports increased and the use of keels diminished, it became its chief source of revenue as the following figures (ignoring shillings and pence) show:

	Keelmen's contributions per tide (including bye tides)	Coal owners' grant
1826	£1,640	£836
1832	£1,020	£823
1834	£686	£770
1836	£924	£910
1838	£847	£1013
1840	£620	£976
1842	£540	£1,015
1845	£571	£1,127
1849	£360	£1,114
1852	£281	£922
1866	£232	£1,856

The numbers of claimants and total allowances to them, including grants towards funeral expenses, were as follows:

---

[27] *Newcastle Courant*, 23 May 1815.
[28] North of England Institute of Mining Engineers, Bell Collection XXII; *Newcastle Chronicle*, 23 and 30 October 1819; *Journals of the House of Commons*, 75 (1819–20), pp.44, 145–6, 354, 423. For the strike see below, Chapter 12.

	Superannuated	Widows	Orphans	Sick	Allowances	Total Fund
1826	146	180	13	38	£2,301	£3,114
1832	126	206	13	41	£1,996	£2,745
1834	113	202	12	37	£1,753	£2,669
1836	114	202	11	26	£1,416	£2,053
1840	92	167	7	16	£1,550	£4,312
1845	78	153	3	23	£1,589	£5,406
1849	90	132	8	20	£1,564	£6,222
1852	89	120	6	25	£1,653	£5,569
1866	83	100	11	17	£2,013	£11,505

The figures given above for the total fund include balances carried over from previous years and interest on sums invested.[29] Since it was prospering largely at the coal owners' expense, and eventually far exceeding the yearly demands upon it, the owners sought to alter their contribution, especially since some of the collieries concerned in the 1820 Act had been worked out and new ones, sometimes much further from the Tyne and under different ownership, had been opened. Thus in February 1854 a bill to limit the tax to coal actually carried in keels (which was estimated at about one-seventh of the total quantity shipped from the river) was introduced in the House of Commons.[30] A correspondent in the *Gateshead Observer* denounced the 'extreme unfairness as well as folly of attempting to benefit the coal-trade by ridding it of the paltry farthing bestowed upon the keelmen' which would deprive their Society of the greatest part of its income.[31] The Guardians of the Society and the keelmen themselves opposed the bill and counsel on both sides argued at length before a committee of the House. Finally it was suggested that instead of immediate abolition, the levy should continue for seven years, and, if the number of claimants on the fund had not then decreased by half, it should remain for a further seven years at the reduced rate of one-eighth of a penny on all coal shipments. The committee amended the bill along these lines, but, although the House then ordered it to be read a third time, no further proceedings took place.[32] Presumably the coal owners decided that it was not worthwhile to procure a measure the effect of which would be so long delayed. Their contributions to the fund therefore continued, but in 1861 the Act 24 and 25 Victoria, cap. 47, abolished dues

---

[29] The account for 1826 is printed in E. Mackenzie, *Descriptive and Historical Account of Newcastle*, II, 552; accounts for 1832, 1845 and 1849 are in the North of England Institute of Mining Engineers D/70, and for 1834, 1836, 1838, 1840 in WAT/1/20; for 1852 see *Gateshead Observer*, 18 March 1854. In this last case the total fund has been calculated from the information given which might be incomplete. The account for 1866 is in TWA 394/57.

[30] *Journals of the House of Commons*, 109 (1854), pp.41, 45, 70.

[31] *Gateshead Observer*, 18 March 1854.

[32] Report of proceedings in the Commons' committee, *Gateshead Observer*, 1 April 1854; *Journals of the House of Commons*, 109, pp.164, 183.

levied by charitable corporations on ships, or on goods carried by ships, with effect from 1 January 1872.[33] The Society of Keelmen was among the charities listed in the first schedule to the Act and was thus deprived of its main source of income when the Act came into operation. Gross annual income which in 1871 totalled £2,732 fell to £1,292 in 1872, and once again expenditure began to exceed income. Besides an unspecified number of sick, the fund was supporting 61 superannuated keelmen, 89 widows and 10 orphans at a total cost of £1,617, plus £158 for management. By 1874 gross income had fallen to £790 while disbursements on 44 superannuated, 87 widows and 2 orphans amounted to £874 with an additional £111 for management.[34] At the beginning of 1875 only 68 keelmen were still contributing to the fund by the tide. A year later the number had fallen to 63, and their occupation was under imminent threat as the swing bridge which would allow ships to pass further up-river was about to be opened. Despite its unfavourable yearly balance, the Society still had capital of £11,254, accumulated mainly from the coal owners' grant and interest from investments, and it was proposed that it should be reconstituted as a friendly society 'more in consonance with the requirements of the present day'.[35] It is not known whether this idea was pursued, but so far as the keelmen were concerned the Society had served its purpose in assisting the many members of their community who fell into need.

The hospital building remained in possession of the society established in 1730, which received nothing from the money raised under the Acts of 1788 and 1820. Even so, according to an account published in 1829, the society was then in a flourishing condition with three hundred members and £600 invested at interest, but, as a result of the 'decay of the keelmen's trade', the stewards announced in 1852 that their institution was now in 'extreme poverty'. They had been obliged to discontinue allowances to the sick and apply the limited resources towards funerals of deceased members. They had no fund for repairs, and as the hospital clock, one of its prominent features, had been struck by lightning they appealed to the public for assistance.[36] In 1890 the society applied to the Corporation for extension of the lease of the ground on which the hospital stood. At least £163 was needed for repairs and the Corporation's Estate and Property sub-committee suggested that the Corporation might immediately buy out all rights of existing members and terminate the lease which was due to expire in 1898. This was evidently acceptable to the society, but, on further consideration, the committee dropped the proposal and the lease continued until its expiry when it was not renewed. The commercial value of each of the fifty-four rooms was then two shillings per week, but the Corporation decided that

---

[33] 24 & 25 Victoria, 1861, *The Statutes of the United Kingdom of Great Britain and Ireland,* 101, pp.163–182.

[34] Press cutting (appended to a booklet by William Brockie, *The Keelmen of the Tyne,* n.d., in the Central Library, Newcastle) with information supplied by the Secretary to the Treasury in response to a request by Joseph Cowen MP relating to the keelmen's charity 1864–1874.

[35] Press cutting on proposals to reconstitute the Society c.1876, *ibid.*

[36] *Account of the Keelmen's Hospital* (Newcastle, 1829); petition of the stewards of the keelmen's hospital to the Mayor, Aldermen and Councillors, 1 September 1852, TWA 394/49.

persons who had occupied rooms for at least twenty years should be allowed
to remain at a weekly rent of sixpence. This concession was extended to the
majority of the existing tenants, former wherrymen and other 'watermen'; by
this time there were no keelmen among the occupants.[37] The building still
stands, a memorial to a remarkable attempt at self-help by a body of workers
well acquainted with poverty and deprivation.

---

[37] Newcastle Corporation Estate and Property sub-Committee minute book, no.1, 5 December 1890,
p.1; 12 January 1891, pp.2–3; 18 November 1898, p.123; 8 December 1898, p.124, TWA, MD/
NC/77/1; Dendy, *Records of the Hostmen's Company*, Surtees Society, CV, introduction, lii.

5

Combinations and Strikes 1710–38

While disputes over the charity were embittering relations between the keel-men and their masters in the early eighteenth century, the men were suffering from a number of serious grievances in connexion with their employment, most of which arose from the unsatisfactory state of the coal trade. Over-production and a saturated market led to cut-throat competition among the Tyneside coal owners, while increasing shipments from Sunderland as well as from a few minor ports in Northumberland, none of which was hampered by imposts such as the Richmond shilling on each chaldron of coal exported from the Tyne, posed a further threat to that trade. Coal owners, fitters, shipmasters and deal-ers, especially the London lightermen, pursued their own and often conflicting agendas by resorting to illegal and clandestine practices which impacted on the keelmen and other workers in the coal trade. The keelmen responded by enforcing strikes, two of which during this period were particularly determined and prolonged, and attempted, albeit unsuccessfully, to form an organization to protect their interests.

In 1708 several principal coal owners on the river combined to regulate their own vend, and by restriction of wayleaves to the river and other methods sought to reduce the quantity marketed by their competitors.[1] This obviously affected the entire workforce, but it hit the keelmen especially hard. The reduc-tion of their employment was aggravated in May 1710 when, in order to raise the price at London, a combination of shipmasters detained the fleet of about seven hundred sail at Harwich, thus completely stopping coal shipments from the Tyne.[2] When at last the colliers arrived in the Tyne some of the keelmen complained that they were 'wrong'd in their turnes in ye worke'.[3] Moreover, for certain tasks the fitters refused to pay them the same rates as formerly. All these grievances added to those concerning the charity led to a strike in June 1710. In a petition to the magistrates, the keelmen pointed out the divergence of interest between the coal owners and those whom they directly or indirectly employed.

---

[1] For detailed accounts of the coal trade in this period see Edward Hughes, *North Country Life in the Eighteenth Century; the North East, 1700–1750* (London, 1952), and J.M. Ellis, 'A Study of the Business Fortunes of William Cotesworth c.1668–1726' (unpublished D.Phil thesis, Oxford, 1976).

[2] The shipmasters claimed that if they had not combined and held up the trade they would have had nothing for their voyage on account of the combination of the coal owners at Newcastle and the lighter-men at London. Cotesworth Papers, CK/3/64; cf. Hughes, *North Country Life*, p.187; Ellis, 'Business Fortunes of William Cotesworth', p.119.

[3] Minutes of the keelmen's grievances, Cotesworth Papers, CJ/3/6.

Whereas the coallowners and fitters hath contracted ore combined more like to raise the coalls in this river to the great prejeduce and hinderance of the coall traide, which great loose and damnage wee poor men are nott able to comprehend as to the great lose of her Majestyes revenous, and also to the great lose of traide in this towne and about it by the great hinderance of poor laboursome men that workes as miners in pitts and carriagemen imployed in the coal traide; but wee that are keellmen cann give a little nearer relation our owne lose, for wee may and dare declaire that it lost every skipper and men imployed in eatch keell above twelfe pounds for eatch keell or keell boat belonging to the river, and is like to lose a great deall more if some speedy course be nott taken for the repressing of soe hard and weighty a matter, for if this contract ore combination goe one, they are like to breake all traide hear and to bring this whole contry to rueine.[4]

They proceeded to demand 'the former uses and costomes of the river' in respect of several contingencies. When a ship to which they had been sent could not take in the coal immediately, they asked for 2s 6d for every lying tide below the Pace, and one shilling for every such tide above that point; if the ship was already fully loaded and they had to bring a laden keel back to the staithe from Shields, they expected 13s 4d, or a proportionate sum for a shorter journey; if they cast only part of the keel-load into one ship and the remainder into another they expected payment in both cases; and when they removed ballast from a ship they demanded the former payment of 13s 4d, irrespective of the quantity. They called for various payments if a skipper and his men were impressed to deal with a wreck, and demanded that no fitter should employ pan-boats (craft connected with the salt pans) for any work in the coal trade – another threat to their employment – on pain of forfeiting the dues to their hospital. As they were 'all like to be lost for want of beer' when they loaded a ship, they asked for the former beer allowance, or 1s 8d per keel instead. If liquor was given it was to be of good quality, for, they complained, if they received any at all, 'the seamen aboard of severall vessells gathereth all the grounds of theire drunke out bear and puts in one caske and gives us poor workemen to drinke, if never soe hott, which is the death and rueine of many [a] poor man'. Finally, they made representations about their charity as stated in Chapter 2.

In a paper evidently drawn up for William Cotesworth, secretary to the coal owners' Regulation, a person well acquainted with the keelmen explained some of their complaints and demands in greater detail.[5] In several cases they were paid in public houses kept by the fitters' servants who obliged them to buy drink, 'or they will stopp some of their money for it, and sometime for trash licq[uor] (which they must leave as well as the money for it) altho they have but one or two tides to receive'. When a ship to which a keel had been sent could not take in the coal, instead of 13s 4d the fitter would give the men only 5 shillings, out of which they had to pay one shilling 'for the cann [i.e. drink] and loaders'. They used to be paid 2s 6d for lying tides, if a ship could not be

4   TWA 394/57; cf. 394/3.
5   Cotesworth Papers, CJ/3/6.

immediately loaded, but now they received nothing. If they removed fewer than eight chaldrons of ballast from a ship, 'the fitter will pay them but what he pleases, p[er]haps 6s 8d or 10 shillings, whereas it is known and provable that they ought, and used to have, 13s 4d if they get but 1 or 2 chalders because it costs them a tide'. Thus, 'some part of these dues are lessen'd, and so not wholly paid by some of the fitters, and some of them wholly denied by all'. The fitters claimed that this was in accordance with a complicated scale of payments approved by the Common Council of Newcastle in March 1705.[6] The keelmen were to receive only 5 shillings for bringing a laden keel back to the staithe, but, if they were then ordered to another ship, they were to be paid up to a further 13s 4d, according to the location of the vessel. If they cast eight chaldrons of ballast out of a ship they were entitled to 13s 4d, but only a proportion of that sum for a lesser quantity. Some of the keelmen were said to have agreed to this scale, but the majority now contended that it had been 'clancularly done' and refused to work until they were 'righted therein'.[7]

The keelmen proceeded to block navigation of the river in a 'riotous and tumultuous manner', and 'threatened to pull down houses and to comitt other great disorders' unless their grievances were redressed.[8] The magistrates were insulted and 'opposed in a hostile manner' when they read the proclamation against riots. The Common Council petitioned the Queen for military assistance to suppress the tumults, and, to strengthen their case, pointed to the resulting 'total destruction of Her Majesty's duties and customs', but their real concern was the 'diminution of the coal trade ... to the great damage of this Corporation and the freemen and inhabitants thereof'. They therefore seized the opportunity to attack the Regulation, 'a contract ... whereby many of them [the keelmen] and their families are reduced to great necessities for want of employment', and begged the Queen to take into consideration 'such unlawful contracts and combinations ... tending to the destruction or diminution of the coal trade'.[9] The underlying problem affecting all parties was, as Professor Hughes points out, 'a glutted market, intense competition and redundant numbers', but, although the keelmen's grievances were, as he says, 'many and various', his conclusion that 'their famous strike in the summer of 1710 was not caused by the recent combination among the coal-owners' does not accord with the facts.[10]

The coal owners' policy provoked hostility in other quarters. Some of the shipmasters complained that the London lightermen would not unload their vessels because the Regulation gave a large premium to obtain preference for

---

[6]   TWA, Calendar of Common Council Book, 1699–1718, pp.150–2.
[7]   Cotesworth Papers, CJ/3/6. 'Clancular' i.e. 'secret', 'clandestine', *The Oxford English Dictionary*.
[8]   10 June 1710, Calendar of Common Council Book, 1699–1718, pp. 259–62.
[9]   *Ibid.*, p.260.
[10] Hughes, *North Country Life*, p.173. Ellis considers that the immediate cause of the strike was the shipmasters' stoppage of trade and the Hostmen's mismanagement of the charity, 'Business Fortunes of William Cotesworth', p.120. Both contributed to the unrest among the keelmen, but the strike began after the shipmasters had resumed trading, and the keelmen in their petition put the coal owners' contract at the head of their grievances. The municipal authorities, for their own ends, highlighted the contract as the cause of the strike.

ships carrying its coal. (Cotesworth later admitted that in one year the lighter-men were paid £1,250 for that purpose.)[11] It was alleged (though with what truth it is impossible to say) that shipmasters encouraged the keelmen to strike and donated cash to enable them to hold out for as long as possible.[12] The fitters too resented the restrictions imposed by the Regulation, and some of them were not displeased at the strike. Lancelot Cramlington was said to have declared that the keelmen were 'on the right of it and that the contract was a knavish thing'. Francis Armorer was reported to have said that the keelmen were 'in the right to break the contract, and he would not be the man that shoud bid them go to worke', and other fitters were alleged to have spoken to the same effect. 'I believe everything mentioned here of the fitters incouraging the former mis-chief may be proved', Cotesworth's informant later asserted, 'except that of Andrew Dick, w[hi]ch I cannot yet hear any confirmation of', though several keelmen were prepared to 'oath it' that Dick 'was one, if not the first, that bid them stopp the keeles'.[13] Dick was not involved in the Regulation and might well have been opposed to it, but soon after the strike began he complained of the disruption to his trade.[14]

After the strike had continued for more than three weeks and showed no sign of ending, the deputy Mayor called on the government for troops to assist the local forces:

> Wee have kept up and shall continue our Militia and thereby hope to preserve the town from the insults of the rioters, but cannot expect to make the naviga-con of the river free. The keelmen are in number about sixteen hundred; our Militia consists but of eight companys in the whole raw and undisciplined; if wee should make an attempt upon the rioters with them and be repulsed, wee are afraid it would be of very ill consequence ... We think that eight com-mpanyse of regular troops with our own forces may be able to disperse and suppress the rioters and free the navigacon.[15]

The government promised troops and ordered that the Northumberland militia should be raised. However, the Newcastle magistrates did not think it reasonable to put the County to expense without absolute necessity, and there-fore suggested that the force be disbanded but kept on the alert for instant recall. They wished the Northumberland magistrates to issue warrants for the arrest of vagrants, 'for we are very apprehensive that many Scotch young fellows, who come hither to work att the keels for the summer only, will upon sight of the regular forces make their escape into your County'.[16] These migrant workers

[11] Evidence to House of Commons committee, 1711, Cotesworth Papers, CK/3/64.
[12] Cotesworth Papers, CJ/3/6; Anne Clavering writing to James Clavering, 5 September 1710, declared that the shipmasters had 'spirited up [the keelmen] to rebellion and the fitters [with] them', H.T. Dickinson, ed., *The Correspondence of Sir James Clavering*, Surtees Society, CLXXVIII (1967), p.95.
[13] Cotesworth Papers, CJ/3/6.
[14] 9 June 1710, Cotesworth Papers, CJ/3/2.
[15] Nicholas Ridley to the Secretary of State, 23 June 1710, SP 34/12/101.
[16] Jonathan Roddam, Mayor, to Sir John Delaval, 6 July 1710, SP 34/12/120.

were 'ready on all occasions to raise tumults and riotts'.[17]

Any keelmen who attempted to work were soon intimidated. A mob of more than one hundred women, armed with sticks and clubs, threatened to kill the crew of a keel laden with lead if they proceeded further. Several men boarded another keel and confined one of its crew in the stocks in Sandgate. Another man was beaten and condemned to death by a keelman posing as a judge.[18] Others uttered threats that were bound to raise alarm in the town and neighbourhood. One boasted that they would 'turne levellers' and seize provisions that came into the market; another that they would stop supplies coming in from the countryside and starve the town.[19] The keelmen would not allow pan-boats to proceed to the salt works until their owners or skippers had executed a covenant with a penalty clause against conveying coal to the ships. The covenants were made to John Kerr, steward of the hospital, which illustrates, once again, the close connexion between the charity and the men's industrial concerns.[20] Some colliers left the Tyne and loaded at Sunderland, but the coal owners kept their pitmen at work to prevent them joining the keelmen.[21]

It was alleged that a ballad, 'The Keelmen's Lamentation', printed by Joseph Button, a stationer and bookseller of Gateshead, was 'stirr[ing] up the … keelmen and others to riots and tumults'.[22] Button was a friend and correspondent of Daniel Defoe,[23] who may have been the author of this item. Henry Liddell, probably referring to it, complained that it 'plainly tends to the keeping up of turbulent spirit among the poor thoughtless crew, whilst no reall advantage seems to be designed them'. Later he mentioned that Defoe was suspected to be the author of a 'print' which encouraged 'a refractoriness among that sort of people'.[24] Unfortunately, no copy of the 'Lamentation' seems to have survived.

The magistrates intended to take 'the most proper method for opening the trade and preventing any further mischiefs' as soon as they had the assistance

---

[17] Draft affidavit of John Harrison, 2 November 1711, TWA 394/3.

[18] Affidavits of John Grant, William Cragg, James Weatherhead and Richard Humble, James Johnson and Daniel Mackenzey, June–July 1710, TWA 394/3; Cotesworth Papers, CJ/3/5.

[19] Copy information of John Punshon, Hostman, 23 June 1710, Cotesworth Papers, CJ/ 3/5.

[20] Affidavit of William Varey, Notary Public, 8 November 1711, TWA 394/3. Varey and his clerk drew up the covenants.

[21] Anne Clavering to James Clavering, 5 September 1710, Dickinson, *Correspondence of Sir James Clavering*, p.95. Big ships unable to enter the harbour at Sunderland loaded at sea, which favourable weather allowed them to do. Ever since, 'in the best of the season' they did likewise, 'which hath greatly increased the coal trade at Sunderland', Earl Grey Papers, V, Miscellaneous Book 6, fol. 274c.

[22] Deposition of Thomas Barr, 20 June 1710, quoted Francis Manders, 'The Tyneside Keelmen's Strike of 1710: Some Unpublished Documents', *Gateshead and District Local History Society Bulletin*, No.1 (1969), p.10.

[23] Richard Welford, 'Early Newcastle Typography 1639–1800', *Archaeologia Aeliana*, 3rd series, III (1907), pp.16–17.

[24] To William Cotesworth, 21 November and 4 December 1710, J.M. Ellis, ed., *The Letters of Henry Liddell to William Cotesworth*, Surtees Society, CXCVII (1987), pp.11 and 13.

of regular troops,[25] but even after six companies of the Earl of Hay's regiment arrived, the Mayor had to admit failure.

> We have used all methods as well before as since to oblige the keelmen to goe to work but hitherto we have not been able to doe it for they abscond and goe from their houses. We have secured some of them and hope to take more of those rioters today. We have examined and considered some of their complaints which relates to their wages which they wou'd have encreased beyond what has been paid them these thirty years with severall extravagant demands not in our power to grant them. We have given them under our hands that they shall have their just and usual wages and all other reasonable demands soe far as it is in our power to grant, yet this will not prevail with them to goe to work.[26]

After the remainder of the regiment arrived, the magistrates and officers 'labour'd very much' to settle the dispute and eventually, 'with great difficulty', prevailed.[27] By this time weary of the strike, the keelmen declared that they 'only wanted right concerning their wages', and on being assured that they would be 'wrong'd no more', they agreed to resume their labours.[28] The strike had lasted almost seven weeks and must have involved great hardship for the men and their families in a year when their earnings had already been reduced by the actions of both coal owners and shipmasters. The interruption of the coal supply to London led to an investigation by a committee of the Privy Council on the proper means of furnishing the City with coal and regulating the trade. Representatives of the keelmen who brought their grievances before the committee were said to be satisfied.[29] The coal owners, who, unlike the London lightermen, escaped censure, declared that they had made everything 'so easie' to the shipmasters that 300 sail was ready to depart, while many other ships were being loaded with expedition by the keelmen who were again hard at work.[30]

Following the strike a table of the keelmen's wages was drawn up on parchment and signed by the magistrates and fitters.[31] The sums to be paid according to the distance travelled were clearly set out and provisions were made for various contingencies. The keelmen won some concessions. They were to receive full dues when a laden keel had to be returned to the staithe, and if they cast only part of a keel-load into a ship they were still to be paid in full. Payment for lying tides was also specified, and no fitter was to employ pan-boats on pain of forfeiting the dues to the hospital. However, the keelmen failed to gain any concession on their chief grievance, the curtailment of their employment. On the contrary, about four months after the strike, the members of the Regulation

---

[25] Jonathan Roddam to Sir John Delaval, 6 July 1710, SP 34/12/120.
[26] To the Secretary of State, 11 July, SP 34/12/126.
[27] Roddam to Secretary of State, 21 July 1710, SP 34/12/144.
[28] Cotesworth Papers, CJ/3/6.
[29] Privy Council Register, PC 2/83/24, 26; J.C. Boyle to Roddam, 1 August 1710, SP 44/109.
[30] Privy Council Register, 26 July 1710, PC 2/83/35.
[31] TWA 394/3.

agreed to reduce by 8% the number of keels they employed.[32] This, Henry Liddell believed, would 'contribute to make matters go more glibly in several respects' and help to 'remedy the complaints under which the trade groan'd this last year'. He hoped that by prudent management the keelmen would be 'brought to reason and see what is their true interest, ... the joining in with their owners and endeavoring to serve their interests with zeal'.[33] For the new season 260 keels were to be employed within the Regulation, and fitters who kept more in service than their respective coal owners allowed would receive no rent for them. Likewise, the rent would be forfeit if keels within the Regulation carried any non-members' coal.[34] All these measures directly or indirectly affected the keelmen, but the coal owners left the task of managing them to the fitters. 'The fitters have taken the properest measures with the keelmen from whence I can't but expect the desired success', Liddell wrote, 23 December 1710. ''Tis much better that the owners don't appear in 't'.[35]

Even so, the coal owners were soon in serious trouble. The disruptions to the trade during the past year and price increases in the London market raised public clamour, and a bill was introduced into the Commons to dissolve the present and prevent future combinations of coal owners, lightermen, masters of ships and others to advance the price of coals. The coal owners raised a fund and sent William Cotesworth to London to safeguard their interests.[36] They petitioned against the bill, which, they claimed, would put them under insuperable difficulties and tend to discourage the trade.[37] The keelmen were at first included among those whose combinations were to be prohibited, but, as the measure progressed through the House, they were omitted, presumably because they did not act to raise the price of coal.[38] Although it was objected that no provision was made to prevent keelmen or other workers combining to distress the trade in order to gain an increase in wages,[39] the bill was not amended, and finally passed into law (9 Anne cap. 28). It declared all contracts for the engrossing of coals, or hindering their free purchase or sale, to be null and void. From 1 June 1711 coal owners who entered into such a contract became liable to a fine of £100 for each offence, while fitters and shipmasters would incur fines of £50 and £20 respectively.[40]

Before the Act was passed, Cotesworth claimed that the coal owners' combination had been dissolved,[41] but it continued to exist clandestinely until 1716

[32] Minutes of the Regulation, 22 November 1710, Cotesworth Papers, CK/3/9.
[33] To Cotesworth, 4 December 1710, Ellis, *The Letters of Henry Liddell to William Cotesworth*, p.13.
[34] Minutes of the Regulation, 6 December 1710, 6 January 1710/11, Cotesworth Papers, CK/3/11, CK/3/13.
[35] To Cotesworth, 23 December 1710, Ellis, *The Letters of Henry Liddell to William Cotesworth*, p.21.
[36] Minutes of the Regulation, 12 March 1710/11, Cotesworth Papers, CK/3/18.
[37] 13 April 1711, *Journals of the House of Commons*, 16, p.594.
[38] 3 March 1710/11, *ibid.*, p.531.
[39] 'Remarks on the Coal Bill', 21 March 1710/11, Cotesworth Papers, CK/3/50.
[40] *Statutes at Large*, III (London, 1758), pp.768–70.
[41] Rough notes by Cotesworth, Cotesworth Papers, CK/3/54.

and possibly longer.[42] In December 1713 its members again agreed that each of them at his discretion would reduce his keels,

> always remembering that a superfluous number of keels starves their men and forces the skippers to get fit tides of such people as hires none, which enables those people to injure the trade of the gentlemen concerned in the Regulation.[43]

This was unlikely to be understood by redundant keelmen, nor would they, or other workers, appreciate the oft-used argument that without regulation the collieries producing inferior coal would be forced to close, resulting in massive unemployment and throwing the market into the hands of the few owners of a superior product.[44]

Despite the 1711 Act, coal owners and others concerned in the trade continued to form combinations from time to time, and the keelmen inevitably suffered from the restrictions they imposed. Such alliances tended to be highly unstable on account of the conflicting interests of the participants, and the keelmen's hardships were sometimes exacerbated by unfavourable weather as in the 'hard and tedious winter' of 1717–18.[45] When trade tardily began in the spring that year it was further interrupted by storms.

> We have had a new winter begun of late [George Liddell wrote to Cotesworth, 23 March 1717/18]. You know well eno' what great winds we have had of late, yet on Wensday night our keels went down in order to cast on Thursday morning, but finding the wind likely to rise, such as could did cast and severall that could not were sunk and none got up till Friday morning. On Friday night it rained till ten violently and betwixt that and 5 in the morning it snow'd furiously so that it laid a foot thick on the ground and a storm of wind at the East by which many keeles were sunk.[46]

Even when the weather improved, the volume of trade continued to be restricted. The shipmasters wished to establish a system of loading and delivering in turns, and therefore proposed that the coal owners should refuse to supply ships that came without certificates showing compliance with this arrangement, or else impose an additional charge of two shillings per chaldron. George Liddell and some other principal coal owners were not averse to this. Liddell was anxious lest the shipmasters should fall into the dealers' hands, and predicted that 'except something of this kind be done they infallibly will'. The coal owners as

---

[42] Although P. Cromar states that the Regulation broke up through internal disagreements in 1715 ('The Coal Industry on Tyneside, 1715–1750', *Northern History* XIV, 1978, pp.193–207), J.M. Ellis believes that while its effectiveness had diminished by 1716 it continued to exist in some manner perhaps up to 1719, and that the threat of a wayleave bill was more important than disagreements between the parties in its demise (Ellis, 'Business Fortunes of William Cotesworth', pp.128, 138).

[43] Minutes of the Regulation, 10 December 1713, Cotesworth Papers, CK/3/38.

[44] Ellis, 'Business Fortunes of William Cotesworth', p.112. That the contention was not necessarily correct is shown by the fact that, after regulation of the trade collapsed in 1845, inferior coal outsold the best. Paul M. Sweezy, *Monopoly and Competition in the English Coal Trade 1550–1850* (Cambridge, MA, 1938), p.128.

[45] Petition of the keelmen, April 1718, TWA 394/7.

[46] Cotesworth Papers, CP/1/26.

well as shipmasters would then become the dealers' slaves, but he was reluctant to become directly involved in an illegal combination. He therefore suggested that the shipmasters should approach the fitters, who, with the tacit blessing of the coal owners, could make some excuse to avoid loading the ships of recalcitrant masters, or of 'interlopers' who came only 'when the prize is inviting'.[47] Those involved in the trade at Sunderland, whose co-operation was essential to success, agreed to participate in the scheme.[48] Even so, the state of the London market continued to raise problems for the northern producers. 'I am not a little provok't at the Agents above for setting so high a price on coales at the market which has done great disservice to the trade', Liddell wrote, 4 May 1718, '… If they do not lower their price they must break of course, for, as all staiths are full, the whole country would be in a rebellion if ships should not be dispatched as soon as they come in'. The keelmen, he added, were 'ready for a mutiny'.[49]

In a petition to the magistrates they complained that they had suffered the hardships of the winter in hope of a prosperous trade to come, but now their expectations were entirely frustrated, 'for the coaleowners fitters and shippmasters have combined together in a Contrait (as they call it), by which our keeles are not onely consined to lye by for one halfe the year idle, but also when shipps doe come must not be loaden out of their turnes'.[50] Moreover, 'the keeles are obleiged to carry near tenn chaldron for 8, or … sunck 4 inches above the plate that they may make out double coales att London' (which was achieved by overloading the keels so that they sank far over the plate that marked the 8 chaldron limit). To give more for the same rate was obviously a more flexible means of lowering the price than a straightforward reduction which would be difficult to reverse, but for the keelmen it involved much extra labour without pay, besides the danger, especially in stormy weather, of navigating overloaded craft; and, as the ships were filled in fewer keel-loads than normal, the men's earning power was at the same time being curtailed. Thus they denounced the practice as 'contrary to Law and Justice, and not onely to the oppression but to the utter ruine' of themselves and their families.

The magistrates and fitters managed to avert a strike on this occasion, but a year later, in May 1719, they were faced with mutiny on an unprecedented scale. The trouble originated in Sunderland where, 'on pretence [that] their accustomed wages are too small', the keelmen, about 800 in number, struck and made 'such extravagant demands' as all concerned with the trade considered 'not fitt to be complyed with'. The strikers disregarded the proclamation against riots and, as the civil authorities were powerless to curb them, continued to act 'in a riotous and dangerous manner'.[51] Almost immediately the Newcastle keelmen

---

[47] To Cotesworth, 6 April 1718, Cotesworth Papers, CP/1/33; to Sir Henry Liddell, 18 and 20 April, CP/1/38, 39.

[48] George Liddell to Cotesworth, 27 April and 2 May 1718, Cotesworth Papers, CP/1/43, 44. He was, however, uncertain whether the owners and fitters at Sunderland would co-operate fully with the scheme.

[49] Liddell to Cotesworth, 4 May 1718, Cotesworth Papers, CP/1/45.

[50] Petition of the keelmen, April 1718, TWA 394/7.

[51] Mr. Robinson to Secretary of State, James Craggs, 15 May 1719, SP 35/16/ 62(1).

joined in the dispute. 'The keelmen here upon the River Tyne did about four-teen days ago enter into a combination with those at Sunderland upon the River Weere that they will not go to work … without a great increase of their wages … and they insist upon other exorbitant demands', the magistrates reported on 16 May.[52] They sent for those who, they believed, governed the rest, but they either hid or refused to attend. Apart from arresting and imprisoning some who were most active and abusive, the magistrates claimed that they had not proceeded rigorously, as they hoped to persuade the men to return to work. As at Sunderland, the keelmen were too numerous for the townsmen to suppress, and, if they remained obstinate, military assistance would be required; but the magistrates believed that the men's combination was made 'with a view to their private interest only, without any design of disturbing the publick peace of the nation'. This sober assessment stood in sharp contrast to the alarmist view of John Hedworth, a County Durham magistrate, who urgently called on the government to send troops to protect Sunderland.

> Tho' I cannot yet call it a rebellion [he wrote on 15 May] yet as so great a number as eight hundred men upon the Were, and two thousand upon the Tine are above the reach of the civil power, it is uncertain how long such a body made desperate by their obstinacy and poverty may contain themselves within any legal bounds.

He believed the 'rising' was 'calculated w[i]th a further view to distress the City of London by putting an entire stop to the coal trade at a most dangerous time, if it had not pleased God to have disappointed our enemys … I really apprehend that they now want only a leader to hurry them into the most violent extreams'.[53]

The landing of a small Spanish force in Scotland and the rising of some Highlanders fuelled such fears, but, while there was good reason to dread the consequences of a long strike by so large a body of men (though the Tyne keelmen numbered 1,600 rather than 2,000), there was no evidence that they were disaffected or that they sought to exploit danger to the state. William Cotesworth and George Liddell were anxious to contradict such allegations which they suspected had been made to obtain a military force to deal with 'w[ha]t has been called the keelmen's rebellion':

> We understand yt it has been represented the disturbance the keelmen have given at this time is in favour of the rebellion now on foot against the state, the more readly to prevaile for the assistance of the military power. If it prove true yt any have so done, we think our selfes bound to set yt matter in a right light and to pray yt the Lord Justices [of the regency] may be told w[ha]t is the truth, that the keelmen in this river have not at any time in our memory shewn any disaffection to the present Happy Settlement but on

[52] Magistrates of Newcastle to Craggs, 16 May 1719, SP 43/57.
[53] SP 43/57.

the contrary have always expressed a hearty zeal for King G[eorge] and his gove[rnment].

The high proportion of Scotsmen among the keelmen naturally raised suspicions that they might espouse the Jacobite cause, but Cotesworth and Liddell obviously remembered that 700 keelmen had volunteered to defend Newcastle against the rebels in 1715 and had promised to raise more recruits if need arose. Industrial action by the keelmen, or other groups of workers in the north east, was never politically motivated. The 'conspicuous loyalty' of the workforce was a central feature of the region.[54]

Cotesworth and Liddell proceeded to point out the main cause of the strike:

That the keelmen in both rivers have very imprudently and unjustly as well as illegally and yt in concert with each other put a stop to the coal trade of both rivers is very true and have by violence hindered some very small number from working, but it is chiefly on pretence yt they cannot subsist their families without an encrease of their wages by reason of the agreemt the masters and owners of ships are come to to contract their time of trade into less compass.

The fitters had no intention of yielding to the strikers' demand for higher wages. The rates that had been paid time out of mind were always considered to be sufficient, indeed 'very great', they contended, and if increased would probably be more than the trade could bear. To demands that payment for lying tides should be 'as formerly was the custom of this river', and that when a laden keel had to be brought back to the staithe the crew should receive 13s 4d 'as formerly', the fitters replied that the rates settled by the magistrates for both contingencies 'some time ago' had always been paid, and would continue to be.[55] The keelmen, however, categorically declared that payments for lying tides had been abridged 'as of laite'[56] and, despite the fitters' assurances, it seems that the terms of the 1710 settlement were being evaded. As to the complaint about the overloading of the keels, the fitters claimed that the measure given was no greater than usual. If the keels were overloaded at any staithe, they wished that some method could be devised to prevent it, but the keelmen ought to have adopted other means than a strike to gain redress.[57]

The keelmen also complained that the fitters' servants at the staithes abused and oppressed them 'beyond all reason'. They monopolized the keels 'so that another man cannot gett a tyd amongst them', appropriated the craft for their

[54] To Sir Henry Liddell, 24 May 1719, Cotesworth Papers, CJ/3/8–12. According to an endorsement on this copy, Cotesworth wrote the letter but George Liddell signed it 'in both our names'; Leo Gooch, *The Desperate Faction? The Jacobites of North-East England, 1688–1745* (University of Hull Press, 1995), pp.43–4; Richardson, *The Local Historian's Table Book*, I, p.349; Gwenda Morgan and Peter Rushton, *Rogues, Thieves and the Rule of Law, The Problem of Law Enforcement in North-East England, 1718–1800* (London, 1998), p.218.

[55] TWA 394/57.

[56] 'The Second Remonstrance and Demand of the Keelmen', TWA 394/7; another version, with some variations, and comments by Cotesworth, Cotesworth Papers, CJ/3/8–12.

[57] TWA 394/57.

own purposes, and, to the detriment of the regular skippers, employed men for that position who did not have the requisite skill. Lives were being put at risk, as these substitutes were not 'cappable of ther labour'. The keelmen claimed that they had to pay the fitters' men twenty pence 'for every tyd that is served them by any keell or boat out of his masters employment' (a practice known as going 'fitt tides').[58] A well-informed observer confirmed that this was indeed the case, 'the fitters' men recovering 20d p[er] tide for fitt tides or refuse to imploy them, and the same for stirring [i.e. steering] a keel wch is takeing the advantage of the poor men's [necessity]'.[59] The fitters replied that they did not allow their servants 'to take or receive any money of the keelmen for going fitt tydes, and if their servants do receive any such money it is at the desire and request of the s[ai]d keelmen'. However, they promised to prevent such practices, which were greatly disadvantageous to themselves.[60]

In a second and fuller 'remonstrance' the keelmen repeated their demands and complaints, especially that they were 'so much oprest by reason of the long contrak made by our respescktive fitters and masters of ships and others … that we are not able to subsist and maintain our selves and familys, our wages being so low, and the measure so great'.[61] Therefore 'by a generale consent of all and every of our Sosiety of Keellmen', they called for an additional 4 shillings per tide for every full keel-load they cast and 2 shillings for half that quantity. They repeated their demand for full dues (13s 4d) 'that formerly we used to have' when they had to return a fully or partly laden keel to the staithe, and likewise full dues, 'as formerly', for every keel-load of ballast they removed from a ship. They also asked for one shilling for shifting a ship from the quays, and beer 'in time of heaveing the coals' or sixteen pence instead. Finally, they demanded 'that every on[e] of our forsaid Sosiety of Keellmen that is now in close prison, and women besid, shall be released and sett at liberty, and all old feeds and emnitys taken away… this is what we have all consented to, with a generall consent, without any objection at all'. In another version of their 'remonstrance', the keelmen expressed their solidarity in even stronger terms:

> Every one of us has agreed that in case any of our respective fitters make any objection against any thing herein mentioned and take any advantage at any of our forsead Socyiety of Keellmen and discharg that person or persons so accused from his imployment, that in that and such like cases we have agreed that no keell shall move from his place till that person or persons … so objected against be restored to his former station, unless that a mor lawfull reason cane be shewed.[62]

What was this Society of Keelmen which seems suddenly to have come into being? Earlier in 1719 the keelmen had evidently attempted to renew their bid to obtain incorporation, ostensibly for the purposes of their charity. The Hostmen

[58] Second Remonstrance, TWA 394/57.
[59] Cotesworth Papers, CJ/3/8–12.
[60] TWA 394/57.
[61] TWA 394/7.
[62] Cotesworth Papers, CJ/3/8–12.

predicted 'entire ruin not only to this Company but to the Corporation and trade in general' if the keelmen gained such independence,[63] but whatever efforts the keelmen made for that purpose evidently failed, and the Society to which they now referred was an entirely new initiative to form what was in effect a trade union. The keelmen on the Wear, who had no concern in the Newcastle charity, appear to have been the prime movers in the combination under articles drawn up by Richard Flower, a schoolmaster of Bishopwearmouth, who had instigated the strike at Sunderland. The articles were probably destroyed to prevent them falling into the hands of the authorities who were anxious to obtain Flower's draft 'to fix it upon him'.[64] Another piece of evidence that might have thrown light on the affair has also disappeared: only the cover remains of a letter from the Sunderland keelmen to those of Newcastle 'to incourage them in their design of refuseing to work'.[65] There was certainly solidarity between the two bodies. 'Mr Hedworth has been twice at Sunderland to accomodate this difference but without success', wrote John Makepeace, who was involved in the coal trade there,

> for the menn not only insist upon three shillings advance each tyde but that the keelmen's demands at Newcastle be likewise comply'd with, for several [ship]masters to be dispatched offer'd to give it at this time, but they were so farr from embraceing it that they had the impudence to demand bond from them and all masters they load to submitt to this imposition.

Makepiece saw no prospect of a speedy end to the dispute and lamented the injury to his business which had already suffered (as had the keelmen) from the effects of the contract, cross winds and other delays, to which was now added 'the most fatall of these, mutinous keelmen'.[66]

Although the Newcastle magistrates claimed that they had not proceeded with rigour against the keelmen, William Cotesworth considered that their actions had made it more difficult for the employers to achieve a settlement.

> We have taken great pains to bring the men to the labour they bound themselves to last Christmas by fair means [he wrote to Sir Henry Liddell, 24 May] but the violence the magistrates used at the first by comitting them to jayle has so exasperated them yt all our gentle methods have failed, tho' we did yesterday at a meeting the keelmen desired at Pratts in conjunction with a few of the cheife fitters and some of the most considerable [ship]masters agree and promise to redress all their grievances and to comply with every thing except an encrease of their wages, and we also recommended it to them to perform the agreement they had at present subsisting and next Christmas, if they did not like the terms then, not to hire themselves, but nothing we

[63] Hostmen's minute book, 5 March 1718/19, TWA, GU/HO/1/2, f.664; Dendy, *Records of the Hostmen's Company*, p.186.

[64] De La Faye, Secretary to the Lords Justices, to John Hedworth, 23 July 1719, SP 44/281/164–5.

[65] TWA 394/10.

[66] Makepeace to Gilbert Spearman, 17 May 1719, Durham University Library, Archives and Special Collections, Shafto Papers, 494.

could say would take any effect so yt we must now waite to see the issue of the military power and the poor men's better consideration of the kindness we have shewn them.[67]

The central authorities, however, fully endorsed the magistrates' action and ordered that those arrested, 'which it is taken for granted will be as many as you can secure', should be kept 'in safe custody ... and particular care taken that they do not escape'. Informations against them were to be passed to the Solicitor to the Treasury 'that care may be taken for prosecuting the rioters with effect'.[68] Captain Delaval, commander of HMS *Gosport*, was ordered to receive from the magistrates at Sunderland and Newcastle 'such keelmen as they shall have to send on board you for His Majesty's service'.[69] The magistrates, too, considered that impressment of the ring-leaders and 'chief abettors of the tumult', against whom they had issued arrest warrants, together with protection of those willing to work, would be the only means of ending the strike. Negotiations, after a promising start, had ended in deadlock:

> Several of ye keelmen on behalf of themselves and brethren appeared before us complaining of some grievances from the fitters (who were likewise present) which were adjusted by us to all their satisfactions. On these occasions wee pressed on them their duty to his Maj[es]tys Governmt and the hazards they were in by continuing to stop the trade and navigation of this river in so tumultuous and riotous a manner and therefore urged them to work according to their bonds, whereupon some hundreds of them assembled together and after their deputys had reported to them what pass'd with us, they by a vast majority sent us word they would not work till they had additional wages of four shillings p[er] tide which annually in this port would amount to six or seven thousand pounds, a burthen too great for the coal trade to bear as we apprehend, so we are at a loss what to do.[70]

The keelmen too were evidently perplexed as it became clear that they would not gain the four shillings they demanded, while their imprisoned brethren were in danger of impressment into the navy or severe punishment. Thus in a third 'remonstrance' addressed to the magistrates they expressed willingness to return to work provided the keels were not overloaded and that various demands made in their previous representations, mainly for restoration of payments formerly made, were granted. They did not mention their demand for an additional four shillings, but insisted that 'the prisoners must be releiv'd'.[71] This was now their prime concern. 'We have apprehended and committed to prison two of ye keelmen who were esteemed the most active and whose example and authority did very much influence the rest', the magistrates reported on 4 June, 'which had so good an effect that afterwards application was made to us by a considerable

[67] Cotesworth to Sir Henry Liddell, 24 May 1719, Cotesworth Papers, CJ/3/8–12. See n.54 above.
[68] De La Faye to the Mayor and other magistrates of Newcastle, 21 May 1719, TWA 394/7.
[69] Dispatch from Admiralty to Captain Delaval, 22 May 1719, John Robinson, *The Delaval Papers ...* (Newcastle, n.d.), p.144.
[70] Magistrates to Secretary Craggs, 30 May 1719, SP 43/57.
[71] TWA 394/7.

number of them who offered for themselves and the rest to go quietly to work if we would discharge those whom we had committed to prison'. The imprisoned ringleaders were evidently two of four men named in an arrest warrant as the 'cheif & principall promoters, incouragers, aiders & abettors of the said combination, disturbances & tumultuous assemblies' who had collected 'severall sums of money' to continue the combination and support themselves. Two of them had been members of a deputation which, as Cotesworth reported on 24 May, had met the chief fitters and some of the principal shipmasters but refused their terms and held out for increased wages. It is not known, however, whether these were the two imprisoned. The keelmen's demand for the immediate discharge of the prisoners was not confined to their leaders, but included all men and women being held on account of the strike and the disturbances that accompanied it. They also called for pardon of 'all offences given by any skipper or keelmen or by their wifes or any other person in their favour'. The magistrates replied that they had express orders from the government to the contrary, but promised that, if the men resumed work and behaved themselves, they would intercede with the Lords Justices, who in the absence of the King jointly exercised the powers of regent, that all prosecutions against them might be stopped. This undertaking, together with some other concessions, proved sufficient 'After consultation with their fellows', they submitted, and on 3 June the whole body resumed work.[72]

The magistrates did not mention that there had been some hard bargaining. 'Two days past I have been in a bussy place perswading to get the keelmen to goe to work', Thomas Armstrong, one of the negotiators, wrote on 3 June to Cotesworth. The main points of the agreement finally reached were 'that all the prisoners be released upon recognizance, their charge[s] to be referred to the magistrates [to] ease them as well as they can', and that 'all the keels goe to the sev[eral] staiths and load as the king's measure is, as well to please the owner as the [ship]master'. They were to receive payment for lying tides, one shilling for shifting a ship from the quay, and full dues when a ship to which they had been ordered could take in only half a keel-load or had gone to sea. If the shipmaster gave them no drink when they loaded his vessel, the fitter was to allow them sixteen pence, 'but that is as fitter or master pleases'. Shortly before these terms were finalized the keelmen had indicated that they were willing to carry 'the same quantity of coals ... that the Sunderland men carry – the last piece of evidence of the connection between the two bodies.[73]

As soon as the men returned to work, the Newcastle magistrates, as they had promised, sought permission from the Lords Justices to release the prisoners. They suggested that as none of them was charged with a capital offence, the men and women against whom no particular information of any riotous act had been

---

[72] Magistrates to Secretary Craggs, 4 June 1719, SP 43/61; copy warrant for arresting several keelmen 'upon the combination not to work until their wages were increased', TWA 394/7; Cotesworth to Sir Henry Liddell, 24 May 1719, Cotesworth Papers, CJ/3/8–12; list of keelmen negotiators and note of their refusal of terms, 23 May, *ibid*; preliminary agreement and letter Thomas Armstrong to Cotesworth, 3 June, stating final settlement, *ibid*.

[73] Cotesworth Papers, CJ/3/8–12.

made should be released, provided they gave sureties for their appearance at the next quarter sessions, while those who had been most active should give security for their good behaviour and appearance at the next Assizes, 'because the authority of the judges will be a much greater terrour to them than anything we can do, and by this means they may be enabled to support their families who (as we are credibly informed) are by their obstinacy reduced to very great necessitys'.[74] The Lords Justices agreed that the 'ring-leaders and most mutinous' should appear at the next Assizes and the rest at the quarter sessions. As the secretary to the Lords Justices, De la Faye, believed that the magistrates did not wish to punish the offenders, he proposed that they should be persuaded to petition the Lords Justices to stop any proceedings against them, at the same time 'acknowledging their offence and expressing their repentance'.[75] A petition on these lines, supported by the magistrates, was duly presented, and, as 'these poor men' had repented of their 'crime', the Lords Justices ordered the Attorney General to stop the prosecution and authorized the magistrates to drop any local proceedings against them.[76] The County Durham magistrates were likewise advised to organize a petition on behalf of the offenders at Sunderland. Hedworth gladly complied as he believed that 'nothing can conduce more to keep the rest in quietness at their work than an entire discharge of them'. The Lord Justices 'readily granted' the prisoners' petition. They were to be released, and, on appearing at the Assizes, would receive the promised indulgence.[77]

The magistrates were uncertain as to whether clemency was to be extended to the schoolmaster Richard Flower. Hedworth and a colleague, Anthony Ettrick, did not release him with the keelmen, but the Mayor of Durham later accepted bail for him to appear at the quarter sessions, which caused Hedworth to 'despair of any further discovery or information about this matter'.[78] Two weeks later, he confirmed that he could obtain no additional intelligence that Flower might have provided about the combination. He was surprised and concerned when, by a majority of one, the Durham magistrates committed Flower to the Assizes. He was anxious that the proceedings should be dropped, partly because he felt he might be accused of negligence for failing to prepare for the prosecution. To justify himself he declared that he had applied to Ettrick to give security to appear and give evidence against Flower according to information formerly received, but Ettrick 'absolutely refused', and Hedworth was unwilling 'to commit a man of his temper and knowledge in the law' without positive directions from the Lord Justices. Ettrick may have taken this stand because he did not wish to become involved in a case in which a 'strong party' was calling for Flower's discharge, but he may also have been influenced by the antagonism which evidently existed

[74]   Magistrates to Craggs, 4 June 1719, SP 43/61.
[75]   De La Faye to magistrates, 9 June and 2 July 1719, TWA 394/7.
[76]   De La Faye to magistrates, 21 July 1719, TWA 394/7. The Admiralty also cancelled the orders for the impressment of the strikers, 3 June, Robinson, *Delaval Papers*, pp.144–5.
[77]   De La Faye to magistrates, 2 July 1719, TWA 394/7; De La Faye to John Hedworth, 16 June 1719, SP 44/281/62–3; Hedworth to De La Faye, 23 June, 12 July 1719, SP 35/16/139, 35/17/26.
[78]   Hedworth to De La Faye, 23 June 1719, SP 35/16/139.

between Hedworth and himself. 'Indeed I hope Flower is intended to be included in the favour granted to the poor keelmen, as a fresh instance of their excys clemency', Hedworth wrote, 'and which I doubt not, will have a very good effect upon the common people, who now in general repent of their error and own themselves to have been in the wrong'.[79] Three days before Hedworth wrote this, the Lords Justices had intended that Flower should be punished with the 'utmost severity', but the case had obviously collapsed through lack of evidence.[80]

The proposed severity did not extend to the keelmen. 'The Lords Justices are tender of these poor people', De la Faye wrote, 'who are the best, if not I fear, the only well affected mob in England'.[81] After the strike, the Justices recommended that Hedworth and Ettrick should enquire 'whether those poor people have not just ground to complain of oppressions from their masters the fitters, particularly in those matters you mention about cloathing and other necessarys being imposed upon them in lieu of money for their wages, and to do them right, and as far as the law enables you to prevent any injustice being done them'.[82] Hedworth tried to minimize the men's grievances. It could not be expected, he contended, that so few should have arisen among 800 men during the past four years. However, the fitters had promised not to impose necessaries or houses upon them. This, he admitted, was 'truly a grievance', but, as the shipmasters 'generally bring corn the first voyage of the year and oblige the fitters to take it in discount for their loading of coals', the trade 'must as well be carried on by truck as with ready money', and payment of the keelmen in this manner could scarcely be avoided.[83] There were many evils associated with truck payments when imposed by unscrupulous employers. Workers might be compelled to purchase inferior goods, or items they did not need, at inflated prices, thereby reducing their real wages, restricting (or in the worst cases eliminating) their power to purchase elsewhere, and increasing their dependency on their masters. Two magistrates from Newcastle, who had earlier been summoned before the Lords Justices, denied that the Tyne keelmen were obliged to do more work or were paid less than usual and affirmed that they received their wages weekly in money.[84] The Newcastle men did not complain of truck payments on this occasion, though from time to time they grumbled about being paid for certain tasks in liquor. In some cases, however, their discontent arose over the quality of the drink rather than the system itself.

After the strike a new wages agreement for the Tyne keelmen was engrossed on parchment and signed by the magistrates and fitters.[85] Several additions were made to the basic settlement of 1710, especially 'that no keel shall be obliged to load more than 8 chaldrons of coal at a time'. If the crew of a keel cast coal into two ships in one tide they were to receive 2s 8d over and above the usual wages,

[79]   Hedworth to De La Faye, 12 July 1719, SP 35/17/26.
[80]   De La Faye to Hedworth, 23 July 1719, SP 44/281/164–5; Morgan and Rushton, *Rogues, Thieves and the Rule of Law*, p.208.
[81]   9 June 1719, SP 43/61.
[82]   De La Faye to Hedworth, 16 June 1719, SP 44/281/62–3.
[83]   Hedworth to De La Faye, 23 June 1719, SP 35/16/139.
[84]   4 June 1719, SP 43/61.
[85]   TWA 394/7.

but if in so doing they lost a tide, they were to have 8 shillings. If a shipmaster did not provide the usual quantity of beer to the keelmen loading his ship they were to be allowed 1s 4d instead. Despite these provisions the men gained little by the strike. A few weeks later, the Hostmen's Company resolved that the new wages agreement was to continue 'no longer in force than 'till Christmas next', the time for binding, when the fitters presumably intended to alter its terms.[86] As Cotesworth pointed out, the keelmen could refuse to bind themselves under conditions that they did not like,[87] but at the end of a year during which they had been particularly impoverished they were hardly in a position to take such a stand. In subsequent wage negotiations the 1719 agreement was never mentioned, only the settlement of 1710 and another made in 1744. The regulation against overloading the keels, the men's most important gain, was to be flagrantly disregarded according to the exigencies of trade.

The advent of the military and imprisonment of some of the ringleaders, together with the threat that they would be impressed into the navy, broke the strike. Even so, many of those involved escaped into the adjoining counties, since the officer commanding the troops at Newcastle lacked authority to act in the independent jurisdictions of Northumberland and Durham.[88] It appears that doubts had also been raised as to the extent that the military could assist the civil authorities. In a letter to the Mayor, De la Faye declared that although all subjects were obliged to assist the magistrates in the due execution of the laws and preservation of the peace, 'yet, that the military officers may have no scruple in this respect', the Secretary at War had been ordered to write to them 'to that purpose'.[89] The same day, orders were sent to the commander of an infantry regiment at Newcastle to proceed to Sunderland to assist the civil magistrates in suppressing any tumults that might arise there and 'repell force with force in case the said civil magistrates shall find it necessary'.[90] The combination of the keelmen of Tyne and Wear represents one of their most significant attempts to better their working conditions, but the Society of Keelmen disappeared without trace and almost half a century elapsed before another attempt was made to unite the two bodies of keelmen.

Although there is no record of renewed industrial action by the keelmen until 1738, some of the practices of which they complained in 1719 continued to occur at least intermittently during the intervening period as the various parties concerned in the coal trade pursued their often conflicting interests, and dissensions broke out between individuals within these groups. It is not surprising, then, that surreptitious and illegal practices were engendered which proved detrimental to the keelmen. As a modern writer, describing the situation in 1729, observes, 'the cross currents were complex':

---

86   Hostmen's minute book, 1713–30, TWA, GU/HO/1/3.
87   Cotesworth to Sir Henry Liddell, 24 May 1719, Cotesworth Papers, CJ/3/8–12.
88   Mayor and aldermen to the Secretary of State, 6 May 1738, SP 44/130/343–4.
89   De la Faye to the magistrates, 21 May 1719, TWA 394/7.
90   Copy letter Mr Tresby to Colonel Cholmley, 21 May 1719, Cotesworth Papers, CJ/3/8–12.

The ship-owners were trying to squeeze what they could out of the [coal] owners, but looked upon the Lightermen as the real peril, the coal-owners were in difficulties amongst themselves, but had a collective feud with the Lightermen and a grievance against the ship-owners for being so indiscreet as to cause their affairs to be dragged into the limelight. The coal-owners and Lightermen were at each other's mercy on account of the illegal premiums that were extorted by the Lightermen from certain owners.[91]

To enhance their profits the shipmasters sought to delay the start of the coal trade and, as in 1718, establish a strict rota for loading in the North and unloading in the South, but on learning of the scheme George Liddell raised many objections, especially about the effect on the keelmen.

But what I had like to forget, & is very materiell [he wrote to his nephew, Henry Ellison, 14 January 1728/9]. What must become of the poor keelmen? They are a sort of unthinking people that spend their money as fast, nay generally before they get it. They gave over work ye beginning of November & many of them had not then a shilling before hand. They live upon their credit, & a little labouring work, till they get their binding money at Christmas. That money goes to their cred[ito]rs & then they borrow of their fitters to buy provisions & have credit with the runners for a little drink, & so they put of[f] till ab[ou]t Candlemas [2 February]. Now if they are not to begin till ab[ou]t Lady day [25 March], half of them will be starved, for as their time of working will be so much shorter, trades people will not trust them their being no prospect of being rep[ai]d.[92]

There was a surfeit of ships in the trade, he added, many of them commanded by masters 'of great passions & little reason'. Eventually it was agreed that, with a few exceptions, no colliers would be loaded until 3 March. This was 'the beginning of a great piece of work',[93] declared an agent of George Bowes, a coal owner whose policy often differed from that of the Liddells, but George Liddell was not entirely happy with the arrangement, especially that ships without certificates showing that they had delivered in turn were not to be loaded. This illegal procedure, he believed, would inevitably provoke a reaction in parliament.[94]

His fears were soon realized. The shipmasters and Hostmen were attacked with 'great warmth' in the Commons, and a committee was established to investigate loud complaints from the City of London. There was a great deal of 'wrangling' in the committee, but Liddell sucessfully defended the coal

[91] Raymond Smith, *Sea-Coal for London: History of the Coal Factors in the London Market* (London, 1961), pp.43–4. The manoeuvres of coal owners, ship owners and the London coal dealers in the 1780s are described in a well-informed article in the *Gentleman's Magazine*, LX (1790), pp.442–4.

[92] TWA, Ellison Papers, A/32/21. For the sake of clarity the abbreviations 'yt' and 'yn' have been expanded to 'that' and 'then'.

[93] Strathmore Papers, letter book, 24 January 1728/29, reproduced by permission of Lord Strathmore and Durham County Record Office, D/St/C2/3/8.

[94] Liddell to Henry Ellison, 26, 28 January, 1, 13 February 1728/29, Ellison Papers, A/32/ 28, 29, 32, 36.

owners and the Hostmen, whose charter was under threat of abrogation.[95] The Lightermen, accused of being 'great oppressors', threatened to produce letters proving that the fitters were involved in the combination 'at the instance of the [ship]masters', but Liddell managed to prevent this disclosure.[96] Finally, the House resolved against prosecuting the shipmasters and Lightermen even though they were in an illegal combination to enhance the price of coal.[97] Liddell feared that if the Lightermen's Company were dissolved, the shipmasters, many of them 'unreasonable unthinking creatures', would gain excessive power which would be 'tyrannically used'. It was in the coal owners' interest 'to preserve the ballance of power in their own hands, & not to lett either of the contending partys oppress the other'.[98]

The coal owners, however, were far from being united. Liddell and Bowes agreed that nothing but a regulation would heal the trade, but Liddell regarded as a 'dangerous experiment' Bowes' suggestion that to force their rival, Richard Ridley, and others to comply, they should lower the price and refuse to accept Ridley's bills of exchange.[99] In the absence of a regulation the various owners competed against each other by giving more than statute measure. 'Pray watch Lady Clavering's, Mr Ridley's & the rest of the coal owners' measure', Liddell urged Ellison, 18 March 1730/1, 'tor the [ship]masters say they have better measure then from us; nay affirm that they have been offered to be made 15 of a keel the year round' (i.e. that each keel-load, supposedly of 8 Newcastle chaldrons, should be made to equal 15 London chaldrons).[100] Several weeks later, Liddell was 'much concerned' that the measure given at other staithes exceeded his own. He was convinced that the staithmen who supervised the loading of the keels were guilty of 'indirect practices, no doubt by direction from some of their principalls'.[101] Faced with 'the underhand dealings ... by such as can worst afford it', he again looked to a regulation, and was even ready to concur with Bowes' 'desperate remedy' of lowering the price and keeping to statute measure. It was essential to put pressure on Ridley who otherwise would 'out do us with measure'. His 'clandistine dealing' threatened to cut the Liddells out of the London market.[102] While the shipmasters had orders to seek double coal (16 London chaldrons to the keel) or at least measure equivalent to 15 such chaldrons, Liddell ordered Ellison to warn Ridley and others that, if they continued to give greater measure than in the previous year, he was empowered to lower the price. Liddell also wanted any overloaded keels to be noted with a view to prosecution. Threat of a price cut, he believed, might awe Ridley a little, 'at least as to measure, and make him the reasonabler if

---

[95] Liddell to Henry Ellison, 24 April, 4 and 10 May 1729, Ellison Papers, A/32/54, 59, 61.
[96] Liddell to Henry Ellison, 4 and 10 May 1729, Ellison Papers, *ibid.*
[97] Liddell to Henry Ellison, 13 May 1729, Ellison Papers, A/32/62.
[98] Liddell to Henry Ellison, 22 February 1728/9, 10 May 1729, Ellison Papers, A/32/40, 61.
[99] Liddell to Henry Ellison, 23 November 1730, Ellison Papers, A/33/15.
[100] Liddell to Henry Ellison, 18 March 1730/31, Ellison Papers, A/33/36.
[101] Liddell to Henry Ellison, 7 April 1731, Ellison Papers, A/33/43.
[102] Liddell to Henry Ellison, 7 and 12–13 April 1731, Ellison Papers, A/33/43,44.

we come to treat'.[103] Liddell then called on the Commissioners of Customs to order their officers to supervise the measurement of the keels, prevent any new or repaired ones operating without being measured, and stop 'any keel above statute measure' casting her coal the same tide that she came down. He expected an order to this effect to be sent to Newcastle immediately.[104] Yet the evil was not easily remedied. Soon he was expressing surprise at the measure given by some of his partners in the 'Grand Alliance', 'and we be so asleep as to let them load a whole fleet before discovered'. He himself was not above doing as the others did. 'I must recommend it to you', he wrote to Ellison, 29 April 1731, 'to let us give as good measure as our partners do & not let us hold the candle till the season be spent'.[105] The result can be seen from the Grand Allies' minute book:[106]

> June 1731. The measure increased from the top of the plate to an inch & a half or such as would make double.
> December [1731]. To the top of the plate only.
> April 1732. A plate breadth over the top.
> July [1732] An inch & half over.
> September [1732]. A third of an inch, thought by all the steathmen to be suff[icient] as to make 15 a keel. But the measure given by all was much greater.

The keelmen who had to load, navigate and unload the additional coal without extra pay were the victims of these manoeuvres.

Sometimes a strong combination of coal owners could avoid giving over-measure. In 1710 the shipmasters complained bitterly about lack of gift coal and short measure at Newcastle,[107] but, as in that year, the keelmen were still liable to loss by restriction of the vend. This was again the case in the spring of 1738 when the fitters agreed that their vends should be proportioned every month and that those who had exceeded their quota should stop loading until their brethren who had fallen short had vended their share. These proceedings were not recorded in the Hostmen's general minute book but kept in a separate volume, evidently to preserve secrecy.[108] Any brother who exposed the Company's orders was liable to a fine of £5. Although the scheme was operated by the fitters, the coal owners and ship owners were also involved. If a fitter was suspected of having transgressed any rule established for the good of the Company, he had to appear at the next meeting of the coal owners and swear an answer to the charge, two of the Company being present. Three fitters who loaded 'irregular ships' were fined sixpence per chaldron and ordered to inform the ship owners at Scarborough and Whitby that this penalty had been imposed

---

[103] Liddell to Henry Ellison, 12–13 April 1731, Ellison Papers, A/33/44.
[104] Liddell to Henry Ellison, 17 April 1731, Ellison Papers, A/33/45.
[105] Ellison Papers, A/33/46.
[106] North of England Institute of Mining Engineers, GA/2.
[107] Statements of Captain Bowyer and Mr Plaw, Cotesworth Papers, CK/3/64.
[108] Dendy, *Records of the Hostmen's Company*, pp.194–9 and Hostmen's minute book, TWA, GU/HO/2, in which there is additional material.

'to prevent the Company being blamed'. Several other fitters were fined or incurred penalties for breaches of these regulations, among them Joseph Smith, who had declared at the outset that if he exceeded his quota he would not cease vending. He was later fined for loading a ship 'contrary to order', as was Samuel Shields who had loaded several 'irregular ships'.[109]

If the scheme was disadvantageous to some of the fitters, it was much more so to the keelmen, many of whom were subjected to periods of enforced idleness even though ships were waiting for coal. When the vends were proportioned on 30 March 1738, eleven fitters who had exceeded their quotas were ordered to stop loading or taking on any ship without consent of the committee. On 8 April they were allowed to load 'any ship they are concerned in' (i.e. had shares in), but no independent ship without consent. Again, when the vends were proportioned on 27 April, several fitters had to turn over ships to others. No fitter was to load any vessel that had not delivered regularly until ten days after loading the ship that had delivered in turn before her at London, and then no more than three keels of coal were to be cast on her in one tide.[110] All these restrictions obviously curtailed the keelmen's earning power, and at the beginning of May, while the fitters were doing 'everything in their power to contribute to the good of the trade in general',[111] the keelmen enforced a strike.

The men employed by Joseph Smith produced an address to inform him of the reason for the 'stop'.

> It is becaus that the work is not right pearted for ther is sum that gettes to mutch and ther is otheres fitt to sterve so you most endover and other gentel-men fitteres that his thes pour men servantes under them to sie to gett them work that they may live, other wayes yow most suport them with muny till sutch tim they gett work, but we do hop yow will sie the work better perted that every pour man may live.[112]

In a petition to the magistrates, a number of 'indigent, suffering & starving' skippers described their 'most melancholly necessitous circumstances',

> we & our wives & families being at the point of starving for want of the necessary supplies of life by reason of the want of busyness, & trade in our busyness having been worse this winter than ever was known in ye memory of any now alive, and continues so to be, to our utter undoing & ruine.[113]

The coal owners and Hostmen were so strongly denounced in another petition to the magistrates that some keelmen dissociated themselves from its 'too rigorous terms'.[114] The petitioners alleged that they were being denied their ancient dues as settled in 1710, and that the combination of coal owners and

---

[109] Dendy, *Records of the Hostmen's Company*, pp.195, 198; Hostmen's minute book, 18 and 25 May 1738

[110] Dendy, *Records of the Hostmen's Company*, pp.195–6, 198–9.

[111] *Ibid.*

[112] TWA 394/57.

[113] 4 May 1738, TWA 394/9.

[114] Affidavit of John Higgons, Richard Brewhouse and John Berkley, skippers, 9 May 1738, TWA 394/9.

Hostmen had prevented them working 'at all times that ships required coales'. Therefore they prayed that 'all minoplyes in trade combinations and privet contracts may be set aside, seing they are so ditrementall to some thousands of his Majestyes loyall subjects and only for the intrest of a sett of men that preffers a privet intrest before a publick good'. They hoped that the magistrates would not allow them to labour any longer under 'a barbarity abhored by Jewes, Turks and Infidales'. Such was the cruelty of the coal owners and Hostmen that they would starve the men's innocent wives and children. Since the Hostmen had 'no regard to honour and honesty', the petitioners begged the magistrates to oblige them to give bond to the keelmen to pay the ancient dues.[115]

The author of the petition, which set forth various other grievances, was John Blair, one of the skippers, who brushed aside his colleagues' protests at the strong expressions it contained. 'What need you be affraid of such expressions to the magistrates', he contended, 'when the like have been delivered to the King and Parliament'. Three skippers from different employments declared in an affidavit that Blair had been directed to write nothing beyond what was included in a parchment relating to their wages (the settlement of 1710) and that all the skippers then present wished to alter the wording but Blair had prevented it.[116] Blair was one of the signatories of the petition of the indigent and starving skippers quoted above and this, too, may have been his work. A 'villainous fellow' among the keelmen wrote for them, declared William Scott, one of the fitters, shortly after the strike. 'He did not spare the C[oa]l O[wne]rs', but 'by some informations made before the magistrates', the keelmen 'cleard themselves of what these gentlemen were chargd with'.[117] Scott expected that Blair would be prosecuted, but he realized that caution was necessary. 'What this scribe will say for himself when he's calld on I cannot tell, but as yet it wod not be prudent of the magistrates to give him any trouble'.[118]

Although some keelmen considered that the petition had been too rigorously expressed, they did not deny that combinations by coal owners, fitters and shipmasters reduced their employment. Moreover, they had numerous other grievances which they represented to their respective masters. 'The pan men [those employed in boats belonging to the salt pans] tak our brid from us', some complained, 'by taking balest out of ships at ounder wadges and lickwayes by taking fitt tides [to load coal] so that we stop them till their masteres give us a bound of ther handes that they wil do so no mor'.[119] A similar complaint had been made in 1710 when it had been agreed that no fitter should employ pan boats on pain of forfeiting the dues to the keelmen's hospital. Again, many keelmen did not receive a customary allowance of fire coal each year. The skippers employed by Henry Atkinson were particularly aggrieved on this

---

[115] 9 May 1738, TWA 394/9.

[116] Affidavit of John Higgons *et al.*, TWA 394/9.

[117] Scott to George Bowes, 12 May 1738, Strathmore Papers, reproduced by permission of Lord Strathmore and Durham County Record Office, D/ST/C1/3/42 (2).

[118] *Ibid.*

[119] Keelmen to Joseph Smith, TWA 394/57.

account and, 'being poor men & not able to sue for justice at law', called on the magistrates for redress.[120] Others complained that payment for lying tides was being evaded, and that, as in 1719, they were paid only 5 shillings instead of 13s 4d when they had to bring a laden keel back to the staithe.[121] As usual there were many complaints about the beer that they were supposed to receive from the shipmasters. 'Self intrest hath so hardned the shipmasters' harts', declared the keelmen employed by William Selby, 'that we neither have no[r] cann get anie justice doon us by them'.[122] Other keelmen alleged that the shipmasters had wronged them in unspecified ways. As in 1719, the keelmen made many complaints against the staithmen. Their oppressions were 'so great we cannot bear with them', Selby's men declared, and men from other works echoed these sentiments. The staithmen charged sixpence for use of a spout if the keels were loaded by this means instead of by hand, and the keelmen complained that they were obliged to pay this charge when only a small quantity of coal was put aboard in this manner, while delays at the spouts often caused them to lose a tide.[123] (It was later alleged that the staithmen deliberately contrived delays in order to gain the 'spout sixpence' and this cost the keelmen 13s 4d through loss of their tide.)[124] Moreover, when they were forced to 'make in' coals at the staithe, the staithmen gave them nothing but drink. Selby's men claimed that they had 'no satisfaction' at all for this work: 'Who reaps the benifite we know not, but we bear the opresion'. As we shall see, the mode of payment for the 'making in' of coal remained a matter of contention long after 1738. Finally, the keelmen complained that they did not receive the shilling to which they were entitled for each keel-load cast into a ship at the quay, nor the shilling due to a man who had to travel from Shields to Newcastle for new orders. Not all the above grievances appeared in each of the representations that the keelmen made to their respective masters, but in some cases there is enough similarity in content and expression to indicate collaboration between the men of different employers. That there was no complaint of overloaded keels on this occasion suggests that the existing regulation of trade by coal owners and fitters was preventing recourse to this expedient.

Soon after the strike began, the magistrates, several of whom were concerned in the coal trade, summoned the fitters and representatives of the keelmen.[125] Perhaps overawed in the presence of the magistrates and their employers, most of the men made no complaint and indicated that they were willing to work. However, they were soon intimidated by the 'mutineers', and the strike continued with the ever present threat of disorder. A few days later, the magistrates promised that if those 'unlawfully assembled in the present tumultuous manner' returned to work, 'the severall complaints delivered to their fitters

---

[120] 4 May 1738, TWA 394/9.
[121] Skippers and keelmen to Francis Simpson, 4 May 1738, TWA 394/9.
[122] William Selby's skippers and keelmen to the Mayor and Aldermen, 5 May 1738, TWA 394/9
[123] *Ibid.*
[124] Petition of keelmen, 1750, TWA 394/19.
[125] 2 May 1738, TWA 394/9.

in writing shall be fully considered and justice done therein'.[126] When this failed to end the strike, the magistrates reported it to the central authorities. As some keelmen appeared willing to work but were afraid of being ill-treated by 'others of their own fraternity', the magistrates believed that a little military force might preserve the peace and re-open trade. They emphasized that the commanding officer must have power to act in the separate jurisdictions of Northumberland and Durham, otherwise 'the end of their march may be fruitless as happened about 20 years ago, upon the like occasion, when a military force was sent to aid the civil magistrates, notwithstanding which for want of the above mentioned power many of the principal offenders escaped by flying into these countys'.[127]

Before the military could arrive, the magistrates and fitters met on 9 May and decided to encourage the few skippers who were willing to work to take their keels downriver the next day. A large crowd assembled to see the result. The strikers manned several keels to stop the attempt, whereupon William Scott called on his fellow fitters to behave like men and assist those prepared to work. He and his colleagues then threatened those who were trying to obstruct the working keels, some of which managed to proceed. 'This gave such a turn, & so suddenly', wrote one observer, Captain Gomeldon,

> that the others who were for stopping their brethren & countrymen, set sail also crying one to another 'What shall we be forced to this without soldiers, sure there never was such a thing before', & in less than an hour there were 200 keels under sail & not one left on the key. Perhaps there never was so great a body of men, after the magistrates had used their utmost endeavours & to no purpose, brought to their duty by so lucky a turn & without the least mischief committed to anyone[128]

Intimidation, evidently by a minority, was the main obstacle preventing a return to work once the various grievances had been brought to the magistrates' attention, and when Scott's courageous intervention dispelled this fear, the strike crumbled. If, as some of the petitioners claimed, they were on the verge of starvation, they could not have endured a prolonged stoppage. Scott's own account was self-effacing: 'The fitters prevailed with the willing part of the keelmen … to make a push for work … the mutinous part opposd them but after some bustle wee go[t] them all afloat and so it continues'.[129] No permanent remedy of the men's grievances was achieved, but, although it was rumoured that the keelmen would soon strike again, they did not do so. Two years later, however, Newcastle experienced 'the greatest riot and outrage of the keelmen and

---

[126] TWA 394/9.
[127] 6 May 1738, SP 44/130/343–4.
[128] Captain Gomeldon to George Bowes, 12 May 1738, quoted Hughes, *North Country Life*, pp.249–50.
[129] Scott to Bowes, 12 May 1738, Strathmore Papers, reproduced by permission of Lord Strathmore and Durham County Record Office, D/ST/C1/3/42(2).

pitmen ever known in this part',[130] though on this occasion the keelmen's protest was not about their working conditions.

[130] Ralph Gowland to his brother, 27 June 1740, Newcastle Society of Antiquaries, transcript in 'Annals and Historical Events, Newcastle', II, 1701–83, Northumberland Museum & Archives, SANT/BEQ/8/1/2.

6

The 'Villainous Riot' of 1740 and its Aftermath

The winter of 1739/40 was marked by a frost of extreme severity which continued unabated for three months. Virtually all trade along the east coast came to a standstill and there was widespread distress among the poor. The coal industry, already disrupted by bad weather during the summer and autumn, was now crippled by the prolonged frost. According to the *Newcastle Courant* of 26 January, coal in Newcastle had for some time past been 'as scarce as money', and had not Alderman Ridley given away small coals to all who fetched them, 'great numbers of poor families in Sandgate and in other places must have starved from excessive cold'.[1] The City Corporation gave money for distribution among the needy and several wealthy individuals made donations for that purpose,[2] but these welcome initiatives could have but limited impact. The keelmen would normally have started work at the beginning of February but were unable to do so on account of the frozen state of the Tyne. On 11 February the Grand Allies employed about two hundred men to cut a channel, over a mile long, from their staithes which enabled some keels to get under way, but attempts to open other parts of the river in this manner were abandoned when two men were drowned. Soon ice-floes blocked the channel already made thus halting coal shipments until the end of the month.[3] Further disruption to trade followed when persistent gales in April prevented the colliers reaching the Tyne, and the problem was compounded by war against Spain which brought danger to shipping from privateers and the risk, especially to seamen, of impressment into the navy.[4] While these circumstances were impeding trade and so reducing the earnings of keelmen and other workers, they were faced with rising prices of grain and other foodstuffs. Continuous rain in August and September 1739 had damaged the crops both before and after reaping, and farmers had to thresh earlier than usual to provide fodder for their cattle during the long frost. By the end of March local supplies were nearing exhaustion, and prospects for the next harvest were not good as the frost was followed by drought. 'To the great oppression of the poor', speculators throughout the land bought up large quan-

---

[1] *Newcastle Courant*, 26 January 1740, quoted Brand, *History of Newcastle*, II, p.520; Joyce Ellis, 'Urban Conflict and Popular Violence, The Guildhall Riots of 1740 in Newcastle upon Tyne', *International Review of Social History*, XXV (1980), pp.332–49; Alderman Ridley's account of the riots, Northumberland Museum and Archives (hereafter NMA), ZRI 27/8.

[2] Richardson, *The Local Historian's Table Book*, I, p.396.

[3] *Ibid.*, I, pp.396–7; J. Sykes, *Local Records of Remarkable Events* (Newcastle, 1833), I, pp.159–60.

[4] T.S. Ashton and J. Sykes, *The Coal Industry of the Eighteenth Century* (Manchester, 1929), p.117; Ellis, 'Urban Conflict', p.336.

tities of any grain they could obtain for export to lucrative markets overseas.[5] As the dearth increased prices rose steeply, far beyond the remarkably low ones of the past decade. During the first half of the year, the price of rye and oats, of particular importance in the north east, almost doubled,[6] and hunger, combined with outrage at those who were pursuing profit at the expense of the poor, led to outbursts of protest in several towns in the region as well as in other parts of the country.

On 20 May a large throng in Stockton, including many women, who swore that they would rather be killed or hanged than die of starvation, prevented exports of corn. Disorder continued and on 6 June, rioters seized a boat loaded with wheat and assaulted the dealer. Hundreds of protesters later threatened to murder him. The aged sheriff of the county, fearful of the responsibility that would fall on him if there was bloodshed, reluctantly raised the *posse comitatus*, the assemblage of the able-bodied male inhabitants. Order was restored without loss of life, but the force soon disintegrated and the prisoners it had taken escaped. Eventually the two MPs for the county sold six hundred bushels of corn to the poor at a low price and, presumably at the direction of the magistrates, proclaimed a ban on the exportation of grain from the locality.[7] On 14 June several persons were wounded in Durham City when the crowd seized wheat from the farmers who refused to lower the price to 8 shillings per boll (two Winchester bushels). A week later, protesters in Sunderland commandeered wheat and sold it at the above price.[8] Pitmen and their womenfolk were largely responsible for these eruptions of direct action.

At Newcastle, too, the first protests were made by women who blocked removal of grain from the city.[9] On 19 June more serious disturbances broke out there. In the early hours of the morning the pitmen at Heaton Colliery, on the outskirts of Newcastle, stopped work and went into the city to 'settle the prices' of grain; some of them were determined 'to take corn where they could get it'.[10] By 5.00a.m. a multitude had assembled in the market place on the Sandhill and with loud huzzars called for the reduction of prices. During the morning several hundred men, women and children, stirred up by 'turbulent spirits' in the Wearside collieries, who alleged that the Newcastle merchants had retained large quantities of corn to sell 'at a great[ly] advanced price', joined the throng.[11] The magistrates ordered that the ringleaders should be

5   Order of the Lords Justices in Council, 26 June 1740, printed in *Newcastle Courant*, 12 July 1740. About the bad weather and the harvests, see letter from 'Philalethes' in the *Newcastle Journal*, 19 July 1740, strongly defending the allegedly 'voracious' corn dealers.

6   Ellis, 'Urban Conflict', p.334.

7   T. Richmond, *Local Records of Stockton and Neighbourhood* (Stockton, 1868), pp.63–4; Bohstedt, 'The Pragmatic Economy, the Politics of Provision and the "Invention" of the Food Riot Tradition in 1740', in Randall and Charlesworth, *Moral Economy and Popular Protest: Crowds, Conflict and Authority*, pp. 55–92.

8   Sykes, *Local Records*, I, pp.162–3.

9   Ellis, 'Urban Conflict', p.340.

10   TWA 394, Minutes of confessions of prisoners: confessions of George Laverick, Robert Clewitt and John Todd.

11   Ridley's account, NMA, ZRI/27/8.

arrested, but their officers were roughly handled and forced to abandon the attempt. The main body of protesters remained on the Sandhill, but others proceeded 'tumultuously through the town', demanding money and terrifying the inhabitants with 'wicked oaths and curses'. They seized grain that was being removed after purchase, as well as unsold corn stored in various inns, and over forty bushels of wheat from a granary. Sacks of stolen grain were piled up on the Sandhill and guarded by the throng.[12]

The magistrates made several attempts to negotiate, and eventually the protesters appointed four pitmen, three waggonmen and one keelman as their deputies. The magistrates also summoned the corn merchants and urged them to adopt 'some reasonable method' of alleviating the distress. They reluctantly consented to sell the grain in their stores at cost price; some produced invoices to prove what they had paid.[13] It was agreed that wheat should be sold at 8 shillings, rye at 6 shillings and oats at 3 shillings per boll, which represented a reduction of almost a quarter of the current rate for wheat and over a third for rye and oats.[14] The deputies signed the following declaration:

> We whose names are hereunto subscribed, do on the behalf of ourselves and the rest of the pitmen, waggon men &c now complaining of the present high price of corn, agree to the above mentioned regulation and undertake that all persons shall be contented therewith and immediately return to their respective habitations and employments.[15]

The Mayor issued a proclamation of the reduced prices and the crowd dispersed, but almost immediately the agreement began to break down. Those who sought to buy found many corn shops shut. The dealers, it was said, had 'absconded through fear', but an apologist for them claimed that although they sold what they had at a loss of 2 shillings per quarter, most of their supplies had been taken by force.[16] It had been agreed that the stolen corn should be deposited in the public weigh-house and restored to its owners, but the next morning the protesters reassembled and shared it out among themselves. More stores were raided, large quanties of wheat seized, and a paper demanding even lower prices for grain, and stipulating the price of peas, beans, cheese and butter, was presented to the magistrates.[17]

The pitmen, who were demanding increased wages, did not return to work as their deputies had promised, and, as the Mayor pointed out on 20 June, the cutting-off of the coal supply was likely to have dire repercussions:

> We are under great fear of a want of coals for keeping our keelmen employed and supplying the ships, the consequence whereof is of greatest moment, for they on wanting work will be too apt to joyn those rioters which will make

[12] *Ibid.*; Brief for the King (against the rioters) TWA 394/56 and other papers concerning the riot, TWA 394/10–14, 394/51–53.
[13] Ridley's account, NMA, ZRI 27/8.
[14] Ellis, 'Urban Conflict', p.342.
[15] TWA 394/10.
[16] Richardson, *The Local Historian's Table Book*, I, pp.398–400; letter from 'Philalethes', as in n.5.
[17] Brief for the King, TWA 394/56.

a most formidible body not to be restrained by any civil authority as hath in
these parts been experienced.

He therefore begged the government to send a military force with authority
to act in the neighbouring counties lest the end of their march should be frustrated, 'as has happened heretofore on the like occasion'.[18] There was bound to
be delay before troops could arrive, even if this urgent appeal were to receive
an immediate response, which was by no means certain. Meanwhile the Mayor
summoned the inhabitants to watch and ward, and called on those concerned
in the coal trade to muster as many of their employees as possible to guard the
town. The Grand Allies promised to raise a force but failed to do so. Alderman
Ridley, however, immediately complied with the request, and by 6.00a.m. on 21
June sixty men 'well mounted, and above three hundred on foot, well provided
with good oaken cudgels', assembled and joined the citizens who had obeyed
the Mayor's summons. The magistrates appointed officers, issued arms, and
posted parties to guard strategic places. Ridley and his men were positioned on
the Sandhill where their presence caused the majority of the protesters to drop
their weapons and pose as 'idle spectators'.[19] A few who continued to be unruly
were arrested and committed to prison. The City gates were guarded by night
and the next few days passed without incident.

Sales of corn were resumed, but, as the low prices attracted people from
distant parts and supplies would soon be exhausted, it was announced that corn
would not be delivered to persons unknown without a certificate from a fitter,
staithman or church warden.[20] The corn dealers had no intention of augment-
ing their existing stocks. After the agreement of 20 June, Ralph Carr, one of
the principal merchants, wrote: 'To pacifie them [the rioters] we are obliged to
let them have what quantity of corn we have upon hand at very low prices, so
will not do to buy in without a prospect of higher prices'.[21] Accordingly he dispatched urgent messages to his agents abroad to stop purchasing grain on his
behalf and to sell, or divert to other ports, any already bought. He re-directed
to Amsterdam cargoes about to be dispatched from the Baltic to Newcastle.[22]
Moreover, despite the protesters, he continued to export grain from the City.
'On account of Ramsays cargo I am much the object of their resentment', he
declared on 22 June, 'for they affirm it was shipped of[f] for Spain', and he
later stated that if Ramsay had returned to Newcastle the mob would certainly
have burnt his ship.[23] Such exports were obviously provocative, even though,
according to the above-mentioned apologist for the corn merchants, the quantity sent overseas did not exceed 315 quarters and was within the terms of the
statute 1 William and Mary cap. 12, which offered bounties on the exportation

[18] Cuthbert Fenwick to Secretary of State, 20 June 1740, SP 36/51/127–9.
[19] Ridley's account; on the failure of the Grand Allies see James Clavering to his son George, 24 June
      1740, in Dickinson, *The Correspondence of Sir James Clavering*, p.226.
[20] 24 June 1740, TWA 394/10.
[21] Ralph Carr to J. Gee, 20 June 1740, Northumberland Museum and Archives, ZCE 10/13.
[22] Carr to Alexander Coutts & Co., 22 June 1740 and to John Trotman, 24 June, *ibid*.
[23] Carr to John Coutts & Co., 22 June and 1 July 1740, *ibid.*

of grain when the home price fell below certain levels. The total sent from Newcastle to other markets in England was, he claimed, 800 quarters of wheat, 1,030 quarters of oats and 300 quarters of barley, far less than in previous years. Even so, at a time of scarcity any diminution of the local supply, no matter what the destination, was bound to provoke anger.

On 25 June a guard composed of members of the Merchants' Company delivered meal to the poor at a low price, but that evening the City was left unprotected. The Mayor had 'thought proper to go into the country' and no one else had authority to issue the necessary orders. Before dawn the next day, a great body of pitmen, waggonmen and others broke open the gate of the tower on the bridge, released the prisoners, and marched through the town 'with bagpipes playing, drum beating and dirty clothes fixed upon sticks by way of colours flying'.[24] Soon the magistrates' worst fears were realized as the keelmen, 'in terrible numbers, arm'd with all sorts of weapons', entered the town, terrifying the inhabitants with threats of 'entire destruction'.[25] In the Guildhall, close to the market place where the multitude had gathered, the magistrates, now throughly alarmed, resolved to reassemble the militia. Fearing that the mob would seize the weapons intended for that force, they decided to create a diversion by selling a cargo of rye on a ship lying at the quay – a rumour that it was about to sail was naturally provoking anger. Two of the ringleaders agreed to arrange a guard to ensure that the rye would not be stolen, but soon they reported that 'the people were all mad and they cou'd not get them to hear reason'. Some of the gentry, armed with muskets brought by stealth into the Guildhall, thereupon volunteered to guard the ship. Most of their weapons were merely charged with powder, but a few were loaded with partridge shot. As Ridley led the volunteers out, they were surrounded and jostled, as it was probably suspected that they were being deployed to enable the vessel to slip away. In the confusion some of them were knocked down and wounded, whereupon the others, panic-stricken, opened fire, killing one man and wounding several more.[26] Immediately, the mob launched a violent assault on the Guildhall.

> Stones flew in among us from without thro the windows like canon shot from which our lives were in hazard every moment [the Mayor reported];[27] and at length the mob broke in upon us in the most terrible outrage. They spared our lives indeed but obliged us to quit the place. Then fell to plundering and destroying all about them. The several benches of justice were immediately and entirely demolished. The Town Clerk's office was broke open and all the books, deeds and records of the Town and its courts thrown out of the windows amongst the mob without doors where they were trodden under foot, torn and most of them lost and the rest defaced and made useless.

---

[24] Ridley's account, NMA, ZRI 27/8.
[25] Fenwick to Secretary of State, 27 June 1740, SP 36/51/198–9.
[26] Ridley's account, NMA, ZRI 27/8.
[27] Fenwick to Secretary of State, 27 June 1740; Ridley's account, NMA, ZRI 27/8.

Ridley managed to lead some of the rioters to the ship and promised to stay there until all the grain had been sold, but, now evidently intent on plunder, they soon left him almost alone.[28] The nine locks on the treasury containing about £1,500 proved a stubborn obstacle, but at last they yielded to the onslaught. Leaving the Guildhall, 'a large and beautiful fabric', almost a 'perfect ruin', the rabble patrolled the streets and threatened to burn or plunder several houses, especially Ridley's, as it was believed that he had given the order to fire, an allegation that he vigorously denied.[29] No doubt he feared not only for his property but for his life. A few years earlier, Captain Porteous, who had allegedly ordered his troops to fire on a mob in Edinburgh, had been tried for murder and sentenced to death. Although he was later reprieved, a body of insurgents broke open the prison, dragged him out, and lynched him.[30] The case had serious implications for magistrates and commanders of armed forces dealing with rioters. The sheriff of County Durham had 'a contentious debate' with the magistrates as to who, if it became necessary, should order the posse to open fire. The magistrates of Newcastle were likewise perplexed, and, according to Ridley, the rioters believed that the Porteous case afforded them a measure of protection. Before the destruction that they had threatened could begin, three companies of soldiers, fortuitously on their way from Berwick to Stockton, reached Newcastle by a forced march from Alnwick, where the magistrates' urgent appeal for help had reached them. Although vastly outnumbered, they confronted the throng with loaded muskets and fixed bayonets, whereupon, realizing that, despite the Porteous precedent, they were in imminent danger, the rioters scattered and fled.[31] Ridley declared that they 'chiefly consisted of keelmen', but 'Crowley's crew' from the iron works at Swalwell, who had come into town at the keelmen's behest, also took a prominent part in the riot and were the largest group among the 213 arrested. The second largest number of captives were keelmen together with women (many of whom were probably keelmen's wives and daughters).[32]

Such violence and destruction by Tyneside workers was unprecedented. Strikes by keelmen were often accompanied with violence, but it was directed not against the magistrates but against any of their own number who attempted to work and others employed to break the strike. The municipal authorities, well aware that their militia was no match for these hundreds of robust men, wisely avoided confrontation on such occasions, at least until the regular forces were present in sufficient strength. The shooting that provoked the assault on the Guildhall was not premeditated but arose from the panic of those who feared for their lives. Newcastle normally possessed a well-stocked market and a food

[28] Ridley's account, NMA, ZRI 27/8.
[29] Fenwick to Secretary of State, 27 June 1740; Ridley to *Newcastle Courant*, 28 June 1740
[30] About Captain John Porteous see *DNB*.
[31] Bohstedt, 'The Pragmatic Economy', pp.71–3; Ellis, 'Urban Conflict', p.339; Ridley's account, NMA, ZRI 27/8.
[32] Brief for the King, TWA 394/56; Ridley's account; Ridley to [the Earl of Carlisle], July 1740, Historical Manuscripts Commission, Carlisle, p.195; Ellis, 'Urban Conflict', p.347..

riot had not occurred before. The price of corn had sometimes been higher than in 1740, but in that year a combination of particularly unfavourable circumstances curtailed the earnings of those dependent on the coal trade, while dearth, aggravated by exportation of grain from the region, resulted in soaring prices and widespread distress. The actions of those perceived by the crowd to be profiting at the expense of the poor in a life-threatening situation generated great anger and provoked direct action. Representatives of the keelmen who urged 'Crowley's crew' and men from Winlaton to join them argued that unless they assisted in seizing the corn still in Newcastle it would be 'shipped off in the night' and, like the keelmen, they would be starved for want of bread.[33]

There were some forty-five food riots in England in 1740 and many similar uprisings during the second half of the eighteenth century. As stated in the Introduction, E.P. Thompson explained them in terms of the moral economy of the poor, in essence a demand for social justice and a fair price. He considered that proceedings in Newcastle conformed to this concept until the corn dealers failed to sell at the promised rates and the fatal shooting provoked violence.[34] Until this catastrophe, despite the looting of grain, the protest had been, on the whole, disciplined, and the negotiations to set the price of corn and other foodstuffs accord well with his model. John Bohstedt, however, one of a number of historians who question Thompson's analysis – his rival concepts of a pragmatic economy, politics of provision and protocol of riot have also been described in the Introduction – sees the seizure of food and prevention of exports rather than regulation of the market as the factors that governed the uprising. He regards the protest at Newcastle, before the final outburst of violence, as the 'most structured bargaining of 1740 between a formidible corps of proletarians, experienced in forceful collective bargaining with large scale capitalists' on the one hand and the City authorities, divided by political and business rivalries, on the other.[35] There is no evidence to suggest that the protesters were motivated by party political considerations on this occasion, but there were certainly sharp divisions on this account among the ruling elite, especially between the Mayor's brother, Nicholas Fenwick, Tory MP for the city, and Alderman Ridley, who was to stand as a Whig at the approaching parliamentary election. Ridley naturally gained popularity with the citizens when his band of men, each wearing a green bough in his hat like an election cockade, quelled the disturbance on 21 June, and it was believed that the Mayor failed to keep up the militia to prevent him from profiting further. 'On acc[oun]t of Parliamentary Party the Militia of the Town was disbanded', Ralph Carr declared, 'wch gave the mob an opportunity of entering undisturbed till it was too late to get a sufficient force'. Everything would have been well, he later asserted, if 'our wise majestrate had not disbanded the militia on partie

---

[33] David Levine and Keith Wrightson, *The Making of an Industrial Society – Whickham 1560–1765* (Oxford 1991), p.386

[34] Thompson, 'The Moral Economy of the English Crowd in the Eighteenth Century', and *Customs in Common* (1991).

[35] Bohstedt, 'The Pragmatic Economy'.

affaires'.[36] Ridley, however, believed that the Mayor's behaviour resulted from a quarrel with the corn merchants.[37] Disagreement may well have arisen over the supply and price at which the various sorts of grain were to be sold, or on account of merchants who, despite the local scarcity, were still prepared to export corn from the city. Again the failure of the Grand Allies to provide the force they had promised may have been due to their rivalry with Ridley in the coal trade or to other business concerns.[38]

Carr and Ridley believed that from the outset of the disturbances the crowd had been intent on plunder, but, before the shooting, the focus was on the price of corn and other provisions and plunder was confined to grain. However, once serious violence erupted, the riot gained its own momentum and plunder became the principal objective. Ridley thought that 'the old levelling principles' were at work, but, although the devastation of the Guildhall and threat of further destruction manifested contempt for authority and desire for revenge, the magistrates were not harmed and most of them were even escorted home in a sort of 'mock triumph'.[39] Although elements of the concepts proposed by Thompson and Bohstedt can be discerned, the complex events at Newcastle do not conform to any single model. What began as a fairly typical and reasonably orderly protest became complicated by underlying tensions within the ruling elite, but, had bloodshed been avoided, a peaceful solution might have emerged.

Ironically on the very day of the Newcastle riot, the Lords Justices of the Regency (during the King's absence abroad) issued a proclamation ordering strict enforcement of laws passed in the reign of Edward VI against the engrossing of corn (the buying up of large quantities to sell at a high price).[40] In recommending speedy and effectual execution of the proclamation, the Bishop of Durham strongly condemned those who by 'avaritious and illegal practices' put private gain above the lives of thousands of labourers and their families, and thereby provoked disorder.[41] The dealers, however, were not worried by the central authorities' edict. 'Last post brought us a proclamation from the Regency by way of forbidding the export', Ralph Carr wrote on 4 July, but 'without a new Act of Parliament no person need regard it'.[42] Even so, the Newcastle merchants bowed to expediency, and, that 'mobs may be prevented',

[36]   Carr to J. Coutts & Co., 1 July 1740 and to Nathan Yelloly, 5 July 1740, Northumberland Museum and Archives, ZCE 10/13; Richardson, *The Local Historian's Table Book*, I, p.400; Ellis, 'Urban Conflict', pp.344–5. The green boughs in Ridley's men's hats are mentioned in his account.
[37]   Ridley's account, NMA, ZRI 27/8.
[38]   Ellis, 'Urban Conflict', p.343.
[39]   Ridley's account; Carr to John Burnett, 1 July 1740, 'Their sole intentions was to plunder', NMA, ZCE 10/13.
[40]   The order is printed in the *Newcastle Courant*, 12 July 1740.
[41]   Edward Chandler, Bishop of Durham, 'A Charge delivered to the Grand Jury at the Quarter Sessions held at Durham…16 July 1740 concerning Engrossing of Corn and Grain, and the Riots that have been occasion'd Thereby'. The Bishop also condemned the riots, which, he argued, were in any case counter-productive.
[42]   Carr to William Norton, 4 July 1740, Northumberland Museum and Archives, ZCE 10/13. On incorrect interpretation of the order see Bohstedt, 'The Pragmatic Economy', p.61.

those who still had corn on hand resolved to sell at home 'even under prime cost'.[43] The protest had thus achieved a measure of success. Such modification of the property rights of farmers and food dealers and the 'exertion of force at the margin of legitimacy and illegality' by the insurgents was, as Bohstedt puts it, 'a real if limited exercise of political power', a view with which Thompson agreed.[44]

Once peace was restored the municipal authorities made every effort to discover and prosecute the offenders, and the corn dealers offered a reward of £5 for information leading to the conviction of each one involved in the theft of their grain.[45] Altogether 304 arrests were made, 91 in respect of the disturbances of 19–21 June, and 213 on account of the riot on 26 June, but 87 were discharged, and proceedings were dropped in a further 79 cases.[46] The Attorney and Solicitor Generals were consulted on the form of the indictments and on the composition of the jury. Since the stolen cash belonged to the Mayor and Burgesses it was advised that a jury of non-freemen should be empanelled to obviate possible objections on this account.[47] Of 138 indictments, true bills were found in 40 cases for felony and in 70 for riot and assault.[48] The fatal shooting was never mentioned by the Mayor when he informed the government of the onslaught on the Guildhall, nor did it appear in the brief for the crown drawn up in preparation for the subsequent trials of the prisoners.[49] Fears were raised that if the soldiers were removed from the area during the Assizes 'fresh tumults' might break out, as the keelmen and others had threatened to release their brethren from gaol. The magistrates authorized the guards to 'repel force by force', but no rescue attempt was made.[50]

The punishments of those eventually found guilty were lenient by the standards of the day. Seven convicted of felony, which could have incurred the death penalty, were sentenced to transportation for seven years; others merely received short terms of imprisonment, yet at the same Assizes a horse stealer was sentenced to death. As one historian remarks, the sentences may have reflected a 'realistic assessment of the power of organized labour on Tyneside' where the authorities had to 'tread a careful path between enforcing respect for law and restoring some measure of social harmony to the area in which they themselves had to live'.[51] This was the magistrates' policy when dealing with offences committed by keelmen during their strikes, and at the Assizes the

[43]   Carr to John Coutts & Co., 1 July 1740, NMA, ZCE 10/13.
[44]   J. Bohstedt, *Riots and Community Politics in England and Wales 1790–1810* (Cambridge, MA and London, 1983), p.221; Thompson, *Customs in Common*, pp.293–4, quoting Bohstedt and adding that riot was always 'a profoundly political as well as an economic event'.
[45]   25 June 1740, TWA 394/10.
[46]   Ellis, 'Urban Conflict', p.347.
[47]   Opinion of Attorney-General Sir Dudley Ryder, and Solicitor-General Sir John Strange, 31 July 1740, TWA 394/10.
[48]   Ellis, 'Urban Conflict', p.347.
[49]   TWA 394/56; SP 36/51/198–9.
[50]   Draft letter [Mayor of Newcastle] to [the Duke of Newcastle], 19 July 1740; warrant issued by the magistrates, 11 July 1740, TWA 394/10.
[51]   Ellis, 'Urban Conflict', p.348; *Newcastle Journal*, 16 August 1740 and 8 August 1741.

judges evidently paid heed to local concerns. As mentioned above in Chapter 3, the magistrates organized a census of keelmen soon after the riot.[52] They were particularly concerned to discover the settlements of those who had come from Scotland or elsewhere and the length of time they had lived in Newcastle. If this was a tacit recognition that poverty had been at the root of the disturbances, the intended remedy was to clear the indigent out of the city.

This 'worst breakdown of civil order in Newcastle's history',[53] made a lasting impression on the authorities. Thenceforth in times of scarcity and rising food prices they tried to take pre-emptive action to avert disturbances. In 1766 Lord Ravensworth earnestly called on ministers for a bill to allow duty-free importation of rye, 'so necessary for the sustenance of the north', and, in 1772 Sir Edward Blackett and Sir Thomas Clavering, MPs for Northumberland and County Durham respectively, introduced a bill to prohibit the export of home-grown rye when the price reached 28 shillings per quarter.[54] In June the previous year, when the keelmen and pitmen on both Tyne and Wear struck partly on account of the high price of corn and other foodstuffs, the Privy Council took steps to procure the importation of rye, the news of which the Mayor of Newcastle hastened to publicize by handbills and notices in the press.[55] Imports of rye from the southern counties of England and from the Baltic were essential, as that grown in the north east was inadequate in quantity for the industrial population, besides being 'very inferior' in quality.[56]

There were several years of scarcity in the 1790s and early 1800s. An Act of 1791 imposed high duties on imports of foreign grain and promoted exports while restricting local markets. When the magistrates found that the 'very scanty' stock in Newcastle would soon be exhausted, they urged the Privy Council to permit imports of rye at low duty, and allow the sale of a large quantity of foreign rye, then 'under the King's locks' in the city, to preserve 'public tranquillity' in this 'alarming crisis'.[57] On 7 May 1795 pitmen assembled nearby

---

[52] 16 July 1740, TWA 394/10; some of the returns are in TWA 394/ 11–12 and 394/57; see above Chapter 3.

[53] Levine and Wrightson, *The Making of an Industrial Society – Whickham 1560–1765*, p.383.

[54] Hughes, *North Country Life in the Eighteenth Century*, p.303.

[55] Copy Aubone Surtees, Mayor, to Duke of Northumberland, 29 June 1771, letter book, TWA 592/1, fols 114v–115. Other letters concerning the disturbances, fols 113–115v.

[56] Draft petition of the magistrates to the Privy Council, n.d., TWA 394/35.

[57] *Ibid.* The Act for regulating the Importation and Exportation of Corn and the Payment of Duty on foreign Corn imported and the Bounty on British Corn exported, 31 George III cap. 30, 1791, offered a bounty of 5 shillings per quarter on the export of wheat when the price was below 44 shillings per quarter and 3 shillings per quarter on rye when under 28 shillings per quarter, and imposed a duty of 24s 3d per quarter on imports of foreign wheat when the domestic price was under 50 shillings per quarter and 22 shillings per quarter on rye, peas and beans when the price was below 34 shillings per quarter. If the price of wheat and rye rose above 54 shilllings and 37 shillings per quarter respectively, the duty fell to 6d per quarter for wheat and 3d per quarter for rye. *Statutes at Large*, XVII, 1788–1792 (London, 1811), pp.498–553. The magistrates argued that although the price of rye grown in the locality was only 24s 2d per quarter, the better quality rye for which there was a demand in the shops was fetching between 32 shillings and 36 or 37 shillings per quarter, and rising. The latter figure would allow imports at the low duty, but the government inspector's returns showed only the price of the local grain. According to the apologist for the corn dealers in 1740 (cited in n.5) the quantity of rye and barley grown locally was insufficient to serve Newcastle for two months in the year.

at Byker and complained that supplies of grain were being withheld from sale by dealers who had purchased large quantities in order to sell at an enhanced price, a practice known as forestalling or regrating the market. To deal with the threatening situation, a large number of special constables were sworn in, and the magistrates, accompanied by a party of light dragoons, then negotiated with the protesters. By promising to do all in their power to prevent the alleged malpractices they persuaded the men to return to work. This and a similar confrontation that took place slightly earlier on Gateshead Fell have been described as 'highly ritualized affairs' in which the protagonists played their roles in conformity with a pattern of expectations. The magistrates' authority was unchallenged, no hurt or damage was done, grievances were aired and remedial action promised – an example of Bohstedt's 'protocol of riot'.[58] The remedy evidently proved ineffective, for six months later, protesters seized provisions in several Newcastle markets and sold them at reduced rates: wheat at 12 shillings per boll, the price that had obtained in previous years, butter at 8 pence per pound, and potatoes at 5 shillings per load. This was done in the presence of the municipal officers, no one was injured, and the owners received the proceeds of the sales. 'That great abuses and enormities have been practised here by forestallers we must avow as a notorious fact', the *Newcastle Chronicle* commented, though it deplored the direct action that resulted.[59]

The keelmen were probably involved in this action though they are not specifically mentioned in the reports. There was an obvious correlation between rising food prices and their demands for increased wages. After a strike in 1791 they gained a new wages settlement on account of the high cost of provisions,[60] and in February 1800 they struck again for higher pay. The citizens feared that a riot was imminent, but the magistrates brokered a settlement whereby each crew would receive an advance of 2s 6d per tide while the average price of wheat remained above 14 shillings per boll and rye above 8 shillings.[61] This 'bread money' became a permanent part of the keelmen's wages.[62] Even so, in 1812, 'in view of the high price of corn', the fitters resolved to render aid to certain keelmen's families.[63] Although in years of dearth the keelmen were apt to make wage demands, this was not always the case. They did not do so in 1740 nor in other years during the next two decades when food was scarce. Most of their strikes resulted from grievances arising out of their employment as in the case of the two vigorous ones of 1744 and 1750 which we shall now consider.

---

[58] *Newcastle Chronicle*, 9 May 1795; Morgan and Rushton, *Rogues, Thieves and the Rule of Law*, pp.191–3.

[59] *Newcastle Chronicle*, 14 November 1795; E. Mackenzie, *Descriptive and Historical Account of Newcastle*, p.72. The proceedings conform well with Thompson's model of the moral economy of the crowd.

[60] See below, Chapter 9.

[61] *Newcastle Courant*, 15 February 1800.

[62] This was stated to be the case in 1809, see below, Chapter 11.

[63] D.J. Rowe, 'The Strikes of the Tyneside Keelmen in 1809 and 1819', *International Review of Social History*, XIII, part I (1968), pp.58–75, quotation p.66.

7

The Strikes of 1744 and 1750

It has already been shown how the coal owners' difficulties tended to result in hardships being imposed on the keelmen. Competition between the coal owners became extremely fierce in the early 1740s as Matthew Ridley, who had succeeded his father as one of the principal coal owners in the area, remained outside the Grand Alliance, and rivalry between the various parties resulted in losses for all. 'But in truth this has been the worst year I ever saw', Ridley declared of the 1744 season, 'the coal trade having met with many repeated obstructions, & the ugly differences among the persons concern'd here has occasioned lowering of prices or advance of measure, which has been great drawbacks from the profits'.[1] Towards the end of July 'advance of measure' provoked a strike by the keelmen who had been obliged to carry up to ten chaldrons of coal instead of the usual eight, an increase of over five tons, without additional pay. The men grew turbulent, the magistrates ordered the proclamation against riots to be read, and four companies of soldiers were sent to keep order in Sandgate.[2] To settle the dispute, a new wages scale was drawn up and signed by the magistrates and twenty-four fitters.[3] The critical clause was that 'no keel shall be obliged to take more than the king's measure' – i.e. eight Newcastle chaldrons each of 53 hundredweights according to statute, on which customs duties were assessed. Ridley, who in January 1744/5 had declared that everyone was 'sick by this time of throwing away their money',[4] eventually joined in a regulation of the vend in 1747. According to William Brown, an eminent colliery engineer, the agreement was 'inviolably observed' for three years, mainly on account of the respective parties' self-interest, 'for by this Regulation there is as much profit arises at the vending 10,000 chalders as 30,[000] when a fighting trade, when one undersells another so that some sells cheaper than they work and then the ship master makes a fine time'.[5] At the beginning of 1750, however, the breakdown of negotiations for renewal of the Regulation sparked off unbridled competition:

[1] Ridley to Henry Norris, 5 January 1744/5, letter book, 1741–9, Northumberland Museum and Archives, ZRI 35/12.
[2] Richardson, *The Local Historian's Table Book*, I, pp.412–13.
[3] The original document has not been found but it was seen and described by Andrew Mitchell in his *Address to the Keelmen of the River Tyne with a Correct Statement of the Dues of the River* (Newcastle, 1792).
[4] Ridley to Henry Norris, NMA, ZRI 35/12.
[5] William Brown of Throckley to C. Spedding, 13 January 1749/50, letter book, North of England Institute of Mining Engineers, Brown/1.

Every owner begun to undersell another tho' not in price fair but in giving extraordinary measure of coals (vizt) 9 or 10 chalders of coals instead of 8 and recd no more for them then for 8. This sort of dealing begun to lie hard upon the keelmen so that they could scarce keep the keel above water ...[6]

Naturally the keelmen complained that their 'taskmasters' had broken the agreement of 1744, and this, combined with other grievances, led to one of the most prolonged strikes of the century.

On 19 March a band of skippers and keelmen at Newcastle quay struck work and forcibly brought all keels to a standstill. The next day parties of strikers proceeded to Shields, boarded several keels, burst open the cabins, smashed the shovels and other tackle and intimidated any crews who were prepared to work. By 22 March all the keelmen either from conviction or fear had joined the strike, and for several weeks to come no keel passed down the river, thus disrupting not only the coal trade but all local industries dependent on coal.[7] 'Trade is intirely stagnated', Brown wrote on 30 April,

cash grows scarce, especially with the coal owners, nothing is heard but complaints ... the river looks dejected or rather deserted, nothing is seen but a few wherrys going up and down instead of keels to the number of 5 or six hundred, [the] harbour full of ships but empty ones ... Sunderland makes a fine sett out and would have done much more but the wind has been against them very much.[8]

The strikers presented a list of grievances to the magistrates but were informed that many of their complaints were 'hardly understood even by the gentlemen coal owners themselves', or, as they bitterly remarked, 'any body else except we who are the sufferours and such as are the gainers by the practices complain'd of'. They therefore explained their grievances at some length in a second petition. They were not complaining of all the fitters, they declared: several had not imposed any hardships upon them and were willing to hear and redress their grievances, 'if they cou'd prevail on the rest to be unanimous therein'.[9] The fitters as employees of the coal owners were not primarily responsible for grants of overmeasure. They did not receive payment for carriage of the extra coal, and overloading was liable to damage and endanger their keels. However, fitters who held shares in the colliers could gain from the practice,[10] and it is probable that some of the fitters had interests in these ships at the time. By 1766 it was said that the fitters both at Newcastle and Sunderland had 'of

---

[6] Brown to Spedding, 30 April 1750, *ibid.*

[7] 'The King against the Keelmen Rioters', TWA 394/24.

[8] Brown to Spedding, 30 April 1750, as in n. 5. The shipmasters, he states, were not unhappy at the stoppage, as the price of coal at London had fallen so low that if the strike had not occurred they would have been obliged to lay up their ships or turn to other branches of business. However, when the price began to rise rapidly, he believed they would grow 'uneasie' if they were not loaded soon.

[9] Petition of the keelmen, TWA 394/19.

[10] The fitter did not pay the coal owner for the extra coal, but he lost the fittage for its carriage. Evidence of Edward Mosley, *Journals of the House of Commons*, 32, p.778.

late years' become owners of ships 'to a very great extent'.[11] The staithmen, who supervised the loading of the keels, may have contributed to the keelmen's grievance, for by exceeding their instructions at the behest of the shipmasters they had opportunity to make clandestine gains. The overloading of the keels was a complex matter with various interests involved, but the keelmen naturally blamed their immediate employers, the fitters. Their first response to the men's complaint was that any allegedly overloaded keel should be brought to the quay and examined by the 'King's Inspector', but the keelmen dismissed this proposed remedy as 'much worse than the distemper' since the customs officer was not obliged to answer a call either from them or their masters. Besides, they contended, the King's measure was 'so self evident and plain' by the mark or nail on each keel that it was 'impossible for us or any person to err in the observation of it'. This was not entirely true as the depth to which a laden keel sank could vary according to a number of circumstances, but when the keels were greatly overloaded, as they evidently were before the strike, there could be little room for doubt.

Several of the keelmen's other grievances concerned the 'can houses' in which their beer was supplied and their wages paid. 'Every five shillings of market money we receive there is 3d. stopped from each of us', they complained, but, besides the deduction of 'can-money', they were

> oblig'd to spend more of our money than we can afford in waiting at these houses for orders, and if we refuse to wait or [are] slow in drinking we are abus'd & threaten'd by the can-house keepers, who are all the fitters servants, to be turn'd out of our keels, and as this rank of our masters (for we have many degrees of masters), as we are inform'd, have no other wages but the benefit of these can-houses, they make it as considerable a perquasite as possible, for which reason we have not the same liquor as the other customers but a certain other liquor is brew'd for us, which they call savage beer or beer for savages, at the same time doing us the honour to take the gentleman's price for it.

Even without the alleged threats of the can-house keepers, these establishments were bound to tempt many of the keelmen to drink to excess, despite the poor quality of the liquor. Again, as in 1710 and 1738, they loudly complained of the shipmasters, who, instead of giving them good beer to the value of 1s 4d or the money, 'sometimes order their servants to give us a small quantity of stuff, sometimes sowr and sometimes yeast which if we venture to drink it is ready to kill us [and] has killed some of us, on account of our being over heated with hard labour'. They had yet another drink-related grievance, though in this case their main concern was the delays and consequent loss of earnings associated with it:

---

[11]   Petition of owners or masters of ships belonging to Whitby and Scarborough, 13 February 1766, cited in a brief to oppose the second reading of a bill for regulation of the coal trade of Newcastle only and to support one for regulating the trade in Newcastle and Sunderland c.1788, TWA 394/55.

Touching the spout sixpences, there is one shilling of our money which is allow'd by the coal owners to each keel each tide which shilling is sunk in the following manner; we are oblig'd to fill two quarts of bad drink for one sixpence & we must carry the other sixpence to the steath for two loaders to help us, but the steathmen to engross this perquasite to themselves oblige us to ly at the steath a whole day for the luire of this dear sixpence & then we are forc'd to goe down to Shields in dark and stormy nights to the danger of our lives beside the loss of our tides, so that to gain them sixpence we often lose 13s. 4d., and the steathmen themselves have oftentimes acknowledg'd that they made £50-0-0 a year by this perquasite, &, say they, who but savages wou'd complain of this.

The keelmen had made a similar complaint in 1738. It appears that by delaying the keels, the staithmen, one of the keelmen's 'many degrees of masters', forced them to use the spouts to load their craft (for which the charge was sixpence) and thereby gained the money that should have gone to the loaders. Delay in despatching the keels was not always against the coal owners' interest. On one occasion Matthew Ridley regarded the interruption caused by 'prodigious stormy weather' and a 'great fresh' in the Tyne as 'lucky' because it would 'help the ships unsold at mark[e]t'.[12] As suggested above, a dishonest staithman might on occasion give overmeasure for his own advantage, and in other ways he could profit by 'setting his own interest at variance with that of his employers'.[13] The keelmen were the immediate victims. They complained of another 'great imposition' put upon them by the staithmen and fitters' servants, who did not allow them time to take the least refreshment when they returned wearied to the staithes but obliged them to make in coals and help with barrows, which was not part of their duty as keelmen. They had made a similar complaint in 1738, though their main objection then was payment in liquor instead of cash. Again, as in 1738, they claimed that the shipmasters often refused to pay them a shilling for 'shifting' a ship from the quay, though they 'earned it very hard':

---

[12] 16 February 1768, letter book, 1767–77, Northumberland Museum and Archives, ZRI 38/2, p.38.

[13] Memorial of A. H. Matthewson, staithman at Dunston, 1819–33, reproduced by permission of Durham County Record Office, Clayton and Gibson Papers, D/CG6/1247. 'A hundred inconveniences follow when a staith man is knave and fool or either', declared Charles Montague writing to George Baker, 16 May 1699 (Montague family letter book, microfilm in Central Library, Newcastle). The working and leading costs of the coal that arrived at the staithes were calculated by the 'ten', a measure that could vary from colliery to colliery. The 'making out' of the tens into chaldrons (usually 15 to 20) for sale took place at the staithes, and the higher the number of chaldrons the greater the profit would be. (Ellis, *Letters of Henry Liddell to William Cotesworth*, pp.270–3.) This gave the staithman opportunity to benefit both his employers and himself by dishonestly manipulating the 'makings out'. In the letter cited above, Montague mentions 'a rascally staithman' at Lemington who would make out 18 or 20% [more], sometimes 25%. He also describes how the staithman attached to another Tyne colliery was given small increases in his salary when he made out more than usual. The coal owners 'pitched upon 25% [increase]'. By changing staithmen, when 'every one tried to out doe his predecessor', the target was attained and they found 'an honest able staithman'. The staithmen also manipulated the loading of the keels according to the coal owners' instructions, but, as suggested above, some keels may have been overloaded as a result of clandestine arrangements between staithman and shipmaster.

for when a ship lyes aground alongside of the key, we have a stage to hang with roaps & two of our men must stand in the keels hold and throw the coals to other two of our men who stand on the stage who throw them into the ship's hold, and when we are deny'd payment (which is often the case) we only receive our holliday title of savages.

The skippers, who as usual led the strike, had a grievance peculiar to themselves. They were entitled to twenty pence more per tide than the other men, they claimed, 'but the fitters to engross this perquasite likewise to themselves make a practice of enticeing a common man to stirr [i.e. steer] keels for their benefite for a groat extraordinary so that the fitters have sixteen pence each of these stirr'd keels'. The fitters charged the keelmen's wages to the shipmasters, which explains how they could gain by putting 'common' men in charge of the keels. According to the petitioners, two-thirds of the keels on the river were subject to this practice. Some fitters, they alleged, had keels so manned in accordance with the number of their children, horses or dogs. In 1719 the strikers had complained of the danger arising from the employment of men as skippers who were not capable of the work, but money was now the petitioners' concern. 'As these perquasites is the right and property of the skippers only', they declared, 'we cannot help looking upon it as a very great encroachment upon us & a great discouragement to such as spend their lives & labours to enrich those that oppress us'. The obvious bitterness was directed not against the keelmen who were supplanting them but against their employers. Over forty years later, when the differential between skippers and ordinary keelmen was still causing 'trouble & confusion', it was proposed that skippers should receive a shilling per tide more than the others plus four pence for providing proper gear for the keel.[14] The right to twenty pence extra which the petitioners so confidently claimed in 1750 had disappeared.

The strikers complained of 'considerable loss' by another measure of economy practised by the fitters, who often sent large numbers of keels to Shields after noon on Saturdays because they would not pay for lying tides on Sundays, although, the petitioners declared, 'we are both kept from our familys and likewise from publick worship which is our desire to attend however we may be deriaded for it'. Religious observance was not characteristic of the majority of the keelmen, but vestiges of presbyterianism may have survived among those who came from Scotland. Their alleged desire to attend Sunday worship may also reflect the influence of John Wesley who was well received when he made the first of many visits to Sandgate in 1742. By the end of the century Methodists and other Dissenters were said to have attracted considerable numbers of keelmen into their ranks.[15]

The petitioners demanded a shilling for a man who had to travel from Shields to Newcastle and back with fresh orders, a very moderate claim of three farthings per mile which had been made but evidently not granted in 1738, and

---

[14] Anthony Hood, fitter, to Nathaniel Clayton, 1 January [1792], TWA 394/30.
[15] *Wesley's Journals*, Everyman edn, I, 374–5; Baillie, *Impartial History of Newcastle upon Tyne*, p.143.

they repeated another complaint then made that many of them did not receive an allowance of fire coal, although the fitters agreed that each crew was entitled to a chaldron per year. They called for payment of their wages on Saturday mornings, otherwise they had to go to market at a great disadvantage both as to quality and price of provisions. They concluded with the following plea:

> Upon the whole when what is above represented is duely weigh'd and considered we hope the just part of mankind will be of opinion that all our grievances ought to be redress'd and such methods taken to adjust and settle our demands as to prevent any necessity of further complaints so that the coal trade may be carried on with quietness and expedition to accomplish which our laborious endeavours shall never be wanting.

The magistrates sent for representatives of the keelmen and their masters and, according to the Mayor, redressed the men's 'just complaints' immediately, but they refused to return to work without an increase in wages, 'which were very extravagant demands and could not be complied with'. As the strike became prolonged, the magistrates feared that many poor families would be reduced to the 'utmost necessity'. They again ordered the keelmen to work and promised to enforce rigorously obedience to the agreement made in 1744, but the keelmen remained obdurate.[16] Both coal owners and fitters suffered increasing financial loss. 'I have not rec[eive]d one shilling from the trade for these 5 weeks by the keelmen refusing to work', Matthew Ridley wrote on 20 April, '& have been obliged to pay £400 a week to the workmen [i.e. the pitmen]'.[17] Meanwhile, the keelmen sought to provide for themselves by casual labour. On 28 April, therefore, twenty-five fitters published the names of some eight hundred keelmen with the warning: 'Above is a list of the keelmen which are bound to us; and we desire that you will not employ any of them in any work or service whatsoever; for if you do, we shall call upon you for such a satisfaction as the Law will give us'.[18] At about the same time twenty-two fitters each began proceedings against one of their skippers in the Sheriff's Court.[19]

The magistrates were determined to break the strike, the more so when they received a report that on 27 April several persons who appeared by their dress to be keelmen were seen in Elswick Fields near Newcastle gathered around a stile from which one of them proclaimed Prince Charles King of England, to which at least four said 'Amen'. The magistrates immediately offered £100 reward for information leading to the conviction of those concerned. 'We shall leave nothing that is in our power undone to get to the bottom of the affair', the Mayor declared, adding that there were six companies of soldiers quartered in the town whose commander was ready to assist the civil power in case of

---

[16] Robert Sorsbie to Duke of Bedford, 30 April 1750, SP 36/112 /331; order of magistrates, 21 April 1750, TWA 394/25.

[17] To John Dobson, letter book, 1750–63, Northumberland Museum and Archives, ZRI 35/12.

[18] Handbill in J. Bell, 'Collections relative to the Tyne, its Trade and Conservancy', I, Central Library, Newcastle.

[19] Bill to the fitters for proceedings against the skippers, TWA 394/18.

necessity.[20] Despite statements made by some historians, there are no grounds to suggest that the keelmen at large were disaffected or that the incident in which very few persons were involved was anything more than a prank, as the *Gentleman's Magazine* later described it,[21] but the central authorities so interpreted the Mayor's report that little or no distinction was made between the industrial dispute and sedition. The Lords Justices of the Regency offered a further reward of £100 and a free pardon (except to those who actually proclaimed the Pretender) to any involved who revealed their accomplices, and the commanding officer at Newcastle was ordered to assist the civil powers to quell the 'very insolent disturbances amongst the keelmen' and bring its authors to speedy justice.[22]

When the skippers against whom proceedings had been commenced came to court they produced a document setting forth their defence and pleading for redress:[23]

> We the poor persecuted and oppressed keelmen of Tyne River having first represented our grievances to the worthy magistrates of this Town and County and afterwards explained them do now in obedience to your commands come to attend your court, but certainly under the greatest disadvantages, awed by the dignity of officers and superior fortunes, as well as unable to argue with gentlemen of more generous education, nor will (we believe) any gentleman that professes the law here chuse to incurr the resentment of our opponents (made formidable by the sweat of our brows) by appearing to speak in our behalf.

Even so, they were not without legal advice, as the following argument shows:

> The Contract or Articles in 1744 now insisted on was broke only by our various taskmasters without regarding the injustice done to us and dishonour done to your worships who then vouchsafed to be their guarantees. If it was a contract it was mutually binding, and if it is no tye upon those who signed it, it can never be interpreted an obligation upon us who did not sign it; and if our being hired for a year is insisted on – we affirm the covenants of that hireing are likewise broke by our taskmasters.

It was obvious that their masters intended to starve them into compliance with whatever hardships they resolved to impose upon them, the representation continued, evidently referring to the fitters' bid to prevent anyone employing them,

[20] Sorsbie to Bedford, 30 April 1750, and enclosure, SP 36/112/331.
[21] *Gentleman's Magazine*, XX (1750), p.233. Kathleen Wilson implies that there was extensive disaffection among the keelmen when she writes that 'suspicions …were borne out in 1750 when a group of them proclaimed Charles Edward king', *The Sense of the People: Politics, Culture and Imperialism in England 1715–1785* (Cambridge, 1995), p.335 n.59; and Nicholas Rogers likewise implies that the keelmen as a whole were involved when 'they proclaimed Charles Stuart'. He sees this, however, as 'a theatre of threat…than any sustained commitment to the Stuart cause', *Crowds, Culture and Politics in Georgian Britain* (Oxford, 1998), pp.52–3.
[22] R.N. Aldworth to Mayor of Newcastle, 3 May 1750; Aldworth and R. Leveson Gower to Andrew Stone, 4 May 1750, SP 44/318/10–11, 12–14.
[23] TWA 394/19.

'and how far these may extend after the laws of justice have already been by them openly trangressed is hard to determine'. The Articles of 1744 did not cover various other grievances of which they now complained. These were 'in justice and reason' entitled to redress, but they had been denied the liberty to explain and publish them 'in opposition to that so much contended one of the press', or to vindicate themselves in that manner against the 'false aspersions' which caused the government to send troops by forced marches against 'innocent oppressed men'. According to William Brown, the magistrates called troops into the town 'for fear of a great disturbance', but the 'false aspersions' were evidently that the keelmen were disaffected, which, as we have seen, the central authorities were quick to believe. Significantly, 'God save King George' appears at the end of the keelmen's representation, though added in a different hand. Although the keelmen claimed that they had been prevented from publishing their case, Brown states that they displayed 'printed bills in the public places of the Town showing wherein they are greavd and the terms they require to go to work' and that the fitters responded in like manner, but as the strike became prolonged the authorities must have barred the keelmen from seeking public support in this manner or in the newspapers.[24]

The representation ends with a plea for justice, expressions of solidarity and a veiled threat:

> As we act from the first principle of nature, self preservation, so we doubt not of finding some of both power and influence sufficient to support our just claim as well as to represent it in a true and publick light in which we hope this court will be found to have acted with impartiality honour & justice, for we are determined rather than have a hand in our own ruin, to apply to the courts of earth and heaven where we shall either find or not need advocates. This is the sense of all of us and we will continue unanimous in it. And as the honour of this court can never allow a stumbling block to be laid in the way of our ignorance so we are resolved not to intrapt our selves by entring upon arguments beyond what is here contained.

Sixteen skippers, each belonging to a different fitter, signed this document, though as the last sentence quoted above implies, these self-confessed ignorant men were not its authors. It was obviously the work of someone with legal knowledge and acquaintance with political philosophy, as the reference to 'the first principle of nature' and appeal to the court of heaven suggest. Locke used the latter phrase in the sense of recourse to battle (hence advocates would not be needed).[25] The author was unable to represent the keelmen in person at the magistrates' court because he himself was in danger of arrest. 'A person who calls himself Herdman, and pretends to be a lawyer of Edinburgh, has been extremely instrumental in advising and spiriting up the keelmen', the Mayor reported, 'but at present he conceals himself in the neighbourhood of the Town

---

[24] Brown to Spedding, 30 April 1750, North of England Institute of Mining Engineers, Letterbook, Brown/1.

[25] *Two Treatises of Government. . . . the true Origin, Extent and End of Civil Government* (London 1690), II, paragraphs 241–2, pp.269–70.

and out of the limits of our jurisdiction. However, we hope to apprehend him soon'.[26] William Dollar, the 'writer or scrivener for the keelmen at the request and by the directions of Mr Herdman', was reported to be surprised that the magistrates had not sought to arrest him as well.[27] The central authorities were anxious to capture Herdman for 'stirring up the keelmen to sedition', and the Duke of Bedford, Secretary of State and one of the Lords Justices of the Regency, dispatched a messenger to Newcastle with a warrant for the arrest of Herdman 'upon suspicion of High Treason'.[28] The Mayor also issued a warrant for Herdman's arrest to answer several informations made against him for 'high crimes and misdemeanours'. The officers employed in the search for him were authorized to break down doors and seize his papers, but he evidently evaded capture.[29] His involvement is one of the intriguing aspects of the strike. Presumably he expected to be well rewarded for his services, but it is unlikely that a lawyer with an established practice in Edinburgh would travel to Newcastle to risk aiding the insubordinate keelmen. Though his representation included strong radical expressions they were by no means treasonable, but the proclamation of the Pretender by a few men who may have had too much to drink gave the authorities opportunity to accuse him of fomenting disloyalty.

The magistrates were not impressed by his arguments. 'The men have remained idle without doing any mischief', the Mayor reported on 30 April, 'and we are proceeding upon the Act of the 20th of his present Majesty and have committed sixteen of the offenders to prison, and shall go on in the same way and hope to bring the men to their duty'.[30] The Act (20 George II cap. XIX) 'for the better adjusting and more easy recovery of the wages of certain servants and for the better regulation of such servants', specifically included keelmen and other workers in the coal industry. In cases of disputes it empowered magistrates to order payment of wages and to commit servants found guilty of 'misdemeanour or miscarriage or ill behaviour' to the House of Correction for a period not exceeding one calendar month.[31] It is not known whether out of the twenty-two prosecuted the sixteen imprisoned were exclusively the signatories of Herdman's document, but obviously most of them were. The arrests failed to intimidate the rest of the strikers nor, as had been expected in some quarters, did they provoke a rescue attempt or riot by the 'rabble part ... so as a military force might have been turned upon them and obliged them to work'.[32]

Having prosecuted the ringleaders and taken steps to prevent the keelmen supporting themselves by casual employment, the fitters proceeded to recruit sailors, waggonmen and others to man the keels, even though there was a con-

---

[26] Sorsbie to Bedford, 30 April 1750, SP 36/112/331.
[27] Deposition of Joseph Dixon, Serjeant at Mace, 27 April 1750, TWA 394/26.
[28] R.N. Aldworth to [Sorsbie], 3 May 1750, SP 44/318/11–12; instruction to Richard Lucas, Messenger in Ordinary, 4 May 1750, SP 44/85/183–4.
[29] Warrant for arrest of Mungo Herdman, 6 May 1750, TWA 394/24.
[30] Sorsbie to Bedford, 30 April 1750, SP 36/112/331.
[31] *Statutes at Large* (London, 1758), V, pp.538–9.
[32] Brown to Spedding, 30 April 1750, North of England Institute of Mining Engineers, Letterbook, Brown/1.

siderable risk to the craft when navigated by inexperienced men. There was an even greater risk from the enraged keelmen, who, after trade had been carried on for several days in this manner, assembled in great numbers by the riverside on 4 May. Many put out in keels and intercepted those that were attempting to pass. They smashed or jettisoned the tackle, threw some of the crews overboard, and 'barbarously' beat and abused others. William Cole, a waggonman, was lucky to escape with his life.[33] Such violence would have prevailed had not the military been called to the scene and protected the substitute workers. Powerless in face of armed men, the keelmen were forced to allow trade to continue, and their strike, which had lasted seven weeks, quickly ended.

The articles of 1744 were reaffirmed,[34] whereupon the principal coal owners pursued their rivalry by lowering their prices instead of overloading the keels. Some cut their price by as much as 5 shillings per chaldron, William Brown reported, and it was expected that further reductions would follow. 'In short', he concluded, 'trade never had [so] bad appearance in my time as it has at present; how long it may continue is uncertain, tho' it is generally believed the owners will come to a new Regulation in a little time'.[35] Neither combination by the coal owners nor the articles of 1744 provided a lasting remedy for the men's principal grievance. Twenty years later they bewailed the oppressions they had endured on account of overmeasure 'under their masters' contrivance or connivance'. Many keelmen, they alleged, had been 'long imprisoned or turned out of bread with infamous characters' when they represented their grievances and used lawful means to obtain redress;[36] and 'when the said oppressions became general or intolerable and the keelmen unanimously resolved to be relieved, or desist from carrying such overmeasure (which was lawful for them to do), armed soldiers have been drawn up and marched against them, and several keelmen have been killed or wounded by the military, contrary to the laws of this kingdom, under pretence of quelling a riot when no riot was intended or effected by keelmen'.[37] The events of 1744 and 1750 were evidently being recalled here, though there is no record of keelmen being killed on these occasions. We have seen, however, that the authorities avoided mention of the fatal shooting in 1740, and it is possible that, in the course of other tumults which certainly occurred, the military injured keelmen who subsequently died of their wounds without the fact being recorded.

The other grievances about which the keelmen complained were not redressed. The abuses connected with can houses and part payment in liquor continued at least until 1791 and probably well beyond that date.[38] The strike exhibited the keelmen's steadfast determination and solidarity, but

---

[33] 'The King against the Keelmen Rioters', TWA 394/24.
[34] *Newcastle Courant*, 12 May 1750; *Gentleman's Magazine*, XX (1750), p.233.
[35] Brown to Spedding, 12 July 1750, North of England Institute of Mining Engineers, Letterbook, Brown/1.
[36] Keelmen's Resolutions, 5 January 1770, TWA 394/29.
[37] *Ibid.*
[38] See below, Chapter 9.

the prolonged stoppage must have involved great hardship for the men and their families. Indeed, a writer in the *Gentlemen's Magazine*, puzzled by their endurance, suggested that the strike had been provoked to keep up the price of coal at London, 'because otherwise it is unaccountable how such a number of people could subsist seven weeks without work'.[39] The men were certainly not paid to remain idle as the writer implied, but such a view would appeal to Londoners forced to pay higher prices resulting from the scarcity of coal. Far from paying the strikers or redressing their grievances, the fitters were intent on prosecuting the offenders. Thus, 'for preventing the like disturbances for the future' it was agreed 'that the leading men ... and such as sufficient evidence could be procured against should be prosecuted at the Assizes', and, subsequently, the Hostmen's Company paid £154 15s 11d, the charges of the prosecution.[40] However, only those charged with assault or damage, not the skippers who led the strike, were tried at the Assizes, and the sentences passed on those convicted were not severe. Two were imprisoned for three months, four for one month, and all were bound over to keep the peace for three years. The leniency of these sentences contrasts with others passed at the same Assizes. For stealing a piece of flannel a man was sentenced to transportation for seven years, and another found guilty of assault and robbery was sentenced to death but was reprieved to be transported for life.[41]

There were no strikes by the keelmen during the next eighteen years, but, as their lament quoted above indicates, they did not remain content. Some left the Tyne to work as coalheavers on the Thames, allegedly on account of the overloading of the keels,[42] and in 1768 the keelmen embarked on an attempt to procure a statutory remedy for this persistent grievance.

[39] *Gentleman's Magazine*, XX (1750), p.233.
[40] Dendy, *Records of the Hostmen's Company*, p.203.
[41] *Newcastle Courant*, 18 and 25 August 1750; Dendy, *Records of the Hostmen's Company*, pp.203, 256.
[42] Evidence of Thomas Price, George Purvis and Thomas Oughten, 1770, *Journals of the House of Commons*, 32, p.777.

8

The Appeal to Parliament

Towards the end of 1767 the north-east coal trade was in depression. Prices were very low, most of the staithes were full as contrary winds had interrupted sailings for much of October, and in several places the workmen were 'uneasy'.[1] The new year did not bring improvement. A correspondent in the *Newcastle Journal* declared that the trade was in a 'most languishing condition' through 'clogs and abuses' at Billingsgate, 'where those Harpies, the coal buyers, crimps, &c ... are making immense fortunes on the wreck of every branch of trade in these parts'.[2] They exacted an illegal premium of sixpence or a shilling per chaldron from the coal owners, a further douceur from the shipmasters, and by custom had one free chaldron in the score.[3] It is not surprising that this period of depressed trade led the coal owners to resort to grants of overmeasure, as the most flexible means of price reduction. Towards the end of March, the keelmen, 'being for some time very heavily oprest with Over Measure which we are not able to subsist with', enforced a strike. 'We all with one voice desire no other terms then King's Measure which is eight chaldron [to the keel]', they declared in a petition to the Mayor, and 'with one consent' would serve on those terms 'so never to be oprest no more'.[4]

The magistrates, most of whom were directly involved in the coal trade, immediately summoned the fitters and a skipper from each employment. The fitters agreed that for the future no keelman was to take in more than 8 chaldrons, and the magistrates passed a resolution to the same effect,[5] but it was the intervention of Thomas Harvey, an attorney, rather than these assurances that ended the strike. Harvey promised the keelmen that he would endeavour

> to settle them under such regulations as would establish good order and peaceable behaviour amongst them, remove the occasion of their complaints, and tend to the good of the coal trade in general, as far as a *certainty of measure* would effect so salutary an end.[6]

Whether he offered his services to the keelmen, or whether he had already been engaged by them, is not clear. He claimed to have been 'an utter stranger' to the contents of their petition to the magistrates, and solemnly denied that

---

[1]   Matthew Ridley's letter book, 1767–77, 2 and 9 October 1767, pp.17-18, Northumberland Museum and Archives, ZRI 38/2.
[2]   Letter from 'Anglo-Novicastellensis', *Newcastle Journal, 2* April 1768.
[3]   *Newcastle Journal*, 23 April 1768.
[4]   TWA 394/29.
[5]   *Ibid.*
[6]   Evidence of Thomas Port, *Journals of the House of Commons*, 32, pp.775–6; letter to the *Newcastle Courant*, 7 May 1768, defending Harvey's conduct.

he had encouraged them to strike. As several gentlemen had acknowledged the reasonableness of the men's complaints, he did not see how his promise to assist them could give offence. This statement, published in defence of his conduct, suggests that he had no dealings with the men before the strike, but this is not certain.[7]

Harvey proceeded to organize the keelmen into a society with the dual purpose of providing for their indigent brethren and regulating the conditions of their employment. To establish the society on a firm foundation and to deal with the question of overmeasure he proposed to apply to Parliament, and it was agreed that a levy of 3 shillings should be imposed on each keel-crew to meet the consequent expense. Most of the keelmen soon donated half that sum, but those in one employment refused to contribute. 'At present there is a total stop to the trade here', Matthew Ridley wrote, on 29 April, 'by some of the keelmen refusing to work and [preventing] those that are well inclined from working unless they will come in to pay so much per keel to Mr Harvey, an attorney, for business that is to be done for them'.[8] This new stoppage, which began on 25 April, was accompanied by violence. A mob seized Henry Robson, a non-contributor who was also accused of carrying overmeasure, bore him through the streets astride a pole – a punishment often employed by strikers and known as 'riding the stang', – and beat him severely. Two men were arrested for this 'stanging', and a warrant was later issued for the arrest of several others.[9] After this initial outburst the violence subsided, but a few days later several keelmen, 'unlawfully and riotously assembled', stopped a keel which was being brought down the river. The magistrates offered a reward of five guineas for information leading to the conviction of those involved, and warned that any who committed the like offence, or who disturbed the peace of the City, would be punished with the 'utmost rigour of the law'.[10] The draft notice included the further threat that those who refused to work for the usual wages would be arrested as idle and disorderly persons. If they were legally settled in Newcastle, they would be sentenced to hard labour in the House of Correction, while the others would be punished as vagrants and sent to their respective settlements.[11] However, this section of the draft did not appear in the published version. According to the Mayor, 'a very worthless few' were intimidating the 'sensible part' of the keelmen who were willing to work. It was amazing, he declared, that 'such numbers who know so much better can suffer themselves to be so shamefully impos'd upon'.[12]

The strikers attempted to bargain with the magistrates for the release of the two imprisoned keelmen. In an address to the Mayor they acknowledged

---

[7]   *Ibid.*

[8]   To George Ward, Ridley's letter book, 1767–77, NMA, ZRI 38/2, pp.44–5.

[9]   Notes by Edward Mosley of evidence to be given to the committee of the House of Commons, including copy warrant for arrest of five keelmen, 2 May 1768, TWA 394/29.

[10] *Newcastle Courant*, 7 May 1768.

[11] Draft 'advertisement for discovering riotous keelmen', TWA 394/29.

[12] Copy of Mosley's 'intended advertisement about Harvey (not executed)', TWA 394/29.

that he had 'righted' them to their entire satisfaction in respect of their 'great oppression', and begged that the two men might be pardoned.[13] 'They now make a point to have some that are in custody for beating and ill-using of their brethren discharged and they will go to work', Ridley observed, 'but I presume the Magistrates will not comply with a demand of that kind; a few days must determine peace or war with 'em'.[14] However, the two culprits themselves soon urged their fellows to end the strike, 'for it will give little satisfaction for people to distress themselves & families for us'.[15] This made it easier for the strikers to accept defeat and they soon returned to work. Harvey expressed abhorrence at the riotous and illegal proceedings that had occurred.[16] The Mayor, Edward Mosley, himself a fitter, was extremely annoyed that Harvey had stirred up the keelmen with 'vain expectations'. In a disparaging rejoinder to Harvey's defence, which he drafted but did not publish, he expressed the hope that Harvey was sincere in his professed concern for the laws of the country and the general good, 'notwithstanding what he has done has produced so very disagreeable effects'. He could not imagine what service Harvey could render the keelmen, 'who are under so good regulations, and perhaps are ye best paid labouring people in the kingdom'. The magistrates were always ready to redress their grievances upon the first just complaint, as they had recently done to the men's declared satisfaction.[17]

As shown in Chapter 3, the magistrates and fitters were alarmed at the power Harvey had acquired over the keelmen and the secrecy that cloaked his proceedings. One of the fitters, William Cramlington, learned that the keelmen had signed a deed whereby they were to be sole judges of the load to be carried and 'not to be subject to any controul from the offputter or fitter's serv[an]t, & that, if any keel take in more than what may be adjudged proper measure by them, each man on board such keel to be subject to a fine of 5sh'.[18] This was soon put into effect. Alexander Williamson, a skipper employed by Mosley, was served with a notice signed by Harvey stating

> that information upon the oath of 3 persons is made that you, John Turner and Andrew Galloway have each of you incur'd the payment of 5s. apiece for loading your keel on ye 30th Inst August with coal at South Moor staith an inch over the plate at ye head and a quarter of an inch over the plate at the stern and for navigating the said keel loaded as aforesd, & unless you and each of you pay ye sd 5s. within 14 days after the delivery hereof you will be sued for the same.[19]

The accused men swore that the keel was correctly loaded to her marks (half plate at the bow and to the underside of the nail at the stern). Mosley told them

[13] Copy address to the Mayor, TWA 394/29.
[14] Ridley to George Ward, 29 April 1768, Ridley's letter book, 1767–77, NMA, ZRI 38/2, pp.44–5.
[15] Copy note from George Turnbull and Charles Miller, 30 April 1768, TWA 394/29.
[16] *Newcastle Courant*, 7 May 1768.
[17] 'Intended advertisement', TWA 394/29.
[18] Copy Cramlington to Mosley, 3 August 1768, TWA 394/29.
[19] Copy, 31 August 1768, TWA 394/29..

to ignore the notice; but Andrew Galloway's mother, fearing that her son, who had been threatened by some of his fellow workers, might come to harm, tried to reason with Harvey. When she declared that the Mayor had forbidden her to pay anything, Harvey retorted that if the fine of 15 shillings on the crew was not paid he would send to London for a writ which would involve costs bringing the total to 23s 10d. Williamson and Turner also approached Harvey, but, on hearing that the charge would soon be increased, they paid the demand.[20]

Disputes could easily arise among the keelmen themselves as to whether or not a keel was overloaded. On 5 September 1768 a party of keelmen stopped a laden keel, but 'the wind blowing then high', which made it difficult to examine her marks, they removed her to a creek where they declared her to be overloaded, even though, since they had all boarded her, 'such additional weight & the movement of the keel & water ... rendered the ascertaining the just quantity of coals in her an impossibility'. A member of the boarding party threatened to throw one of the keelmen overboard, and all swore they would inform Harvey who would fine each of the crew 'for breaking thro' his bond'. The skipper believed that the keel was not overloaded, and the Collector of Customs and two other officers later confirmed his opinion, but he was so intimidated by threats that he preferred to carry less than measure 'when the roughness of the water prevents a certainty'.[21]

Soon after the stoppage on the Tyne, the keelmen on the River Wear enforced a strike, probably on account of overmeasure from which they also suffered. 'The keelmen at Sunderland have carried their cause to such a height that everyone there is obliged to comply with their demands as soon as asked', one of the London newspapers reported with considerable exaggeration,[22] but this account was probably coloured by the fact that the strike coincided with violent outbursts in Sunderland and Shields by sailors in pursuit of higher wages. Much damage was done to property, but a detachment of troops curbed a march that threatened Newcastle.[23] Harvey sought to include the Wearside keelmen in the application to Parliament against overmeasure, and in September 1769 he sent the Beadle and other officers of the Newcastle Society to Sunderland to gain their support. The emissaries stayed at a tavern where, it was alleged, they drank day and night and kept open house 'in the same manner as is done at elections'. Many keelmen came to them under cover of darkness through fear of dismissal.[24]

The petition to the Commons that Harvey drew up referred to existing statutes regulating the admeasurement of keels, the customary keel-load of 8 Newcastle chaldrons, each weighing 53 hundredweights, and the excess loading that occasioned great loss to the keelmen, who, 'notwithstanding such overmeasure are paid after the rate of 8 chaldrons by the keel only'. Customs

[20]   Notes by Mosley, *ibid*
[21]   Affidavit of John Hymers, skipper of the keel, 14 October 1768, TWA 394/29.
[22]   *Westminster Journal*, 16 April 1768.
[23]   Duke of Northumberland to the Principal Secretaries of State, 12 April 1768, SP 44/142/47–49.
[24]   *Journals of the House of Commons*, 32, pp.774–5.

and other duties assessed on that basis were at the same time diminished. The second part of the petition concerned the charity (see Chapter 3) and the petitioners begged leave to bring in a bill to restrict the measure to 8 chaldrons per keel and to establish and extend their society.[25] Harvey had intended the petition to be signed by the keelmen of both rivers, but the Beadle and his companions failed to obtain any signatures at Sunderland. Harvey therefore added a note stating that the petition was

> at the particular request, and for and on behalf of upwards of four hundred skippers and castors, employed upon the River Wear, who durst not, but with the greatest hazard of their respective employments ... be seen or known to subscribe their respective names.[26]

He was closely questioned about this when the petition was considered by a committee of the Commons in February 1770. He admitted that he wrote it at the request of the officers of the Society after their return from Sunderland, and claimed that Sunderland keelmen had told him it represented the general sense of the men employed on the Wear. He refused to name these individuals lest it prejudiced their employment.[27] The committee resolved that, on the evidence submitted, the note at the bottom of the petition was not well founded. Moreover, a counter petition of over three hundred keelmen had arrived from Sunderland, and although it concerned the charity and not the question of overmeasure, the committee concluded that the men on the Wear had no prior knowledge of the Newcastle petition, had never given it their authority, and that misrepresentation in a petition to Parliament was 'a dangerous practice and ought to be discouraged'.[28]

Although weakened, the petitioners' case was not destroyed, and the committee proceeded to deal with the complaint about overmeasure. Harvey produced a printed paper setting out the dues of the river as settled in 1744 and stated that the keelmen wished for a law to limit the keel-load to 8 chaldrons, king's measure, the basis on which they were paid. From accounts of loadings at Newcastle and their 'makings-out' at London he had found that overmeasure had constantly been sent there during the previous three years. He also alleged that the Customs were defrauded by the practice, especially in respect of cargoes sent overseas.[29] Edward Mosley, on behalf of the fitters, admitted that in some instances the keels had been overloaded, but not considerably so. He believed that the keelmen's complaints at the time of the strike in 1768 were well founded, but could not be certain.[30] He produced an impartial list of the 'makings-out' at London of all the ships loaded by his own keelmen during the period 1765–67 which showed that some ships had taken in 'less than measure', though it also revealed that other vessels had received considerably

25 *Ibid.,* p.644; TWA 394/29.
26 *Journals of the House of Commons*, 32, pp.774–5.
27 *Ibid.*
28 *Ibid.*, p.775.
29 *Ibid.*, pp.775–7..
30 *Ibid.*, pp.777–8

more.[31] He declared that the keelmen were 'by no means to be trusted', and the fitters therefore employed servants to ensure that they loaded the proper measure at the staithes and cast it all aboard ship. Without supervision they would 'never or rarely take in ye statute or King's measure', and would 'frequently imbezel and dispose of coals in their way down to Shields'. As customs duties on coal shipped coastwise were paid at the port of delivery, it made no difference to the revenue whether the keels were overloaded or not. However, when coal was to be shipped overseas, the duties were paid beforehand and a revenue officer inspected the keels before allowing the coal to be cast into the vessel.[32] He believed that the officers were very diligent, but George Purvis, a coalheaver who had formerly been employed on the keels, claimed that the officers did not always attend and that he had seen overmeasure cast into a ship in their absence.[33]

Several other former keelmen, most of whom had quitted the Tyne to work as coalheavers on the Thames, gave evidence about the imposition of overmeasure and the impossibility of gaining effective redress from the Newcastle magistrates who were themselves concerned in the trade. Nine of the twelve City magistrates were either coal owners or fitters.[34] Despite their promises, some keels were still being overloaded after the strike of 1768. Individual keelmen were afraid to complain to the magistrates lest they should 'lose their bread and be turned away as vagabonds'.[35] After hearing all the evidence, including some concerning the difficulty of ascertaining the true keel-load, the committee resolved that the existing Act governing the admeasurement of keels was not effectual and ought to be amended. The House subsequently gave leave for a bill to be introduced for that purpose and also for the relief of the keelmen, their widows and children, in and about Newcastle.[36]

Harvey drafted a bill for both these ends. The section concerning the charity has been described above in Chapter 3. The part relating to overmeasure set forth that many skippers and keelmen, under fear of losing their employment, had frequently been obliged to carry excess quantities of coal without receiving additional pay. Removal of this oppression would 'tend greatly to their quiet and relief' and enable them to afford the contributions to the charity. It was therefore proposed that no keel on the Tyne or Wear should be loaded beyond 8 chaldrons at a time, 'allowing 53 hundredweights to every chaldron according to the King's measure', and that, 'notwithstanding such regulation', the skippers and keelmen should not be paid less than the usual rates. The employer

---

[31] TWA 394/28.
[32] 'Part of Mr Mosley's Evidence', TWA 394/29. These notes by Mosley of proceedings before the Commons' committee give more details than the report in the Commons' *Journals.*
[33] *Ibid.*
[34] *Journals of the House of Commons*, 32, pp.777–8.
[35] Evidence of Thomas Price, *ibid.*, p.777; draft advertisement 'for discovering riotous keelmen', TWA 394/29.
[36] *Journals of the House of Commons*, 32, p.779.

as well as the crew of any keel found to be overloaded was to be fined and the proceeds applied to the charity.[37]

The fitters resolved that if the bill was brought before the Commons it should be opposed 'in every particular',[38] but Mosley believed that it would not proceed that far. Objections would have to be presented to the House before the bill was admitted, and these, he considered, would be 'sufficient to defeat Mr Harvey's designs'.[39] Harvey himself, evidently realizing that his bill would fail, soon abandoned it and joined Rose Fuller, MP for Rye, who proposed to introduce a bill dealing solely with the question of overmeasure.[40] Fuller, a 'landowner and iron-master in Sussex and one of the biggest planters in Jamaica', frequently spoke on a variety of topics in the House.[41] At first, to the fitters' relief, he declared that he did not intend to pursue the matter immediately,[42] but Mosley soon began to doubt this. 'I waited upon Mr Fuller this morning [he wrote, 27 March 1770] who still seems determined to bring in his Bill. I find Harvey was with him yesterday and hangs much about him, and if more material business did not put him of[f] he said he would move for his Bill today, which if he does, don't apprehend he will succeed'. Mosley thought it might lie on the table for the consideration of 'the gentlemen in the country', and perhaps be taken up later. He hoped it might not proceed further, but no one could predict 'an old man's possitive humour who has been used to a West Indian imperious life where he was governor for 20 years and the assumption of which power seems not to have left him'.[43] Two days later, Mosley reported that Fuller had sought leave to introduce his bill. His motion was seconded by Herbert Mackworth, MP for Cardiff Boroughs, who had industrial interests in copper and coal and, Mosley believed, was 'under the influence of Lady Windsor', one of Harvey's supporters.[44] Mackworth, however, was 'thoroughly independent' and, like Fuller, often spoke on a wide range of subjects.[45] The Commons granted Fuller leave to bring in a bill to explain, amend and make more effectual the existing Act concerning the admeasurement of keels.[46] Two north-east MPs, Matthew Ridley and Sir Thomas Clavering, pressed Fuller hard to waive, or at least postpone, the measure until it could be 'well considered by the gentlemen in the North', but he seemed determined to continue and, if possible, finish it that session. 'He has deceived us', Mosley wrote angrily, as Fuller had assured him

---

[37] Copy of Harvey's bill, TWA 394/29.

[38] J. French to Mosley, 9 March 1770, TWA 394/29.

[39] Copy Mosley to [French?], 6 March 1770, TWA 394/29.

[40] Note by Mosley endorsed on copy of Harvey's bill, TWA 394/29; J.Airey to Mosley, 24 March 1770, TWA 394/29.

[41] Sir Lewis Namier and John Brooke, *History of Parliament, The House of Commons, 1754-1790* (London, 1964), II, pp.477–80.

[42] Note by Mosley and letter J.Airey to Mosley, 24 March 1770, TWA 394/29.

[43] Copy Mosley to [Airey?], TWA 394/29. Fuller was never governor of Jamaica but he had been a member of the Council and held high judicial office there for a number of years. Namier and Brooke, *The House of Commons, 1754-1790*, II, pp.477–80

[44] Copy Mosley to J. Airey, 29 March 1770, TWA 394/29.

[45] Namier and Brooke, *The House of Commons, 1754-1790*, III, p.91.

[46] 28 March 1770, *Journals of the House of Commons*, 32, p.838.

and his colleague, Henry Waters, that all concerned would have time to consider the bill and raise objections. Haste obviously suited Harvey who made 'all smooth way' to Fuller and Mackworth.[47] Fuller had behaved 'very ungenteely', one of the Newcastle fitters commented, and gloomily concluded that whatever the bill contained it would be 'attended with expence & inconvenience in this country'.[48]

Mosley, however, soon grew more optimistic. On 6 April he reported that at a meeting of Mackworth, Sir John Turner (MP for King's Lynn), Edward Bacon (Norwich), Matthew Ridley and Sir Walter Blackett (Newcastle), and Sir Thomas Clavering (County Durham), who had been appointed to assist in bringing in the bill,[49] Fuller had been prevailed upon to alter it 'a good deal'. Only keelmen who took in overmeasure were now to be fined (and not their employers); Harvey was to have no part in the matter, the proceedings being left entirely to a magistrate; and, after the second reading, the bill was to be left on the table and printed for the full consideration of those concerned. Moreover, it would drop when the session ended, and Mosley was confident that Fuller would not trouble further about it. Indeed, Mosley believed that had Fuller not sworn that he would 'have a bill' he would have abandoned it immediately. He 'now begins to find Harvey out', Mosley added, but did not elucidate this disparaging comment.[50]

The coal owners and fitters of Newcastle and Sunderland petitioned against the bill,[51] but, as Mosley predicted, it proceeded no further than the second reading. Another eighteen years passed before the keelmen gained a statutory provision against overmeasure, but even that proved ineffectual. Meanwhile they were faced with a development which posed an ever increasing threat to their employment.

[47] Mosley to J. Airey, 29 March 1770, TWA 394/29.
[48] Airey to Mosley, 1 April 1770, TWA 394/29.
[49] *Journals of the House of Commons*, 32, p.838.
[50] Copy Mosley to Airey, 6 April 1770, TWA 394/29.
[51] 27 April a nd 1 May 1770, *Journals of the House of Commons*, 32, pp.904, 908.

9

A New Threat

In June 1771 there was widespread industrial unrest across the north east, mainly on account of the high price of corn and other provisions. On 10 June the keelmen assembled and refused to work. Some pitmen soon followed their example and proceeded to recruit the men of every colliery in the region. The Wearside keelmen also stopped work.[1] By 22 June the Wearside men together with most of the pitmen had resumed their labours, but the keelmen on the Tyne continued their strike and, as usual, forcibly obstructed any working keels and beat and abused their crews.[2] As the strike continued, many of the strikers found work in loading ships at Sunderland. The fitters considered proceeding against their men under the recent Act for better regulating Apprentices and Persons working under Contract (6 George III cap. 25).[3] As in a similar Act of 1747, keelmen were among groups specifically included in its provisions whereby a worker who quitted his employment before the expiration of his contract could be committed to the House of Correction for a term of between one and three months.[4] The Mayor met some of the men on 28 June and, after publishing a resolution of the Privy Council to facilitate the importation of rye,[5] had strong hopes that they would soon resume work, but a week later he had to report that 'such as are these people that tho' several attempts have been made, and such means used as were judged the most prudent to effect it, 'till now they coud not be brought to a sense of their duty'.[6] The strike lasted four weeks and was ended largely through the efforts of Edward Mosley, who, perhaps recalling William Scott's success in 1738, escorted keels manned by those willing to work until all joined them.[7]

The keelmen had prolonged their strike because their employment below Newcastle Bridge was being curtailed. Staithes had been erected from which the coal was loaded directly into the ships by means of spouts. Spouts had long been used to load keels, but not ships, and, although only small vessels able to reach the staithes could be loaded in this way, the keelmen's employment was being increasingly threatened as more coal owners began to adopt this method. 'I have just now erected a spout at Byker for small coasting ships',

---

[1] Aubone Surtees, Mayor, to Duke of Northumberland, 14 June 1771, TWA 592/1, fol.113.
[2] Surtees to Northumberland, 22 June 1771, *ibid.*, fol.113v.
[3] Matthew Ridley to George Ward, 28 June and 5 July 1771, Ridley's letter book 1767–77, p.113, Northumberland Museum and Archives, ZRI 38/2.
[4] *Statutes at Large*, XII (London, 1811), pp.506–8.
[5] Surtees to Northumberland, 29 June 1771, TWA 592/1, fols 114v-115.
[6] Surtees to Northumberland, 8 July 1771, *ibid.*, fol.115v.
[7] Richardson, *The Local Historian's Table Book, Historical Division*, II, p.194.

Matthew Ridley wrote, 14 June 1771, 'as the trade has undoubtedly a claim to be excused the expence of keel hire when they can be better dispatched without, both in saving the coals from being so much broken, & also dispatcd'.[8] That argument was to be much repeated in the course of the bitter disputes that eventually ensued, but, after failing to win any concession in 1771, the keelmen did not actively resist this encroachment on their employment for another twenty-three years.

As the general cost of living rose, the increasing hardship that the keelmen experienced became acute in 1787, when the shipmasters deliberately delayed loading their vessels for three weeks after they arrived in the Tyne.[9] The coal owners and fitters arranged relief for those who were consequently unemployed, but this temporary expedient did not address the long-standing problem of poverty among the keelmen. In a strongly worded petition, a group of skippers and keelmen from Whickham and Swalwell asserted that since the first establishment of their wages 'manifold imperfections' had crept in 'till our privileges are annihilated, our interest ruined, our credit marr'd, [and] ourselves made worse than the slaves in foreign countries'.[10] They went on to complain of 'tyrannical power over injured and oppressed innocence', their ever present poverty, and the small effect of many humble addresses presented to their masters. Moreover, they alleged, they were wronged by under-agents, probably without their superiors' knowledge – an echo of earlier complaints made by the keelmen about their 'many degrees of masters'.[11] Instead of beer provided when they loaded the ships they called for 1s 4d in cash, 4d of which they were prepared to assign to the recently established charity, but they were strongly opposed to a greater contribution. They resented deductions amounting to 2s 4d from their nominal wages, whereby for a journey [from Scotswood] to Shields they received 13s 4d instead of 15s 8d. (In works above Newcastle bridge 1s 4d per tide 'steerage money' was deducted for purchase of equipment for the keel, and together with a further deduction of 'can money', this swallowed up the 'owners' wages' element of the men's pay.)[12] 'As we never gave any consent to such stoppages', they argued, 'we consider them as illegal and no way binding upon us'. Finally, they complained of many fraudulent practices concerning 'stirred keels' (about which the skippers had objected in 1750) 'to the great hurt not only of the keel-owners, but of all those keelmen who do not come under such denomination'. It is not known what response, if any, their employers made to this remonstrance, but the catalogue of complaints shows

8   Ridley to Ward, 14 June 1771, Ridley's letter book, 1767–77, NMA, ZRI 38/2, p.112. The difference between the costs involved in the two methods of loading is provided by the following example: in 1813 a ship took in 112 chaldrons of Wallsend coal by spout at the total cost of £2 16s, and 64 chaldrons by keel which cost £6 17s 4d. William Richardson, *History of the Parish of Wallsend* (Newcastle, 1923), pp.230-1.
9   *Newcastle Courant*, 24 February, 3 and 10 March 1787. See above, Chapter 4.
10   Petition to the Mayor and those concerned in the coal trade, c.1788, TWA 394/29.
11   Petition of the keelmen, 1750, TWA 394/19.
12   Resolutions of coal owners and fitters, 26 September 1791, TWA 394/10.

that considerable discontent was brewing among the above-bridge men, even though they were not directly affected by the spouts lower down the river.

About three years later, in September 1791, the above-bridge keelmen struck for an increase in wages and the strike soon became general. 'Some little enormities' were committed by individuals, but there was no riot.[13] The Mayor called a general meeting of the coal owners and fitters and, 'after much deliberation', they resolved that new regulations would be adopted when the keelmen's bonds expired at Christmas, as their existing wages were 'not adequate to support them on account of the high advance of the necessaries of life'.[14] The below-bridge employers agreed to abolish the deduction of one shilling per tide 'can money' from each crew and payment of 'spout sixpences' to staithmen for use of the spouts, and resolved that every keelman might purchase liquor wherever he pleased and 'not at any particular Can or Public House'. Each crew was to receive 1s 4d instead of beer from the shipmasters, and payment for 'making-in' at the staithes was likewise always to be in cash. Allowances for 'shifting keels' and lying tides were to be paid at the fitters' offices with the keelmen's other wages, evidently in recognition of the difficulty the men experienced in securing these payments from the shipmasters. The above-bridge employers agreed that the foregoing regulations were to apply to the keelmen employed between the River Derwent, which entered the Tyne just below Blaydon, and the bridge, a distance of about three miles, and that only 4d per tide (instead of 1s 4d) would be deducted from 'owners' wages' as the skipper's allowance for furnishing proper gear. Each crew was to have a further increase of 1s 2d per tide, and for those employed higher up the river this was raised to 1s 6d. The coal owners unanimously resolved to make regulations at their respective staithes to 'secure the accustomed use of the spouts with the greatest impartiality'.[15] Clearly problems were anticipated when 'spout sixpences' were abolished. 'Afraid that the staithman will not load with the spout' runs a rough note,[16] indicating that the staithmen might make the keelmen load by hand.

These proposals received a mixed reception. All the below-bridge men were prepared to accept them; those from staithes above the River Derwent wanted a greater wage increase; those employed between the Derwent and Newcastle bridge, except the men belonging to two works, were satisfied, while those who occasionally went to staithes further upriver expected the same as the men stationed there. Representatives of the keelmen contended that the 4d per tide 'for finding the geer' should be granted to every skipper (not merely to those employed above the bridge). They called for the final settlement to be printed and certified by the Town Clerk, and a time-limit imposed for it to be

[13] *Newcastle Chronicle*, 24 September and 1 October 1791.
[14] Resolutions of coal owners and fitters, 26 September 1791, TWA 394/10. The quotation is from Andrew Mitchell's *Address to the Society of Keelmen of the Tyne*, see below, n.21.
[15] *Ibid*.
[16] TWA 394/33.

engrossed on parchment and signed and sealed as in 1710 and 1744.[17] Ignoring this obvious distrust, the employers agreed to these demands. The terms were printed and preparations made to have them set down on parchment.[18] The skippers' wages caused some difficulty, as one of the fitters pointed out to the Town Clerk:

> Several fitters & others that vend their own coals from above bridge have promised to stand w[ith] me in the distribution of the wages according to the mode which was unanimously agreed to, viz 'that the skipper sho[ul]d have 1s. per tide more than a common man, exclusive of 4d for finding geer'. I submit therefore to your better judgement whether the present situation of things does not require that this division of the wages sho[ul]d be engrossed upon the parchment as the most proper way to prevent any further trouble & confusion. Indeed I believe it will be but partially signed if this is not inserted. Some of the works above have bound on these conditions, more than 1/3 of ours have done the same & I have great reason to think the rest will follow their example, if they only see that we are firmly resolved not to do otherwise.[19]

Three days later the new wages settlement engrossed on parchment and signed by seven magistrates and seventeen fitters was authenticated with the Corporation seal. A clause concerning skippers' wages was included but left deliberately vague, merely recommending that the skippers be paid a shilling more than the other men, besides the 4d gear money.[20]

Although the settlement fell short of what many keelmen had hoped to secure, they had obtained an increase in wages, which they had failed to achieve since 1710, and the removal of abuses and commutation of liquor payments into money also represented a financial gain. There was, however, room for doubt as to whether these latter concessions would be permanent. According to Andrew Mitchell, a schoolmaster in Sandgate, people were prepared to wager that in a few years 'cans would be filled and liquor taken at staiths and sixpences given for spouts as formerly'. Indeed, soon after the settlement, some keelmen were said to be already yielding to temptation. They were all in danger of being brought back to their former situation by 'mean ignorant men', Mitchell warned in an *Address* to the keelmen which he published, despite being told that they were 'such a set of men as few cared to trouble themselves

---

[17] Report of representatives of the keelmen, 26 September 1791, TWA 394/33.
[18] Nathaniel Clayton, Town Clerk, to John Erasmus Blackett, n.d., TWA 394/29.
[19] Anthony Hood to Clayton, 1 January [1792], TWA 394/30.
[20] 'Further Regulations as to the Dues of the River and Owners' Wages, 3 January 1792, TWA 394/34; printed copy, 394/36. The dues, which varied according to the distance the keelmen conveyed the coal, were charged by the fitter to the shipmaster. Owners' Wages, which also varied according to the position of the staithes, were paid by the coal owners for the keelmen's beer, and steerage money (the skipper's allowance to purchase equipment for the keel). The keelmen did not receive much in cash from this source until the beer allowances were commuted.

with'.[21] If they did not regulate their drinking so that they spent their money where and when they pleased, he imagined them saying:

> We are worse than ever we were; we get nothing at the staiths for our work but drink, and that very bad, and our can houses are as bad as ever, giving us both bad usage and bad drink, and if we go in to get a glass to ourselves, we must sit behind backs, or possibly go to a room where there is no fire, … and be snuft and sneer'd at, as if we were dogs.

The strenuous nature of the keelmen's work obviously generated thirst and many keelmen were probably reluctant to forego the beer allowances that had hitherto been made, even if the quality of the liquor was bad. It is not surprising therefore that to a large extent Mitchell's gloomy predictions were realized. A staithman who worked at Dunston from 1819–33 stated that the keelmen's 'making-in money' (for loading the keels) 'was never considered by them as any part of their earnings, for they got nothing for it but drink', the cost of which at his staithe amounted to between £300 and £400 annually. By using spouts he reduced this expense to £100 but encountered 'much abuse & personal danger' in the process. The workmen, he added, were paid part of their wages in drink at public houses kept by the agents of the colliery proprietors.[22] Again, in 1849 it was alleged that when the keelmen employed by the Stella Coal Company loaded by hand they were compelled to take tickets from the staithman for liquor or tobacco in lieu of money.[23] A correspondent in the *Gateshead Observer* commented that from time immemorial the keelmen had received ale for 'loading away' and that the giving of tickets for beer was still the rule at most staithes for this work; 'the reverse is the exception', he declared.[24] It seems that the regulation of 1792 had been almost entirely forgotten.

No mention was made in that settlement about the loading of the colliers by spouts. Indeed, after 1771, as the keelmen themselves admitted, the matter had 'lain dormant', though they still regarded it as a grievance. Meanwhile, this method was making 'amazing progress'. By 1794 nine staithes below Newcastle bridge were loading ships of up to thirteen keels (104 chaldrons) burthen in this manner. Still more spout-staithes were being erected and the keelmen complained that besides threatening their livelihood these structures impeded navigation of the river.[25] The stewards of the charity at their annual meeting that year unanimously agreed to petition the coal owners about 'the many evils arising from this practice'. A few days later, to the surprise, it was claimed, of the majority of the keelmen, a strike began, presumably enforced

---

[21] Mitchell, *Address to the Society of Keelmen*. 'I some time ago signified in a company my surprize that during the time your masters and you did not understand one another about the grievances you complained of, none appeared to give a public view of them, as they had done to some others in like circumstances. But I was told you were a set of men as few cared to trouble themselves with'.

[22] 'Memorial of services rendered to his employers from 1819-1833 by A.H. Matthewson', reproduced by permission of Durham County Record Office, D/CG6/1247.

[23] *Newcastle Journal*, 7 April 1849.

[24] *Gateshead Observer*, 24 April 1849.

[25] 'Address to the Public from the Keelmen employed on the Tyne', *Newcastle Courant*, 16 August 1794.

by the below-bridge men. The stewards were unwilling to continue to act in an industrial dispute and the keelmen therefore chose other delegates for that purpose. They petitioned the Mayor to call a meeting of coal owners, fitters and ship owners to hear their grievances, but, when he did so, the ship owners failed to appear, 'notwithstanding their former promises to stand by the keelmen'. The delegates contended that the keelmen's employment was being so much reduced that they could not earn sufficient to support their families 'at the advanced prices of the necessaries of life'. Many in 'very indigent circumstances' were making a serious drain on the charitable fund.[26]

The coal owners and fitters unanimously rejected a demand to stop loading by spouts as 'a direct infringement of property' and violation of their legal right to ship their coals in 'the most eligible way that the situation of their works admitted'. A concession on this matter could not be made without exposing all property to claims 'equally incompatible with justice'.[27] Charles Brandling, one of the principal coal owners, informed the delegates of this decision, and, as many keelmen believed that he was solely responsible for the rejection of their demand, thirteen coal owners and fitters hastily published a handbill stating that they entirely concurred that it would be 'unjust to remove the spouts erected *at any staiths* on the River Tyne'.[28] The keelmen had expected that at least an enquiry would have been made into the extent of their distress with a view to granting them temporary relief and that a further investigation would then have been instituted into their complaints.[29] Faced with their employers' outright refusal to compromise, some of the men resorted to direct action.

On 14 July a party of keelmen demolished the spouts serving Brandling's Main, Walker, Wallsend and Usworth Main colleries. They stopped the work at several pits in the vicinity and threatened violence to the pitmen if they attempted to resume their labours. The magistrates called for military aid, and a party of the Earl of Darlington's Durham Rangers was brought in to assist the North and West York Militia already quartered in and near Newcastle. Two troops of the Lancashire Light Dragoons later arrived after a rapid march from Derby.[30] These deployments, the delegates bitterly complained, raised an alarm as if the keelmen were intending to 'turn the world upside down', when all they wanted was work to support themselves and their families. Their 'highest ambition' was always 'to work freely and to spend as freely'. Most of the keelmen, they claimed, were opposed to disorder, but 'horse and foot were employed to chase and affright women and children and no regard paid to guilty or innocent'.[31] The *Newcastle Courant*, too, attributed the disorder to

---

[26] *Ibid.*
[27] Notice to the public from Charles Brandling, *Newcastle Courant*, 2 August 1794.
[28] Charles Brandling to the Duke of Portland, 19 July 1794, enclosing two handbills issued by the coal owners, 11 and 15 July 1794, HO/42/32, 325–7. Brandling declared that the mob remained in a state of 'sulky discontent' and the well disposed believed 'that a little success in their demands woud induce them to come forward and avow principles of the worst kind'.
[29] Keelmen's Address to the public, as in n. 25.
[30] Brandling's notice to the public, as in n. 27; *Newcastle Courant*, 19 and 26 July 1794.
[31] Keelmen's Address to the public, as in n. 25.

those 'more turbulent than the rest', but it praised the 'spirited exertions' of the magistrates and conduct of the military. More than one hundred special constables were sworn in 'at this peculiar crisis', and many more gentlemen offered assistance if the disorder continued.[32] War with France and reports of the dire excesses committed there generated more than usual alarm at the keelmen's proceedings.

The coal owners and fitters responded to the destruction of the spouts by issuing another handbill asserting their intention 'to persevere in loading coals at our respective staiths and spouts both into keels and ships in the usual manner'.[33] This the keelmen stigmatized as disrespect for 'the cry of the poor' and the admonition of Holy Scripture on such conduct.[34] After a general meeting, the keelmen's delegates proposed that wages should be increased by two shillings per tide, that no ships bound for London should be loaded at the staithes, and that for every keel-load of coal shipped by spout sixpence should be paid to their charity. The employers rejected these propositions,[35] and, it was alleged, the majority of the keelmen themselves did not approve of them, 'for nothing would satisfy them but their first object'.[36] Still, many realized that 'however enormous their grievances' they would not obtain redress by continuing the strike, but others stubbornly maintained the contrary view. In an attempt to break the impasse, the stewards of the charity were called to attend a meeting of magistrates and employers who strove to convince them of their 'error' (which was not difficult as the stewards were opposed to the strike), and repeated their promise to redress any real grievance. They advised that the men should serve the rest of the year on the existing terms and seek better ones at the next binding. The keelmen held a general meeting on 28 July and, 'after some pains to convince one another', agreed to return to work the next day.[37] They still hoped that their employers might act to prevent the 'growing evil' of the spouts, but the coal owners and fitters remained steadfast in their determination to resist 'every illegal and compulsory attempt on their *Rights and Property*'.[38] Later that year, they rejected a proposal made by the Guardians of the charity that to increase the fund a levy of three farthings per chaldron should be imposed on coal loaded by spout.[39]

The keelmen did not immediately resume the contest, but their battle against the spouts was by no means over. Meanwhile they had to meet another threat, but this time their employers, whose interests were equally at stake, were on their side.

---

[32] *Newcastle Courant*, 19 and 26 July 1794.

[33] Brandling's notice, as in n. 27; HO/42/32/326.

[34] Keelmen's Address to the public, as in n. 25, citing 'that awful but certain text, "Whoso stoppeth his ears at the cry of the poor, he also shall cry himself but shall not be heard"'.

[35] Brandling's notice, as in n. 27.

[36] Keelmen's Address to the public, as in n. 25.

[37] *Ibid.* The Address does not make it clear whether the magistrates or the keelmen themselves ordered the stewards to attend the meeting, but on the whole it seems most likely that the magistrates did so.

[38] Brandling's notice, as in n. 27.

[39] Minute book, 22 November 1794, TWA 394/54.

10

The Impressment of Keelmen

The right of the Admiralty to impress men to serve in the Royal Navy when need arose was derived from 'a prerogative inherent in the Crown, grounded upon common law and recognized by many Acts of Parliament'. This pronouncement of the legality of impressment made by Sir Michael Foster, Recorder of Bristol, in 1743 was never overturned.[1] Even in peacetime sufficient volunteers could not be obtained to man the ships of the navy, and on the outbreak of war the need became acute. To meet the demand, press gangs organized by the Admiralty's Impress Service would descend on seaports or other towns and scour the streets, public houses and dwellings to seize those deemed suitable for the service. Seamen were the prime target, but men in other occupations might also be taken unless they had protections from the Admiralty. In a 'hot press' little or no discrimination was observed. The violence and brutality that frequently accompanied this forcible recruitment is well documented, as also is the strenuous resistance offered to the press gangs not only by their immediate quarries but often by the populace of the area concerned. From time to time both sides suffered fatalities. The prospect for those impressed was indeed grim. Torn from their homes and their families (which if deprived of the breadwinner would be plunged into destitution), they were subjected to the notoriously harsh naval discipline, and thrust into the perils of active service for the duration of the war.[2] The Admiralty normally granted protections against impressment to the keelmen, and without this security they refused to work, as in 1653 and 1709 (see above, Chapters 1 and 2). When an attempt was made to impress some of them in 1742, they dragged the Impress Service's tender ashore and threatened the lives of the captain and his crew. 'Few trades were as belligerent as this one', the historian of naval impressment remarks.[3] The *Newcastle Courant* of 10–17 September 1743 reported an incident when, evidently disregarding protections, the crew of a tender tried to impress a keelman:

> On Thursday last a gang of 12 of the said Tender's crew, pursuing a keelman on shore, he, to avoid them, took to the water, and swam to a keel in which

---

[1] Quotation from the case 'Ex Parte Softly', 16 May 1801, 1 East, pp.466–74, *English Reports*, 102. About Sir Michael Foster see *Dictionary of National Biography*. Although the legality of impressment could not be successfully challenged in the courts, irregularities in procedure, such as defects in the press warrants, could be contested with a favourable result. The matter is fully discussed in Nicholas Rogers, *The Press Gang. Naval Impressment and its Opponents in Georgian Britain* (London and New York, 2007), pp.17–35.
[2] *Ibid., passim.*
[3] *Ibid.*, p.40.

were three of his brethren. The press gang in their boat followed him, and a smart engagement immediately ensued, but the intended victim, not willing to wait the event, took to the water again and left the other three to dispute it by themselves, which they did with great vigour, till a reinforcement of 12 more from the Tender came to their antagonists' assistance, and obliged our three heroes to capitulate.

The keelmen were protected from impressment during the war with France, 1793–1802, and when hostilities were resumed after the Peace of Amiens it was announced that protections would again be issued to keelmen, watermen and shipwrights employed on the Tyne, provided that they had not been to sea.[4] The navy had been reduced during the peace and it was now faced with a serious shortage of manpower. The impress service was hastily reconstituted, and in March 1803 the press gangs began operations in North Shields and elsewhere in the north east which provoked strong and sometimes violent opposition from the inhabitants. Even so, large numbers of men of all descriptions, including gentlemen, shipowners and tradesmen, were seized.[5] The considerable brutality and mistreatment of the captives alleged to have occurred in the process was strongly criticized in the local newspapers. The *Newcastle Advertiser*, while acknowledging that impressment of seafarers was acceptable, denounced the 'scandalous outrages' whereby men engaged in useful industry were 'dragged like felons through the streets, beat and cut with hangers [short swords], and put on board a tender, merely because it pleased a set of ruffians called a Press Gang to do so'.[6] The *Tyne Mercury* 'so much incurred the displeasure of some inferior officers of the Impress Service … as to occasion threats of punishment', but its editor was unrepentant.[7]

Less than a month after the announcement that the keelmen were to be protected, Captain Adam Mackenzie, the recently appointed Regulating Officer for Tyneside, received express orders from the Admiralty to disregard existing protections.[8] Thus on 10 May the unsuspecting keelmen, a 'vast body of fine men', found themselves included in a 'remarkably hot press'.[9] 'Captain Skene and I determined to take as many of the younger ones as we could this morning, leaving all skippers', Mackenzie reported. It was the general opinion that 'nothing will be done on the river until the keelmen are again protected', he added, but in the meantime 'we will get all we can'.[10] More than fifty young keelmen

4 8 and 15 April 1803, J. Bell, 'Collections relative to the Tyne, its Trade and Conservancy', II, fols 6–8, Central Library Newcastle.
5 N. McCord, 'The Impress Service in North East England During the Napoleonic War', *The Mariner's Mirror*, LIV (1968), pp.163–80; *Tyne Mercury*, 29 March 1803.
6 *Newcastle Advertiser*, 23 April 1803.
7 *Tyne Mercury*, 3 May 1803.
8 *Ibid.*, 17 May 1803.
9 *Ibid.*, 10 May 1803.
10 Mackenzie to Evan Nepean, Secretary of the Admiralty, 10 May 1803, National Archives, ADM 1/2141. About Nepean (1751–1822) see *Dictionary of National Biography (DNB)*. The keelmen were regarded as able and expert mariners. A naval officer declared that he would prefer as a seaman a man aged twenty-one who had been bred to the keels to one who had been on two voyages to the East Indies. 'Ex Parte Softly', as in n.1

were seized in this sudden swoop whereupon, as expected, the whole body stopped work. The Lords Commissioners of Admiralty approved Mackenzie's action but instructed him to stop the impressment of more keelmen.[11]

The coal owners and fitters, angry at the disruption of trade which was bound to continue as long as the threat of impressment remained, sent one of their colleagues, George Dunn, to negotiate with the Admiralty. He succeeded in persuading the Lords of Admiralty to order the release of the impressed men, but, before Mackenzie received this instruction, the vessel on which they were held had sailed for the Nore.[12] Dunn then obtained a sealed order directed to Lord Keith for release of the men when they arrived.[13] The Mayor issued a handbill calling on the strikers to resume work, 'as there now can be no doubt of the impressed keelmen being discharged immediately on the arrival at the Nore, and as a gentleman will be there *this day* for the express purpose of providing them a passage home'.[14] The keelmen returned to work, but, as the impressed men were being disembarked at the Nore, the Admiralty countermanded the order for their release, as it was alleged that the keelmen were content with the protection of one man and a boy per keel.[15] This idea may have arisen through confusion with the practice on the River Wear 'where only one man goes in a keel'.[16] Dunn, who had been waiting to receive the released men, hastened back to the Admiralty but gained no concession.

On 10 June, several coal owners and others, including Sir Matthew White Ridley and Rowland Burdon, MPs for Newcastle and County Durham, met in London and agreed that 'upon the liberation of those impressed and protections being granted to the keelmen on the Tyne during the war', they would strive to procure within two months eighty 'serviceable men' for the navy, that number being roughly equivalent to one-tenth of the adult keelmen.[17] Supported by the MPs, Dunn put the proposition to the Lords of Admiralty, but they demanded one-tenth of the keelmen or else one prime seaman or two landsmen for every ten keelmen protected. Meanwhile the impressed men would be held lest the required number of substitutes was not provided.[18] Since the Admiralty declined to discuss the matter further, the two MPs appealed to the Prime Minister, who finally ordered that the the original offer should be accepted. Thus through the negotiators' 'most strenuous and persevering exertions', the Admiralty was forced to give way.[19] After being held for almost six weeks, the impressed men (except four who had agreed to join the navy and one who

11 Endorsement on above letter of 10 May 1803.
12 Mackenzie to Nepean, 27 May 1803, National Archives, ADM 1/2141; McCord, 'The Impress Service', p.168.
13 Minutes of meeting of fitters, 30 March 1811, reviewing events of 1803, TWA 394/38.
14 26 May 1803, with copy Nepean to Mackenzie, 23 May, ordering the discharge of the impressed men, Bell, 'Collections relative to the Tyne', II, f.13.
15 Minutes, 30 March 1811, as in n. 13; McCord, 'The Impress Service', p.168.
16 Mackenzie to Nepean, 21 May 1803, National Archives, ADM 1/2141.
17 Copy resolution of coal owners and other interested parties on the best means of procuring the liberation of the impressed keelmen, 10 June 1803, TWA 394/38.
18 Minutes, 30 March 1811, as in n. 13.
19 *Tyne Mercury*, 31 May 1803.

needed medical treatment) were sent back to Newcastle. Strangely enough, their impressment resulted in an unexpected benefit. During their detention they had been put to service on the frigate *Lapwing* which while cruising off the coast of Holland captured a Dutch East Indiaman. Dunn took care to ensure that the keelmen obtained a share in the prize-money arising from the capture which amounted to £65 8s each. For relatively poor men this must have seemed a princely sum. The fifty keelmen later presented a silver cup to Dunn with an inscription recording their gratitude.[20]

A committee of fitters set about finding the eighty substitutes as had been agreed. Advertisements were published offering bounties to volunteers approved for service – eleven guineas for an able seaman, ten for an ordinary seaman and eight for a landsman.[21] The keelmen raised a subscription and paid £5 for each recruit,[22] the employers evidently contributing the rest. Meanwhile Mackenzie suffered an accident and Captain William Charleton who replaced him as Regulating Officer held the position for the next seven years. On 23 June the Mayor informed Charleton that the committee was procuring men 'very fast' and arrangements were being made to have them examined by a surgeon before they received part of the bounty.[23] Charleton had orders to accept 'any able men' delivered under the arrangement. By 28 June the whole number had been raised and the Mayor begged Charleton to send off as many as possible, 'as the keeping of them at Newcastle entails an enormous expence upon the coal trade'.[24]

The agreement covered only the keelmen working in the coal trade. Merchants who employed ballast keelmen, wherrymen and other watermen later sought the same terms.[25] After some delay, Charleton was ordered to accept their proposition 'on the express condition that the men furnished be raised out of the[ir] own body'. He was on no account to discharge those already impressed and was enjoined to take care that 'no imposition' was practised.[26] A further twenty-seven men were raised through this initiative. Charleton wanted instructions on

[20] *Ibid.*, 21 June 1803. Nothing could withstand the 'strenuous exertions' of Sir Matthew White Ridley in the keelmen's favour, combined with the persevering endeavours of Mr Dunn, the paper declared. There is a photograph of the cup, preserved in the Laing Art Gallery, Newcastle, in Frank Graham, *Northumberland and Durham, A Social and Political Miscellany* (Newcastle, 1979), p.11. The sum that the keelmen received was much more than ordinary seamen generally gained from this source. The inequitable distribution of prize-money was one of the mutineers' complaints at the Nore in 1797. For further information on the intricacies of prize business and the vast disparities of rewards between senior officers and those in the lowest ranks, see my article 'Prize-money and the British Expedition to the West Indies 1793–4', *Journal of Imperial and Commonwealth History*, XII (1983–84), pp.1–28.
[21] *Newcastle Advertiser*, 25 June 1803.
[22] Captain Wilson Rathborne to C. Yorke, 24 June 1811, National Archives, ADM 1/2416.
[23] Thomas Clennell to Charleton, 23 June 1803, Bell, 'Collections relative to the Tyne', II, fol.18.
[24] Evan Nepean to Charleton, 24 June 1803, *ibid.* fol.19; Clennell to Charleton, 28 June, *ibid.*, fol.22.
[25] S.W. Parker to Nepean, 20 August 1803; Nepean to Charleton, 14 November; Parker and others to Charleton, 21 November; Nepean to Charleton, 21 November, Bell, 'Collections relative to the Tyne', II, fols 29, 37, 42, 44; Charleton to Nepean, 18 November, National Archives, ADM 1/1634.
[26] Nepean to Charleton, 14 November 1803, Bell, 'Collections relative to the Tyne', II, fol.37.

future arrangements for granting protections on the Tyne, as 'without regular-ity' the service would be subject to 'much imposition'. He understood that in former wars the Lords of Admiralty issued a warrant authorizing the Mayor of Newcastle to grant protections, renewable every three months, on proof that the keelmen and other workers had never been to sea. The business was done in the Town Clerk's office, 'very much to his emolument', and without the presence of naval personnel. Charleton suggested that in future protections should be granted in the presence of the impress officers and should last for a year, to cor-respond with the term of the keelmen's bond, thus avoiding the Town Clerk's fee every quarter. Only men who had subscribed towards raising their propor-tion of substitutes should receive protections, and, if the employers extended the number of workmen beyond their present establishment, they should 'raise for the navy one in ten for every such addition'.[27] The Admiralty's reply con-cerned only the ballast keelmen and, apart from repeating that no imposition should be allowed, ignored Charleton's suggestions.[28] Although Charleton considered that the protection granted to the general body of keelmen did not cover new employees, he did not pursue this policy on the Tyne. On the Wear, however, where the keelmen had also procured substitutes equivalent to one-tenth of their number, he demanded additional recruits annually in respect of men who had entered the work and lads employed in the keels who became liable to impressment at the age of eighteen. The discrepancy between the two rivers continued during the next seven years.[29]

The exemption of the keelmen remained a delicate matter. Rear-admiral Phillip pointed out that the keelmen, and also the fishermen of Scotland, did not provide substitutes from their own body but 'procured men by a bounty from among the seafaring men' who were themselves liable to impressment. This he considered a bad bargain for the service which thereby lost the chance of additional men. Charleton was ordered 'to explain the circumstances'.[30] In September 1807, when a proclamation invited volunteers out of protected bod-ies to assist in navigating surrendered Danish vessels, the fitters resolved that one in every twelve of their respective keelmen should be permitted to vol-unteer on the strict condition that they should not 'by that means be rendered more liable to the impress service for the future than they now are'.[31] They obviously feared that once these men had been to sea they would lose their exemption.

Captain Charleton retired in 1810 and the following year his succes-sor, Captain Wilson Rathborne, began another hot press on the Tyne. To the alarm of all concerned in the coal trade, he seized a number of keelmen who

27 Charleton to Nepean, 18 November 1803, National Archives, ADM 1/1634.
28 Nepean to Charleton, 21 November 1803, Bell, 'Collections relative to the Tyne', II, fol.42.
29 N. Clayton to Charleton, 6 April 1811; Charleton to Clayton, 7 April, TWA 394/38.
30 W. Marsden, Secretary of the Admiralty, to Charleton, 27 February 1805 with extract of letter from Rear-Admiral Phillip, 26 February, Bell, 'Collections relative to the Tyne', II, fols 57–8.
31 Resolution of fitters, 21 September 1807, *ibid.*, fol.77; copy of proclamation, 18 September 1807, *ibid.*, fol.75.

had started work after the protection granted in 1803.[32] The fitters urgently reviewed the circumstances of that arrangement and resolved that the Mayor should appeal to the Admiralty.[33] Accordingly he pointed out that Rathborne's action had caused 'great apprehension' to the coal trade and 'much dissatisfaction' among the keelmen who regarded it as a breach of faith. 'We have reason to dread great public inconvenience will result', he continued, unless the Lords Commissioners ordered the release of those impressed and prevented repetition of the measure. The number of keelmen, he added, had not increased but rather diminished since 1803.[34] Sir Matthew White Ridley discussed the matter with Secretary to the Admiralty John Croker who suggested that the action had been taken because young men who were not truly keelmen had been 'adopted as servants and apprentices by that body for the purpose of this privilege of exemption'.[35] Rathborne, however, had already informed Croker that he had impressed the men because they were not among those who had found substitutes in 1803, thus putting the Tyne keelmen on the same footing as those on the Wear and the fishermen of Scotland who found substitutes every year for those attaining the age of eighteen. From the 'great increase in trade' he believed that there must be more keelmen at work than the eight hundred protected in 1803, besides boys who had since then reached eighteen; but, as those concerned on the Tyne understood that the eighty substitutes then supplied satisfied the Admiralty's demand for the duration of the war, he asked for instructions.[36] The reply confirmed that the Lords Commissioners did not consider any keelmen exempt except the eight hundred who had found substitutes.[37] Thus the Mayor was informed

> that it never could be intended to extend protection beyond the eight hundred individuals who were keelmen at the commencement of the war and who are of course to continue protected during the war; but that on no consideration can any others be protected from the Impress as they become liable thereto, unless they submit to the same conditions.[38]

Rathborne requested lists of those who had entered keel service or grown up in it since 1803 in order that substitutes might be provided, and promised not to interrupt the trade for a reasonable time to enable necessary arrangements to be made.[39] The members of the coal trade had no intention of submitting to this interpretation of the 1803 agreement. The Town Clerk urgently begged Captain Charleton to explain 'what circumstances induced the Impress Service to act so differently towards the keelmen on the Wear & those on the Tyne' during

[32] Rathborne to J.W. Croker, Secretary of the Admiralty, 30 March 1811, National Archives, ADM 1/2416. For Rathborne (1748–1831) and Croker (1780–1857) see *DNB*.
[33] Minutes of meeting, 30 March 1811, TWA 394/38.
[34] Draft, Mayor to J.W. Croker, 30 March 1811, *ibid.*
[35] Ridley to N. Clayton, 2 April 1811, *ibid.*
[36] Rathborne to Croker, 30 March 1811, National Archives, ADM 1/2416.
[37] Rathborne to Thomas Burdon, Mayor, 5 April 1811, TWA 394/38.
[38] John Barrow, 2nd Secretary of the Admiralty, to Burdon, 2 April 1811, *ibid.* About Barrow (1764–1848) see *DNB*.
[39] Rathborne to Burdon, 5 April 1811, TWA 394/38.

his term of office.[40] Charleton, however, politely declined, 'not thinking myself authoris'd to explain such circumstances to the coal trade upon the Tyne', but, he asserted, his conduct over a period of seven years was 'never directly or indirectly construed to be different from the intentions of the Admiralty'.[41] The coal owners and fitters contended that the intention of the agreement was best proved by the conduct of all parties, particularly that of the Impress Service, which was 'in strict conformity' to their own interpretation of it. They earnestly requested the Lords of Admiralty to review the matter, but, if the 'new construction' was upheld, they begged for sufficient time to supply the necessary quota of substitutes.[42] 'Considering the pressing exigency of the service', the Secretary to the Admiralty replied, 'their Lordships conceive their demands upon the keelmen to be exceedingly moderate'. They would allow a month for furnishing substitutes, after which the Regulating Officer was to impress all keelmen liable to serve for whom no substitute had been provided.[43]

This was bad news and worse was to follow. Rathborne informed the Mayor that he had orders to receive one seaman or two landsmen for every ten keelmen not already protected.[44] The members of the coal trade did not immediately appreciate the full implications of this. The task of finding substitutes within the time limit was proving difficult, besides which the bounty was now £60 for an able seaman, though, as Rathborne pointed out, ten men would gain protection at a cost of only £6 each, whereas an able seaman would gladly pay £80 for exemption.[45] The Admiralty granted a further month for raising the substitutes, but, as the shortfall persisted, it was decided to seek recruits from the unprotected keelmen. A number of them volunteered, but, to the dismay of the coal trade, Rathborne refused to accept one keelman as a sufficient substitute for ten, his orders being to take none but able seamen on that basis. 'This appears rather unreasonable on the part of the Admiralty', George Dunn remarked to Nathaniel Clayton, the Town Clerk, 'and I have no doubt when the case is properly represented to their Lordships but they will accede to the measure of taking one *sufficient able keelman* as a substitute for *ten* of their body'. This was 'very material to the interest of the trade'.[46]

In his submission to the Admiralty, Clayton made no mention of numbers, but merely stated that the Regulating Officer had refused to accept keelmen as substitutes for those not protected under the former arrangement and requested that these men should be received if found fit for service.[47] Presumably he hoped that by this approach he might elicit an endorsement of the 1803 agreement, but in this he was disappointed. The members of the coal trade resolved

[40]   Clayton to Charleton, 6 April 1811, TWA 394/38.
[41]   Charleton to Clayton, 7 April 1811, *ibid.*
[42]   Burdon to Barrow, 13 April 1811, *ibid.*
[43]   Barrow to Burdon, 17 April 1811, *ibid.*
[44]   Rathborne to Burdon, 20 April 1811, *ibid.*
[45]   Rathborne to Charles Philip Yorke, first Lord of Admiralty, 24 June 1811, National Archives, ADM 1/2416.
[46]   George Dunn to Clayton, 24 May 1811, TWA 394/38.
[47]   Draft, Clayton to Barrow, 28 May 1811, *ibid.*

to draw up a memorial and earnestly requested Clayton to present it personally to the Lords of Admiralty. On 10 June Dunn pointed out that the time for finding the substitutes would expire in four days, but 'next week being our Race week a number of substitutes will most probably be obtained, provided their Lordships accede to the prayer of the memorial'. Otherwise, the general feeling among the fitters seemed to be that it would be better 'to let things take their course rather than submit to so serious a demand as that of one-fifth of their people being required for the naval service'. None of the keelmen volunteers had been passed before the Regulating Officer, because, if they were not received on the one in ten basis, it would create a precedent that in future wars might occasion 'the most serious & irremediable injury to the coal trade'.[48]

The memorial met with an absolute refusal. The Secretary of the Admiralty informed Clayton that

> their Lordships consider the request to be exceedingly unreasonable, and in the present scarcity of men for his Majesty's service are rather disposed to withdraw the indulgence altogether than to continue it to men who, tho' strictly liable to the impress, are not satisfyed to commute their services by finding one able seaman or two landmen for every ten.[49]

The coal owners and fitters, angry at the refusal to put keelmen on the same footing as able seamen, resolved to send a deputation to the Admiralty. They 'talk of the trade stopping work and London being distressed for coals if their demands should not be acceded to', Rathborne reported, 'but I should hope they would not try the experiment as on the last striking a coal owner informed me it was a loss to him of £150 per diem'. He hoped that self-interest would lead them to 'make their men conform' to the Admiralty's demand.[50] He was confident that the men would be governed by their employers in this matter. It was highly unlikely that the keelmen's employers would induce them to stop work, though fear of impressment was likely to cause them to do so on their own accord. In the event, the dispute was resolved without disruption to trade, the Admiralty conceding that one keelman was equivalent to an able seaman.[51]

The whole episode shows that, despite the increasing use of spouts for loading the colliers, the keelmen were still indispensable, indeed, 'the very sinews of the coal trade' as the *Tyne Mercury* described them in 1803.[52] We shall now see how they fared in the changing industrial conditions of the nineteenth century.

[48] Dunn to Clayton, 10 June 1811, *ibid.*
[49] Barrow to Clayton, 17 June 1811, *ibid.*
[50] Rathborne to Yorke, 24 June 1811, National Archives, ADM 1/2416..
[51] McCord, 'The Impress Service', p.175
[52] *Tyne Mercury*, 31 May 1803.

11

The Strike of 1809: The Keelmen Prevail

Although masters and men were united in opposition to the demands of the impress service, the unanimity did not extend to the question of the keelmen's wages. The continuing rise in prices during the war involved them in increasing hardship, the more so since their employment was in many cases being curtailed. In a petition of 29 August 1809 to the Mayor, Joseph Forster, himself a fitter, and the rest of the trading brethren of the Hostmen's Company, the keelmen argued that even if they had constant employment with as much work as they could do throughout the year, 'the very high price of every article connected with housekeeping' would render their present wages barely sufficient for the sustenance of their families. They therefore requested that the men employed above Newcastle bridge should each receive an additional 1s 6d per tide, and those below the bridge 1s, with 'house and firing'. The petition was couched in deferential terms and 'in full confidence' that it would be received 'with all due attention'.[1]

The fitters met the keelmen's delegates at the Mayor's Chamber on 7 September. The delegates produced memoranda stating that the requested wage increase bore little proportion to the rise in the price of provisions and other necessaries since 1710, nor to the advances granted to other labourers whose wages were proportionate to factors such as exposure to hardships and dangers, or work that was extremely laborious, slavish, or dirty – to all of which the keelmen could plead to a much greater extent. Their wages were irregular, and out of them they had to 'vitual' and pay the boy who made up the crew of each keel and support their own poor through the charity. Moreover, their house rents were 'exorbitantly high'.[2]

Their chief spokesman, Henry Strachan, claimed that apart from 2s 6d 'bread money' and 1s 2d per tide granted to those employed above the bridge, the keelmen's wages had not been increased since 1710.[3] This did not fully take into account the adjustments made in 1792 to the owners' wages element of the men's pay, and it was also objected that 'making-in money' had recently been augmented (though that payment was generally made in drink). However, it was true that the basic keel-dues for conveying the coal from staithe to ship had not been altered during the past hundred years. Strachan stressed the plight of the below-bridge men who were 'particularly pressed at this time for want of work', and cited the case of two employments in which the men had worked

---

[1] TWA 394/37.
[2] 'Memorandums for the Keelmen's Delegates', TWA 394/37.
[3] Minutes of meeting of fitters, 7 September 1809, TWA 394/37.

only sixty tides and four by-tides in one, and a mere thirty-eight tides in the other, during the current season. Formerly 240 tides were regarded as making a 'tolerable year'.[4] Perhaps tactfully, he did not attribute the lack of work to the increasing practice of loading the colliers by spouts, though this was one of its principal causes. He claimed that in the course of the past twenty-five years the wages of every artisan had been doubled, and, consequently, the petitioners had 'much difficulty in keeping their expectations so low'. He considered that men with families needed £2 per week. House rents had 'advanced to such a pitch that there is no getting them paid', he declared, his own being £5 for two rooms in which he lived with his wife and six children. Boys received between thirteen and eighteen pence per tide from the rest of the crew. Fire coal allowances varied: Strachan's employer allowed one waggon-load of small coals per keel; Tanfield Moor Colliery two waggon-loads; and Walker Colliery 4 shillings in lieu of coal.

The fitters adjourned the meeting for a week when the coal owners were requested to attend. After 'serious consideration' by the whole body, a committee was appointed to investigate the grounds of the keelmen's petition and all their circumstances.[5] It reported to a general meeting of coal owners and fitters on 30 September when it was resolved that some addition should be made to the wages of the above-bridge keelmen, but not to those of the men below-bridge who received 'ample payment for their labour'. Their existing dues appeared 'abundant', their employment was less subject to obstructions from neap tides and land floods, and they generally had 'more regular and constant work' than the men stationed higher up the river. The meeting was aware that their employment had lately been 'much abridged', but this could 'only be of short duration' and did not merit a permanent increase in wages. (Strachan had admitted that the previous year had been exceptionally good with about 270 tides worked.) When they were fully employed, as was usually the case, their earnings were 'greatly beyond their due proportion compared with those above bridge'. Having taken all into consideration, including the additions and adjustments made to the wage-scale in 1792 and the 2s 6d per tide 'bread money' granted in 1800 on account of the high price of corn (which, although intended to be temporary, had become permanent), the meeting recommended that from 1 January next there should be 'a progressive advance of owners' wages to the above-bridge men, ranging from 1s to 2s 4d according to the distance between their respective staithes and the bridge. However, it was further recommended that the allowance for house rents be abolished and that the binding money for Stella staithe, the highest up the river, should be reduced to £12.[6]

---

[4] *Ibid.* In each of two other cases Strachan mentioned that the keelmen had worked 120 tides, and there were still three months left of the season. The previous year had been exceptional, with about 270 tides worked. For adjustments to the keelmen's pay in 1792 see above Chapter 9 n.20.

[5] Minutes, 14 September 1809, TWA 394/37.

[6] Minutes, 30 September 1809, Easton Papers, North of England Institute of Mining Engineers, East/4, p.31.

Although some concession had been made to the above-bridge men it fell considerably short of their demand for 1s 6d *per man*, as the owners' wages were always reckoned *per keel* and therefore the increment in them had to be shared between three men and a boy. The abolition of an allowance for house rent was a strange response to the claim that these rents were 'exorbitantly high', and reduction of the binding money at Stella could not be pleasing to the men employed there. The above-bridge men thus had little grounds for satisfaction at the offer which, contrary to what one writer has stated, certainly did not exceed their demands.[7] Most remarkable was the total rejection of the below-bridge men's case, despite their admittedly straitened circumstances. The unsympathetic attitude of the employers is further indicated by the comments of William Chapman, a member of the committee, when forwarding the resolutions to Nathaniel Clayton, the Town Clerk. He had made a slight addition, he wrote, 'throwing the blame where it lies', as the committee had done in their report. 'They imagine that many amongst the keelmen will be actuated by reason, and therefore they think detail necessary, particularly as it refutes the assertion of their ring leaders that no change has taken place since the reign of Queen Anne'. Clayton, however, deleted wording he considered too provocative, and Chapman, converted by Clayton's reasoning, declared he was glad that the 'obnoxious passage' had been suppressed.[8]

The attempt to render the package palatable to the keelmen failed. About two weeks later the below-bridge men enforced a strike backed by threats of violence to any who attempted to work. They also prevented the loading of ships at the spouts. On 22 October a meeting of the magistrates and employers resolved that the fitters should order the below-bridge men to work in accordance with their bonds and, if they refused, warrants should be issued for their arrest.[9] Two days later it was reported that none had resumed work, though some were willing to do so if the rest concurred. Others stubbornly demanded the increase requested in the petition. The keelmen employed at Felling staithe, for example, declared that they were unable to live on their existing wages and would hold out even at the risk of being imprisoned or 'to a man impressed into his Majesty's service'.[10] The magistrates issued warrants for the arrest of the recalcitrants, but, as usual, execution of them proved difficult. George Heads, arrested by four constables on 26 October, was rescued by a band of keelmen including at least two members of his family.[11] The authorities offered a reward of forty guineas for information leading to the arrest of the offenders, but to no avail.[12] The incident persuaded the Mayor that military aid was 'immediately necessary',[13] and an elaborate plan was drawn up to execute numerous

---

7   Rowe, 'The Strikes of the Tyneside Keelmen in 1809 and 1819', citation p.61.
8   Chapman to Clayton, 3 and 5 October 1809, TWA 394/37.
9   Minutes, 22 October 1809, TWA 394/37.
10 William Carp (?) to J.B. Pearson, 23 October 1809, TWA 394/37.
11 Information of Constable Thomas Aiston, 26 October 1809, TWA 394/37.
12 *Newcastle Courant*, 28 October 1809. The reward was still being offered on 30 December.
13 Copy letter the Mayor to lieutenant-general Dundas, 26 October 1809, TWA 394/37.

warrants with that assistance. The next morning parties of dragoons scoured each side of the river from the bridge downwards while corporation boats on the river maintained communications with the armed forces. The aim had been to cut off the keelmen's retreat in all directions and so 'increase their alarm', but the dragoons encountered no 'considerable assemblages' of strikers.[14]

Later that day the magistrates of Newcastle, whose jurisdiction was limited to the boundaries of that city and county, were joined by those of Northumberland and Durham. They promised that, if the men resumed work, they would fully examine the question, and report to the employers 'for their consideration',[15] but the overture, which offered nothing substantial, had no success. Indeed the strikers were now making further demands. In a paper headed 'Omissions of the Keelmen's Petition' they called for payment for lying tides at the same rate as for ballast keels ('the dues for one tide for each day, and double on the Sabbath'); three shillings when they had to travel overland for orders; and, if they had to return a laden keel to the staithe, payment for a full tide without any deductions (a demand often made on previous occasions). They begged the magistrates to grant a patient and candid hearing of their demands, 'as perhaps they may not be properly understood'. Their petition, they believed, would then be found 'not unreasonable'.[16] The magistrates met the keelmen's delegates on 28 October but no settlement was achieved.[17]

Two days later, the employers and magistrates resolved to employ substitute workers to navigate the keels. Ten special constables were sworn in and a deputation was sent to Captain Charleton of the impress service to solicit his 'essentially necessary' assistance.[18] Charleton agreed to co-operate, and the presence of his boats on the river during the next two days 'contributed in a great degree to keep the keelmen in check' while waggon-men, pitmen, sailors and others brought keels down to the ships.[19] The keelmen were becoming turbulent, in some cases violent, and on 3 November the magistrates of the three counties deliberated on how to reduce them to a 'state of subordination'.[20] It was proposed that some should be arrested immediately, but, as it was anticipated that the constables would encounter 'serious resistance', further military and naval assistance was considered essential. The Mayor therefore again begged Charleton to help:

> The disturbances excited by the keelmen have risen to great disorder and some acts of violence have been committed by riotous bodies of them assembled on the water & by forcibly stopping keels which were under way

---

[14] Plan of operations, 26 October 1809, TWA 394/37; *Newcastle Courant*, 28 October 1809.

[15] Minutes of proposition to the keelmen, 27 October 1809, TWA 394/37.

[16] TWA 394/37.

[17] Minutes of meeting, 28 October 1809, TWA 394/37.

[18] List of special constables, 31 October 1809; 9 more were sworn in, 1–4 November, TWA 394/37; George Knowsley to Charleton, 31 October 1809, Bell, 'Collections relative to the Tyne, its trade and Conservancy, II, fol. 90.

[19] Letter from the fitters to the Mayor, requesting him to make a further application to Charleton, 2 November 1809, *ibid.*, fol. 94.

[20] TWA 394/37.

navigated by others. For these acts & for the desertion of their service many
warrants have been issued, and as the civil power is quite inadequate to the
execution of them, it is proposed to call for the assistance of the military,
and the magistrates of the three counties, who are now assembled, direct me
to request that you will lend all the assistance on the water that your boats
properly manned can afford.[21]

Charleton was invited to a preparatory meeting so that the magistrates could
have the benefit of his advice. It was proposed that a company of infantry
would man the boats while a troop of horse and a company of infantry proceeded separately to Bells Close and Lemington and another party of horse and
two companies of infantry controlled strategic points on the south side of the
river. A magistrate and guides would accompany each detachment. The fitters
would attempt to send keels downriver, whereupon the keelmen would probably assemble at places such as Derwenthaugh and Dunston where the guides
would identify wanted men.[22] The Mayor wrote urgently to Sir Edmund Nagle,
commander at Leith, begging him to send a warship to assist the magistrates.
He assured him that the Admiralty would be informed of this request. Nagle
immediately sent HMS *Strenuous*, a gun brig commanded by one of his rela-
tives, 'an active intelligent officer'.[23]

Some arrests were made during the operations of 4 November, and, hoping
that the show of force had sufficiently alarmed the keelmen, the magistrates and
fitters decided to isssue a handbill calling on them to resume work. There were
differences of opinion on the wording of this proclamation. One draft referred
to the 'dangerous and serious situation' in which the keelmen had placed themselves and their families by their violent and illegal proceedings, and earnestly
recommended them to resume work to avoid the 'dreadful consequences of the
law', but the final version merely announced that all bound keelmen who did
not resume work within the next two days would be deemed to have deserted
their service and would be prosecuted as the law directed. 'To remove all pretence of the well disposed being kept from their employments under fear of
violence', a force fully adequate to protect them would be stationed on the
water and both sides of the river till order was restored.[24] A proposal to offer a
substantial reward to be paid on conviction of anyone opposing a keelman in
the discharge of his duty was rejected,[25] but it was agreed to arrange another
demonstration of force, 'merely to shew the keelmen that the magistrates continue to employ the military to assist their endeavours to restore order amongst
them'.[26] The local commander, lieutenant-general Dundas, undertook to provide infantry and cavalry for the purpose. Arrangements were made to billet
small detatchments of infantry in areas where the keelmen lived, and a survey

21 Isaac Cookson to Charleton, 3 November 1809, Bell, 'Collections relative to the Tyne', II, fols 96–7.
22 Plan of operations, 3 November 1809, TWA 394/37.
23 Isaac Cookson to Nagle, 3 November 1809; Nagle to Cookson, 4 November, TWA 394/37.
24 Heads of a proposed handbill; printed public notice, both 5 November 1809, TWA 394/37.
25 Draft of above printed notice where a reward of 50 guineas, altered to 20, was finally struck out.
26 Draft plan of operations for 6 November 1809, TWA 394/37.

showed that 263 men could be quartered in seventy houses situated above and below the bridge.[27]

By the evening of 6 November there was little sign that the keelmen would obey the injunction to resume work the next day. It was therefore proposed that, if they did not, the plan should be put into action and every effort made to execute warrants issued against the below-bridge keelmen, who were regarded as the most recalcitrant. In previous operations the constables had failed to find those named in the warrants, though they had encountered other strikers who were preventing their fellows from working. It was therefore recommended that every bound keelman absent from work should be 'instantly taken into custody'.[28] At least sixteen were apprehended and subsequently sentenced to hard labour in the House of Correction for periods of one or two months.[29] The magistrates had 'great hopes' that the disturbances might now be coming to an end and that some of the above-bridge keelmen would return to work. At a joint meeting of magistrates and members of the coal trade it was resolved that the water-bailiffs' and quay-master's boats should escort keels from the bridge down to Shields. The crews of the escort craft were to be armed with pikes for self-defence and the military were to patrol both sides of the river.[30] Two days later the Mayor asked General Dundas for 180 infantrymen to be quartered as previously arranged, though they were not to act unless the magistrates called for their help.[31]

The troops were provided, but, though these measures may have prevented breaches of the peace, they did not bring the keelmen back to work. Faced with the prospect of prolonged disruption of trade, and probably influenced by a letter from the Home Office calling on the Mayor 'to lose no time' in reporting particulars of the disturbance among the keelmen,[32] the members of the coal trade announced that they were 'anxious to reconsider' the keelmen's requests, provided they returned to work. As soon as they did so, members of the trade would meet and proposals approved by the magistrates of the three counties would be submitted to them.[33] This surprising offer was a tacit admission that the elaborate measures designed to force the men back to work had failed. It was strange that the magistrates had omitted to report the strike to the government, especially as they had enlisted assistance from the armed services, which was normally done through the Home Department. No doubt the desire to off-set this irregularity and make a favourable impression urged the magistrates to meet a deputation of the keelmen on 11 November, after which the Mayor

---

[27] Return of infantry quarters on the north and south sides of the Tyne as taken by order of the magistrates, 5 November 1809, TWA 394/37.

[28] Further plan of operations, 6 November 1809, TWA 394/37.

[29] *Newcastle Advertiser*, 11 November 1809.

[30] Minutes of meeting of magistrates and committee of the coal trade, evening of 6 November 1809; draft letter to general Dundas; further note headed 'Mayor's Chamber 6 November', TWA 394/37.

[31] Draft, the Mayor to general Dundas, 8 November 1809, TWA 394/37.

[32] Isaac Cookson to Richard Ryder, Home Secretary, 11 November 1809, replying to a letter from the Under-Secretary of State, National Archives, HO42/99/593-5.

[33] 10 November 1809, TWA 394/37.

was able to inform the Home Secretary that the conference seemed to have persuaded the keelmen 'to return peaceably to their employment'. The magistrates, he added, believed the country to be greatly indebted to General Dundas and Captain Charleton for their 'zealous & active exertions'.[34]

The keelmen resumed work on 13 November, three days before their employers stated the terms which, with the magistrates' approval, they were prepared to offer. Each crew below-bridge was to receive an additional 1s 6d per tide, while the increase above-bridge was 1s 10d and a further increment of between 1s and 2s 4d according to the position of the respective staithes. Although the new scale would not normally apply until after the expiration of existing contracts, the fitters proposed that 'in consequence of the below-bridge keelmen being much abridged in their work' the addition of 1s 6d per tide should take effect immediately, and (presumably to prevent discontent among the above-bridge men), it was resolved that they should receive the 1s 10d per tide at once, and the remainder commencing on 1 January 1810.[35] The immediate additions were to the 'keel dues', which had not been altered since 1710, but these payments were per keel, not to each member of the crew. The other increases, which applied only to the above-bridge men, were to the owners' wages to which additions had been made in 1792. The amount gained was less than the keelmen had sought, especially in respect of the below-bridge men whose increase divided equally among the three adults in a crew amounted to 6d each (from which a portion would go to the boy) instead of the shilling per man for which they had petitioned before the strike. The above-bridge men fared better, their increase each tide varying between 2s 10d and 4s 2d per keel. Allowing for a small deduction for the boy in each crew, this represents a gain of between 11d and 1s 4d per man, compared with the 1s 6d they requested at the outset.

In a draft proposal, partly in response to the points raised by the keelmen subsequent to their petition, the fitters suggested that 2s 6d (later reduced to 2 shillings) should be added for lying tides; that an additional shilling should be paid to a messenger travelling for orders; and that six chaldrons of coal should be given to each crew per year.[36] These proposals were not included in the terms offered to the men on 16 November, but they may have been granted subsequently. A note concerning binding money states the amounts as follows: All below bridge, £1 per keel; Dunston, £1 10s; Benwell, £2; Denton, Kenton & Lemington, £3; Whitefield, £12. Once again the below-bridge men received the least.[37]

As the annual binding time approached, members of the coal trade evidently feared that the settlement would not endure. On 9 December their committee resolved 'that no coal owner nor fitter shall directly or indirectly treat with any keelman 'till after the next general meeting of the trade … unless the keelmen

[34] Cookson to Ryder, 11 November 1809, National Archives, HD42/99/593-5.
[35] 'Terms agreed on to be offered to the keelmen', 16 November 1809, TWA 394/37.
[36] Fitters' proposals, TWA 394/37.
[37] Ibid.

themselves shall come forward and agree to hire on the terms already offered by their masters'. At the general meeting it was agreed that every fitter should be 'permitted to endeavour to hire his keelmen on ... 30 December on the terms already offered to them'.[38] Despite these implied misgivings, it seems that the binding was achieved without difficulty.

By holding out for four weeks against strong opposition the keelmen achieved a notable victory in gaining an increase in wages. The basic rates then established were still in use forty years later.[39] The sums gained were, however, small, especially in the case of the below-bridge men, the prime instigators of the strike. They were strategically well placed to enforce a stoppage which the better-off above-bridge men may not have been eager to join at the outset or to stay out so long (though the first offer made to them fell below their own demands), but intimidation, if not conviction, persuaded them to comply. Although they were not immediately affected as were the keelmen lower down the river by the spouts, their own circumstances could easily change. Some of their fitters might in the future be contracted to a below-bridge colliery, while individuals might change employers when their bonds expired. Indeed, shortly after the strike, the coal owners resolved 'that no work below bridge shall engage more than one keel's crew from all the works above bridge', thus restricting such movements of labour.[40] The keelmen were undoubtedly aware that the location of their employment might be altered and self-interest as well as intimidation, or memory of their accustomed solidarity, may have played a part in inducing the above-bridge men to make common cause with their less fortunate brethren. It has been suggested that the magistrates made little use of the military and naval forces at their disposal and that they were 'seemingly reluctant to break the strike by all out pressure on the keelmen', but, as shown above, it was not lack of will but the virtual failure of strong-arm tactics that led the authorities to resort to negotiation.[41]

Although the below-bridge men did not on this occasion explicitly complain about the spouts, the major cause of their impoverishment, nine years later a desperate struggle began against the increasing erosion of their employment by this method of loading the colliers.

---

[38]   Coal Trade Minute Book, 1805–1815, pp.127–8, Northumberland Museum and Archives.
[39]   Copy keelmen's bonds to Stella Coal Company, 1852, 1857, reproduced by permission of Durham County Record Office, NCB I/SC/548, 550.
[40]   Coal Trade Minute Book, Northumberland Museum and Archives, 23 December 1809, p.128.
[41]   Rowe, 'Strikes of the Tyneside Keelmen', p.65.

12

The Strike of 1819: A Partial Victory

After the turbulence of 1809 the keelmen settled into a state of apparent tranquillity. They did not join the seamen in their great strike of 1815, much to the relief of the authorities, who had feared that the great bodies of keelmen, pitmen and waggonmen, thrown out of work by the strike, would join the seamen.[1] The prospect was alarming, but, although the strike lasted for six weeks, such a junction of forces did not take place. Keelmen, pitmen and seamen tended not to interfere in each others' industrial disputes.[2] Indeed, stoppage of the coal trade on which so many workers depended for their bread could provoke hostility towards the strikers on the part of those not involved in the dispute.

Meanwhile, vessels 'of almost any burthen' were increasingly being loaded by the spouts and a new device, known as 'the drop', whereby the colliery waggon was lowered over the ship and emptied directly into her hold.[3] The employment of the below-bridge keelmen was thus being steadily eroded, and the revenue of the keelmen's charity correspondingly decreased at the very time that heavier demands were being made upon it. After payments had been made to the superannuated, widows, orphans and the sick, the balance against the fund rose from £47 13s in 1815 to almost £162 in 1818.[4] This was a matter of concern for all the keelmen, not just to those employed below Newcastle bridge.

On 27 September 1819, a year marked by widespread economic and political discontent, the keelmen enforced a strike. In a petition to the coal owners and fitters they complained that they had suffered 'very great privations from want of employment, chiefly owing to the vend by spout having increased so much of late'. They therefore begged that no ship be allowed to load more than six keels (48 Newcastle chaldrons) of her cargo at any spout.[5] This meant in

---

[1] Copy letter, Mayor of Newcastle to Lord Sidmouth, Home Secretary, 7 October 1815, TWA 394/42.
[2] Norman McCord, *North East England, The Region's Development 1760–1960* (London, 1979), pp.84–5; 'The Seamen's Strike of 1815 in North-East England', *The Economic History Review*, new series, 21 (1968), pp.127–43.
[3] The laden waggon ran onto a platform suspended from a long pivoted lever-arm by which it was lowered to the ship's hold. The drop came into use in the second decade of the nineteenth century though it had been invented some years earlier. See Stafford Linsley, 'The Port of Tyne', in David Archer, *Tyne and Tide* (Daryan Press, Ovingham, 2003), pp.176–7; W. Fordyce, *A History of Coal, Coke, Coal Fields...and Iron*, pp.59–60.
[4] Particulars of the keelmen's fund, 1815–18, National Archives, HO 42/196/430. This and many other documents among the Home Office papers relating to the keelmen's strikes of 1819 and 1822 are printed in A. Aspinall, *The Early English Trade Unions* (London, 1949).
[5] 28 September 1819, National Archives, HO 42/196/427.

practice that loading at the spouts would be restricted to small vessels, 'such as formerly could alone go under them'.[6] The petitioners further requested that a penny on every chaldron vended by spout be donated to their charity, which, they claimed, could not continue without their employers' assistance. Finally, they called for enforcement of the eight chaldron keel-load, 'the danger being very great in stormy weather or strong tides if the keels carry more than that quantity'.

At a general meeting on 2 October the employers unanimously agreed to subscribe £300 to the charity as soon as the men returned to work, ordered that no keel should carry more than eight chaldrons at a time, and that, as prescribed by the Act of 1788, the off-putter at each staithe should swear to load the keels fairly to that limit. Any who refused or neglected to take the oath within a week would be dismissed,[7] but there was no reason to suppose that revival of this provision against overmeasure, which had never been effective and had evidently fallen into disuse, would now remedy the keelmen's grievance. Moreover, their complaint indicates that the recent Act of 1815 (55 George III, cap.118) designed among other things 'for preventing frauds in overloading keels and other carriages used in conveying coals for exportation or to be carried coastwise', was also being disregarded. As to the spouts, the employers absolutely refused to make the least concession. To limit the use of these devices or impose a charge on coal loaded by them would be 'a violation of private property and of the principles on which all trade is carried on'. The local press fully endorsed this stance. The *Newcastle Courant*, for example, declared that the keelmen were calling for the substitution of 'expensive manual labour for a cheap machinery already erected and in operation; a demand wholly incompatible with all the acknowledged principles of freedom in trade'.[8]

The keelmen rejected the proffered terms which fell far short of their demands. Even £300 for their charity did not provide the long-term assistance it required. The Mayor, Joseph Forster, immediately reported the stoppage to the Home Office. Although he had no reason to suspect that the men were motivated by political notions, he feared that ill-disposed persons would strive to 'inflame them to mischief', and drew attention to the weakness of existing military and naval forces in the area. In response to his report a warship was ordered to the Tyne.[9] The Mayor was not alone in fearing that political activists would try to promote discord. 'This is not a time for masters to do anything that looks like oppressing their labourers', Joseph Bulmer, an acting magistrate, commented on the overloading of the keels, which he rightly described as a tacit price reduction to the ship owner at the keelmen's expense. As the strike

---

[6] *Tyne Mercury*, 5 October 1819.
[7] 2 October, National Archives, HO 42/196/430.
[8] *Newcastle Courant*, 2 October 1819.
[9] 28 September 1819, National Archives, HO 42/195, and endorsement stating that a sloop of war had been ordered to the Tyne. Joseph Forster had been Mayor when the 1809 strike began and was again almost at the end of his term of office.

continued, Bulmer, who was fond of sending alarmist reports to the Home Office, declared that the keelmen were 'living by plunder, taking turnips and potatoes from the farmer in open day'.[10] William Richardson of North Shields, even more alarmist, could not 'sit still and see the laws and institutions of Great Britain trampled upon'. Reporting that a body of keelmen had forcibly compelled trimmers and waggoners to stop work, he predicted that this was 'only the forerunner of that awful rebellion, plunder and rapine, now in embryo, and which will in a few days shew its daring head if the arm of the law and force civil and military put not a stop thereto'.[11] Nicholas Fairles, a magistrate particularly unsympathetic towards the working classes, feared that the pitmen, 'a numerous and ignorant race', might join the keelmen;[12] and others were apprehensive that the seamen from about three hundred ships then moored in the Tyne, who also had grievances against their employers, might do the same.[13] 'We have the most formidable set of men to contend with', Archibald Reed, the newly elected Mayor, declared, 'consisting of sailors, lightermen [i.e. keelmen], pitmen, and I am truly sorry to add of Radical Reformers'.[14]

Reform Societies had sprung up all over the region and the authorities were alarmed when the reformers proposed a mass meeting to protest against the recent loss of life and injuries caused when troops and yeomanry charged through a huge crowd listening to 'Orator' Hunt and other radicals in St Peter's Fields, Manchester, commonly known as 'the Peterloo massacre'. The Mayor declined a request by the radicals (stigmatized by a local magnate as 'the very lowest class of blackguards')[15] to convene the meeting, but he evidently promised that the magistrates would not interfere with a peaceful assembly. 'Very inflammatory language and seditious writings' were said to be diffused among the keelmen.[16] One such was probably an *Address of the Reformers of Fawdon to their Brothers the Pitmen, Keelmen, and other Labourers of the Tyne and Wear*, which, although recommending restraint, denounced the 'monstrous system of government', attacked the clergy and the rich, and referred to a struggle 'betwixt a starving people and a few shameful, hard hearted Diveses, who first plunder us, without right or reason, and then, when we complain, send the military, either to murder us or awe us into slavery'.[17] 'The small wicked pamphlets must be suppressed, and some restraint put upon the newspaper editors, or the liberties of England will be trampled under foot & that under guise

[10] Bulmer to Sidmouth, 28 September and 8 October 1819, National Archives, HO 42/195, 42/196/423.
[11] Richardson to the Mayor, 30 September 1819, TWA 394/42.
[12] Fairles to Sidmouth, 30 September 1819, National Archives, HO 42/195.
[13] Robert Wheldon to Sidmouth, 2 October 1819, National Archives, HO 42/196/440–1.
[14] Archibald Reed to Sidmouth, 20 October 1819, National Archives, HO 42/197/671–4.
[15] Sir Matthew White Ridley to 2nd Earl Grey, 8 October 1819, Durham University, Archives and Special Collections, Earl Grey Papers, B42/12.
[16] Earl of Darlington to Sidmouth, 15 October 1819, National Archives, HO 42/196/413–14.
[17] Copy in the North of England Institute of Mining Engineers, Bell Collection, XI, 83. It was printed by John Marshall, a notable Newcastle radical.

of preserving them',[18] William Richardson, now a special constable, urged the Home Secretary.

The meeting on 11 October passed off peacefully. Contrary to expectations, the keelmen took little interest in the proceedings, but the authorities were shocked at the vast number of reformers, 'men of the lowest order', estimated at 18,000, who marched in regular array with banners flying and drums beating, to join the throng of spectators, making a total of about 40,000.[19] As another meeting was projected, the Mayor enquired whether the magistrates, aided if necessary by the military, could prevent an assemblage which, although having legal objectives, might 'intimidate or disturb the well disposed and overawe the civil power', and whether they could legally disperse such a gathering under the Riot Act, though no tumult had occurred.[20] R.W. Brandling, a prominent Northumberland magistrate who was also concerned in the coal trade, answered both questions in the affirmative, but doubted the prudence of using such powers. 'The extravagant pretensions of the radical reformers, raised and kept alive by abandoned profligates and men of desperate fortunes, must I think work their own destruction', he declared. Erroneous opinions could be conquered only by force of reason.[21]

Meanwhile, the keelmen refused to yield to what their employers and the authorities regarded as reason. The day after he was installed as Mayor, Archibald Reed courageously ventured to address a full meeting of the keelmen. He believed that he had convinced them of the 'illegality of their proceedings and the impossibility of ... attending to their complaints until they returned to work', but his hopes were dashed when the men resolved to continue the strike. Thomas Clennell, chairman of Northumberland Quarter Sessions, then met about three hundred keelmen, but again without success.[22] A few days later the Mayor attempted to re-start trade in defiance of the strikers. Accompanied by some constables he proceeded downriver in a steam packet, and together with boats from a warship, escorted several laden keels to North Shields. Despite a hostile crowd, he landed there and went to an inn for refreshment. According to Joseph Bulmer, who was not an eyewitness, a large number of keelmen forced those attempting to unload the keels to cease work. Bulmer may have exaggerated the extent to which the keelmen were involved, though they would hardly have failed to resist the attempt to break the strike, but there were certainly others, including, it was alleged, many local radicals, in the throng.[23] The disturbance grew increasingly violent. Those remaining on the

[18] Richardson to Sidmouth, 21 October 1819, National Archives, HO 42/197/32–33.
[19] Fairles to Sidmouth, 12 October 1819; Archibald Reed to Sidmouth, 12 October 1819, National Archives, HO 42/209–10. Lord Darlington, however, put the number of radicals at not more than 7,000. To Sidmouth, 21 October 1819, HO 42/197/577–8.
[20] Draft case, TWA 394/42; Reed to Sidmouth, 22 October 1819, National Archives, HO 42/197/618–9.
[21] Brandling to Nathaniel Clayton, 25 October 1819, TWA 394/42. Brandling (1774–1848) was projector of the Brandling Junction Railway. T. Fordyce, *Local Records or Historical Register of Remarkable Events ... 1833–1866* (Newcastle, 1876), p.240.
[22] Reed to Sidmouth, 5, 6, 7 October 1819, National Archives, HO 42/196.
[23] Bulmer to Sidmouth, 15 October 1819, National Archives, HO 42/196.

steam boat were stoned by boys said to have been incited by women. One of the stone-throwers was arrested but immediately rescued; another prisoner was taken into the inn but it was so violently assailed that it was released. Two boats manned by marines were stoned 'most dreadfully', and, after warning shots only provoked greater violence, one of the marines fired directly into the crowd. Joseph Claxton, a seaman who had arrived just a few minutes earlier, was killed. Believing that the Mayor had given the order to fire, the mob launched a furious attack on the inn. The windows were shattered and the door forced with iron pipes, but the Mayor and his companions escaped by a back exit.[24] He hastened to report the attack to the Home Office and pleaded for an adequate force of warships and marines to be sent without delay and for military strength in the area to be increased. At this point he was unaware of the fatality. 'Some shots were fired by the boats' crews in their own defence', he wrote, 'but as far as I have yet been able to ascertain, only with blank cartridges'.[25] Mobs, terrifying the inhabitants with 'frightful shouts', continued to assemble in North Shields for several nights after the riot. 'Blood for Blood' and other 'terrible and threatening expressions' were scrawled on walls and doors.[26] The Mayor believed that the reformers were 'in a state of almost rebellion', and, typically alarmist, Joseph Bulmer declared that the 'lower orders' were 'ripe for anything'.[27]

In compliance with the Mayor's urgent appeals, four companies of soldiers were immediately sent to Newcastle and other reinforcements were promised. Lord Darlington called out the South Tyne Yeomanry, but Lord Sidmouth, the Home Secretary, obviously fearing a repetition of what had occurred at Manchester, recommended that the yeomanry should not be ordered into action 'except in case of emergency'.[28] Sidmouth, although generally regarded as favouring repression, was not unsympathetic to workers who had grievances against their employers, and in this case he urged that 'when the keelmen shall have ceased to trangress the Law, their complaints shall be listened to with attention and indulgence, and if well founded, the causes of them should, of course, be removed'.[29] In the event, the yeomanry were merely employed in protecting the coal owners' property. Without such protection the spouts would certainly have been destroyed, as had happened on the River Wear in 1815 when the keelmen attacked a recently erected spout-staithe and caused damage

[24]   *Tyne Mercury*, 19 October 1819; *Newcastle Chronicle*, 16 and 23 October 1819.
[25]   Reed to Sidmouth, 14 October 1819, National Archives, HO 42/196. The next day he issued a handbill offering £100 reward for information leading to the apprehension of those involved in the disturbance, HO 42/196/415. On 17 October he sent a further account of the riot and reported that one man had been killed, HO 42/197/656–9.
[26]   *Newcastle Chronicle*, 23 October 1819.
[27]   B ulmer to Sidmouth, 15 October 1819, National Archives, HO 42/196/411–12.
[28]   Quoted in Rowe, 'The Strikes of the Tyneside Keelmen in 1809 and 1819', p.72. Lord Darlington was similarly concerned. The magistrates 'must be responsible if they order the military to act and I have strongly urged them not to do so, unless the civil power is overcome or incompetent', to Sidmouth, 15 October 1819, National Archives, HO 42/196/413–4.
[29]   Quoted in McCord, *North East England*, p.83.

estimated at £6,000.[30] The military had also to guard the coroner, jury and witnesses during the inquest on Joseph Claxton, which lasted for five days. Attempts were made to intimidate the jury into returning a verdict of wilful murder, and, after one of 'justifiable homicide', shots were fired at the houses of two jurymen.[31]

At a Court of Inquest held in Newcastle before Thomas Clennell and a full bench of magistrates (the first time, it was claimed, that this court, established under Henry IV, had been held in the locality), the jurors found that there had been a riot in North Shields and Thomas Gustard, a shoemaker, who had been involved, was fined twenty shillings and bound over to keep the peace. Three keelmen, although absent, were each fined £15 for a riot at Wallsend staithe. That three Englishmen had been declared guilty without opportunity to offer a defence provoked strong criticism in the radical press.[32]

Meanwhile Thomas Clennell had been negotiating with the keelmen and their employers and, after much difficulty, he obtained new terms for the men. Although they still refused to end the strike, which had now lasted three weeks, their sole remaining demand was that work should be provided for between 100 and 140 of their body who were unemployed.[33] The Mayor therefore suggested that the Corporation should employ these men in dredging the river, and the Common Council readily agreed.[34] At a mass meeting on 20 October the keelmen accepted the terms thus enhanced. The £300 which the coal owners offered would be paid to the charity within a week of the men's return to work, and, to benefit the fund still more, application would be made to Parliament for a bill to impose a levy of a farthing on every chaldron of coal shipped from the Tyne.[35] This, it was estimated, would yield about £900 per annum.[36] As the impost was to be on all coal whether loaded from keels or spouts, the issue of a tax on spout loadings, which the coal owners had resisted ever since it was proposed in 1794, was avoided. No overmeasure was to be carried in future, and the off-putters were to be 'immediately sworn to that effect'. Moreover, the keelmen were to be paid within a fortnight for the overmeasure they had carried since the beginning of the year. The payment known as 'makings-in' was fixed at 2s 6d per keel and was always to be paid in money, and the keelmen were not to be compelled to drink at the staithes. They were to receive

---

[30] *Newcastle Chronicle*, 6 November 1819. About the attack on the spouts on the Wear, see below, Chapter 15.

[31] *Newcastle Chronicle*, 23 October 1819; *Tyne Mercury*, 26 October 1819. The inhabitants of the Parish of Tynemouth offered a reward of 200 guineas for information concerning those who fired through the windows of the jurors' houses, and a further reward of 100 guineas was offered by the two jurors themselves, 21 October 1819, National Archives, HO 42/197/69.

[32] *Tyne Mercury*, 19 October 1819; *Newcastle Chronicle*, 23 October 1819. Extract from *The Star*, 22 October 1819, quoted in the *Tyne Mercury*, 2 November 1819.

[33] Reed to Sidmouth, 19 October 1819, National Archives, HO 42/197/664–5; Duke of Northumberland to Sidmouth, 20 October 1819, HO 42/197/667–8.

[34] 19 October 1819, TWA, Calendar of Common Council Minute Book, 1817–24, fols 35–6.

[35] Handbill, 20 October 1819, North of England Institute of Mining Engineers, Bell Collection, XXII; *Newcastle Chronicle*, 30 October 1819.

[36] *Newcastle Chronicle*, 23 October 1819.

a shilling per crew for casting into a ship with port-holes more than five feet above the gunwale of the keel, and a further shilling for every foot that height exceeded six feet. Any disputes about this payment, which was to be made by the shipmasters, were to be settled by the harbour master. All keelmen would be bound for the next year and none of them would be discharged for anything that had happened during the strike. Each keelman on binding was to receive twenty shillings in aid of house rent. The bonds were to be printed and a copy given to each man, but it was to be understood that the covenants might vary according to local situations. In case of any future dispute, two keelmen were to be immediately deputed to apply to a magistrate who was to send the complaint in writing, without naming the complainants, to the secretary of the coal trade.[37]

The settlement was said to be 'almost to the entire satisfaction' of the keelmen,[38] but it did not please some of their employers. The owners or agents of two collieries refused to follow the rest in advancing money to the keelmen to enable them to buy provisions, and the men attached to these collieries did not return to work with their fellows. Fearing that the whole body would strike again, which he could not contemplate without the 'utmost dread of the consequences', the Mayor advanced twenty shillings to each of the men concerned, on condition that if their employers did not repay him the other coal owners would do so.[39] This solved the immediate problem, but less than a fortnight later, the men struck on account of the continued recalcitrance of the owners who had objected to the settlement and attempts by others 'to evade the terms to which they had agreed'.[40] Most of the employers soon settled with their keelmen, and by 9 November, five days after the stoppage began, all except those attached to one colliery had returned to work. The Mayor and Clennell met the men and the colliery agent that day and achieved a settlement.[41] The same evening James Losh, a local barrister who had interests in coal mines, had 'a good deal of conversation with Clennell as to the keelmen' and was satisfied that 'their masters were more to blame than the poor men themselves'.[42] Later, Losh again expressed sympathy for the keelmen:

> Their first demands were certainly just, and had been long refused or evaded, but when they made their stick they got heated, felt their strength, and demanded more. The arrangement made by the Magistrates was I think upon the whole fair, and had the Keelmen well content. But it is quite true that some of the coal owners attempted to evade the new regulations, and this

[37] Bell Collection and *Newcastle Chronicle*, as in n.35.
[38] Duke of Northumberland to Sidmouth, 20 October 1819, reporting on a conversation with Clennell, National Archives, HO 42/197/667–8.
[39] Reed to Sidmouth, 21, 22, 23 October 1819, National Archives, HO 42/197.
[40] Reed to Sidmouth, 4 and 6 November 1819, National Archives, HO 42/198; James Losh to 2nd Earl Grey, 19 November 1819, Durham University Archives and Special Collections, Earl Grey Papers, B40/7/7.
[41] Reed to Sidmouth, 7 and 9 November 1819, National Archives, HO 42/198.
[42] Edward Hughes, ed., *The Diaries and Correspondence of James Losh, 1811–23* (Surtees Society CLXXII, 1962), p.103.

immediately produced great irritation. All however is quiet again and Mr. Clennell told me yesterday that he thought it wou'd continue so.[43]

During the strike Losh had been approached by a deputation of keelmen seeking his 'opinion, or rather advice'. 'In my conversation with them', he later wrote, 'I succeeded in shewing them the folly of their attempting to interfere with the spouts and other machinery, and in preparing them to accede to the first fair & moderate proposals made to them by the coal owners'.[44] This advice they eventually followed. The secure funding of their charity was the most substantial gain they had ever achieved by a strike, even though their bid to have a greater tax imposed specifically on coal loaded by spout had failed. The prohibition against overloading the keels was strengthened by the agreement to pay for the overmeasure previously carried. This was unprecedented in the keelmen's long struggle against this abuse, and shows that the owners had instigated or at least connived at the practice. The regulation about payment for 'makings-in' and drinking at the staithes appeared beneficial, but similar orders had been made in 1792, and it was doubtful whether this new one would be any more effective. The keelmen had often experienced difficulty in obtaining payment from the shipmasters, but it was unlikely that the harbour master would be readily available to settle the disputes that would inevitably arise over demands in respect of extra labour. The offer of employment by the Corporation seemed an important gain, but the dredging of the river was but a temporary expedient. Thus some of the apparent gains were likely to be soon eroded, and the advantages had to be offset against the men's failure to extort any concession on the use of the spouts.

The coal owners resolutely resisted encroachment upon what one newspaper described as the 'dearest and most important of our constitutional rights, the free enjoyment of private property'.[45] However, having represented the keelmen's complaints about the spouts to the Common Council, Clennell declared that a petition to that body would receive 'every attention'.[46] This fudged the issue for the moment. When the keelmen's petition was presented it was referred to the river jury and a committee of the Council, but a deputation who attended to explain and reinforce its arguments was given no opportunity to do so. The jury eventually reported that the petition was unreasonable and ought to be rejected, and with this the committee concurred.[47] Meanwhile the employment provided by the Corporation lasted for only three months. Worse still, the keels were soon being overloaded again, and, 'notwithstanding the indemnity which was promised', several keelmen who had acted as deputies during the strike were dismissed. The keelmen did not now dare to send a deputation to the Mayor

---

[43] Losh to Grey, 11 November 1819, Durham University Archives and Special Collections, Earl Grey Papers, B40/7/6.

[44] Losh to Grey, 19 November 1819, *ibid.*, B40/7/7.

[45] Press cutting, North of England Institute of Mining Engineers, Bell Collection, XI, 81.

[46] Handbill, 20 October 1819, *ibid.*, XXII.

[47] TWA, Calendar of Petitions to Common Council, 1799–1850; Minutes of Common Council, 23 December 1819, fol.139; 4th *Address* of the keelmen, 1822, Bell Collection, XXII.

and had to inform him through 'a confidential person'.[48] Angry at the employers' double breach of faith, and fearful of its probable ill-consequences, the Mayor immediately wrote to the secretary of the coal trade :

> I am extremely sorry to inform you that great discontent prevails among the keelmen in consequence of the overmeasure which they are now carrying, and which, notwithstanding the oath administered to the offputters, is as great now as it was previous to the month of last October. They have other complaints, but it appears to me that a rupture may be prevented if their employers will either lessen the measure or pay for the overmeasure which they carry. You will oblige me by laying this statement before the coal owners.[49]

This evidently had a good effect. The men did not immediately 'rise in a body' as the Mayor feared, and the Home Secretary expressed satisfaction that the coal owners had 'now shewn themselves sensible of the propriety and justice of keeping faith with the keelmen'.[50] Even so, their conditions of employment continued to deteriorate, and two years later they enforced 'the long stop'.

[48] Reed to Sidmouth, 6 April 1820, National Archives, HO 40/12/72.
[49] Reed to John Buddle, 5 April 1820, National Archives, HO 40/12/74.
[50] Quoted in McCord, *North East England,* p.83.

13

'The Long Stop' of 1822: The Keelmen Defeated

On 1 October 1822, many keelmen employed above the bridge stopped work and obstructed any crews about to depart. Nathaniel Clayton, one of the coal owners, ordered the staithman at Dunston to find out why the stoppage had occurred and expressed willingness to redress any well-founded complaint.[1] Discontent spread rapidly, however, and by the following morning the whole workforce had joined the strike. A committee of the coal trade agreed that each fitter should order the men to work and ascertain the reason if they refused,[2] but the strike continued and next day the men presented a petition to the Mayor.[3] Although the stoppage originated above the bridge where no ships could be loaded by spout, the first complaint in the petition concerned this grave issue:

> That your petitioners feel greatly hurt that so many of the keelmen are at present out of employment, by which they and their families have not the necessaries of life, and your petitioners have no prospect of being better, but the contrary; they therefore humbly pray that the gentlemen would please to grant the favour that no more than six keels of coals be put into any ship or vessel by the spout, until the employment get better for the keelmen.

They further called for restoration of binding-money and other allowances, including earnest-money formerly given three months before the binding. In every other respect they were content with their existing terms. According to a newspaper report, the petitioners' complaints were well justified. In one of the above-bridge works, where one hundred keelmen were employed more constantly than most of the others on the river, their wages during the existing year averaged no more than 14 or 15 shillings per week, while in many cases the average below-bridge was only 7 or 8 shillings, 'a sum very inadequate to the support of themselves and families'. Matthias Dunn, who was in a position to be well informed, acknowledged that on account of the spouts many of the below-bridge keelmen had been earning 'very bad wages' which he put at between 10 and 12 shillings per week.[4]

The magistrates met representatives of the keelmen and the coal trade on 4 October. The Mayor complained that by striking before informing a magistrate

[1]   Clayton to Michael Green, 2 October 1822, TWA 394/45.
[2]   Northumberland Museum and Archives, Coal Trade Minute Book, VIII, 1822–23, p.51.
[3]   3 October 1822, TWA 394/46.
[4]   *Durham Chronicle*, 12 October 1822, from a correspondent, also printed in *The Times*, 15 October 1822; diary of Matthias Dunn, quoted by R. Oliver Heslop, 'Keels and Keelmen', North of England Institute of Mining Engineers, D/71. The claim that some keelmen earned only an average of 8s 0d per week, which also appeared in the radical *Black Dwarf* of 27 November 1822, was disputed in the *Tyne Mercury* of 10 December 1822, in which the author of an article contended that some keelmen earned

of their grievances the men had failed to observe the 1819 agreement. Their deputies explained that the strike, which they had tried to prevent, was caused by suspicion that the coal owners were about to impose a general rent-charge for use of the keels, as some had already done. This indicates why the trouble started above rather than below the bridge, though the rent-charge was not mentioned in the petition. In response to the complaint about unemployment, the owners stated that there were now 280 keels on the river compared with 300 previously, and on that basis only 60 out of a total of some 900 keelmen would be redundant, besides which the number employed below the bridge, where the problem lay, was probably less than a third of the total body. This did not satisfy the men's representatives who believed that the number of unemployed was higher. They also complained of obstructions to the navigation of the river by the mooring of ships, often more than two abreast, at the spouts.[5]

The Mayor reported that the men's complaints had been fully examined but found to be 'frivolous and without foundation'. The strike therefore continued, enforced as usual by threats and violence against any who attempted to work. 'They have had the audacity', the Mayor declared, 'to send a deputation to the different spouts on the river … to require them to cease their work, accompanied with a threat of violence if they did not comply'.[6] The magistrates therefore stationed detachments of cavalry at the spouts, and the Mayor begged the officer in command at Sunderland to supply two companies of infantry.[7]

The Duke of Northumberland considered that the Mayor was acting too hastily. He urged conciliation and advised that military force should be deferred 'till the last extremity'.[8] He clearly sympathized with the keelmen, 'this meritorious but misguided set of men', but the magistrates who had to deal with the immediate situation were far from sympathetic. Many strikers had left their homes to escape arrest for deserting their employment, and 'so numerous a body of men scattered up and down in a state of idleness and with no apparent means of subsistence' aroused 'considerable apprehension' among the public. Keelmen were reported to have plundered large quantities of potatoes and turnips from the fields, seized bread from a baker's cart, and helped themselves to vegetables from stalls in North Shields.[9] The magistrates reminded all watchmen, constables and other peace officers of their duty to arrest bound keelmen who were wandering abroad and committing acts of vagrancy.[10]

four or five times as much, and that the yearly average wages of those employed by the Grand Allies was not less than 30 shillings per week. Some keelmen were undoubtedly better off than others, but those who were working only a quarter or even less than 240 tides, regarded by the keelmen as making a 'tolerable year', were unlikely to earn more than the lowest figure stated. In 1809 the keelmen's spokesman claimed that men with families needed £2 per week (see above, Chapter 11).

5   Minutes of meeting, 4 October 1822, TWA 394/46.
6   Draft, Robert Bell, the Mayor, to the Duke of Northumberland, 5 October 1822, TWA 394/46.
7   Bell to the officer in command at Sunderland, 5 October 1822, TWA 394/46.
8   Northumberland to the Mayor, 7 October 1822, TWA 394/46.
9   *Durham County Advertiser*, 12 October 1822; press cutting, 8 October 1822, in North of England Institute of Mining Engineers, Bell Collection, XIII, 606.
10 *Tyne Mercury*, 8 October 1822.

The keelmen were not easy to find and even more difficult to capture, and the behaviour of some of those entrusted with the task left much to be desired. A party of soldiers, who had arrived from Sunderland in compliance with the Mayor's request, were ordered to arrest keelmen at Swalwell but failed to find any after watching all day and night. Some of the troops caused 'great disturbance' by a drunken brawl, and one of the constables, also intoxicated, 'behaved ill'. They 'kept the peace by breaking it', the *Tyne Mercury* wryly commented. Six soldiers arrested for this uproar were confined at Newcastle, but, owing to 'the laxity of the guards', three escaped.[11] Despite these inglorious incidents, the magistrates were shocked when the Commander-in-Chief of the Northern District, Major General Byng, withdrew the force 'without previous communication' with them. The Mayor had failed to consult him when he requested troops from Sunderland, and the magistrates believed that 'it may be owing to that irregularity that we are deprived of the benefit of the presence of the infantry'.[12] The Mayor was convinced that the General had acted out of pique, but Byng explained that the paucity of his force obliged him to preclude detachments being made without reference to him, except in case of actual riot, otherwise troops might be removed from locations where they were necessary to those where there was only a probability of their services being required.[13] The magistrates received no sympathy when they complained to the Home Office but were curtly told that the detachment could not be allowed to remain in Newcastle without material injury to the public service; there were four troops of Dragoon Guards still in the town, and, if infantry was needed, the magistrates should consult the general commanding the district.[14] The Mayor and Town Clerk regarded it as absurd that in the event of an emergency they would have to apply to an officer who might be one hundred miles away.[15] The keelmen would certainly destroy the spouts if they were left unguarded, but it was clear that the magistrates could not call on a large force of infantry to protect the coal owners' property or to assist in breaking the strike. Thus they had to place greater reliance on local forces and the tour of duty of the Northumberland and Newcastle Volunteer Cavalry with a dismounted troop of carabineers was extended from eight to thirty days.[16]

As the strike entered a second week, the coal owners and fitters, alarmed at the frequent interruptions to trade that would inevitably drive their customers elsewhere, resolved to adopt firm but temperate measures to aid the civil power. Those who had not already done so were requested to obtain warrants for the arrest of their keelmen, if they did not immediately return to duty, and all were asked to name employees suitable to serve as special constables. Lists of bound

---

[11] James Atkin to Thomas Forsyth, 8 October 1822, and separate note, TWA 394/46; *Tyne Mercury*, 15 October 1822.
[12] Aubone Surtees to Robert Peel, 9 October 1822, TWA 394/46.
[13] Bell to Nathaniel Clayton, n.d.; Major-general John Byng to the Mayor, 10 October 1822, TWA 394/46.
[14] George Dawson of the Home Office to Aubone Surtees, 12 October 1822, TWA 394/46.
[15] Bell to Clayton, n.d.; draft to Byng, 17 October 1822, TWA 394/46.
[16] *Tyne Mercury* , 15 October 1822.

keelmen were to be compiled and notice published that those harbouring or employing them during the term of their bonds would be prosecuted.[17]

On 9 October the keelmen published an *Address* to explain their case which, they claimed, had been greatly misrepresented.[18] The spouts had become 'a great evil', lately increased by the use of steam boats to tow ships of sixteen or eighteen keels capacity to be loaded by them. Many keelmen, especially those employed below the bridge, had worked only fifty-three or fifty-six tides that year, others fewer still, with consequent privations and distress to themselves and their families. To provide more employment, they were calling for the quantity of coal loaded by spout to be limited to 6 keels (48 Newcastle chaldrons) per vessel. The work provided by the Common Council in 1819 lasted only about three months and thereafter no keelmen had been employed by that body. Before the strike that year they used to receive £2 per keel binding-money and a guinea for a supper, but these allowances had subsequently been reduced and, at the last binding, abolished. The 'good old custom' of *arling*, whereby three months before the bonds expired the masters undertook to re-employ their keelmen and confirmed the bargain with earnest-money, was likewise being set aside. This deprived the men of an opportunity to negotiate better terms and they were now compelled to comply with those dictated to them. Some fitters were demanding 1s 6d per tide as rent for use of the keel, a 'peculiar hardship', especially for those who had little employment, and a principal cause of the strike. During the previous year, £2,583 had been disbursed by their charity to support their sick and aged, thus relieving the parishes in the neighbourhood from burdens that they would otherwise have had to bear; but, if the keelmen's employment was curtailed and their wages and privileges diminished, 'poverty and wretchedness' would overtake them, and they would be unable to support 'this noble institution' which had long been their hope and pride. They wished to meet 'quietly and peaceably' to confer with each other on their own affairs, but the deployment of the military to intimidate them prevented the amicable settlement they desired. They condemned the irregularities committed by some of their body and declared that their object was 'neither rapine nor riot, but to labour honestly … in that state of life unto which it has pleased God to call us'.

The identity of the author of this and subsequent *Addresses* published in the keelmen's name is not known, but he was clearly well acquainted with their concerns. However, reaction in the local press was decidedly negative. One newspaper stated on 'best authority' that the *Address* was full of misrepresentations and had been composed by 'some designing person' to excite sympathy for the keelmen to which they were not entitled:

> What must be thought of a body of 8 or 900 articled servants, who, before the expiration of their present engagements, leave the employment of their

[17] Handbill in North of England Institute of Mining Engineers, Bell Collection, XXII; *Tyne Mercury*, 15 October 1822.
[18] North of England Institute of Mining Engineers, Bell Collection, XXII.

masters to their great loss and inconvenience in order to force them into a better bargain for the ensuing year? The fact is that the labour of this useful body of men is in part superseded by the use of machinery; and until employers can be persuaded to pay a larger sum for human labour, when they can obtain the same effect from the operation of cheap machinery, it is not probable that the redress they seek can be granted to them. Their industry must be turned into some other channel.[19]

Despite its radical stance in politics, the *Tyne Mercury*, in consequence of its strong adherence to the economic doctrines of the day, was unremittingly hostile to the strikers. The keelmen had broken their contract and were mistaken in supposing that their employers were under any obligation to sacrifice their property to relieve them. They were mistaken too in thinking that their wages were to be reduced by a charge for use of the keels. One or two collieries had 'imprudently' made this proposition which their keelmen had accepted, but, when they 'repented', they had been released from the agreement. The strike increased the likelihood that the employers would resort to the use of steam power which posed a new threat to the keelmen.[20] The *Durham Chronicle* of 12 October 1822 likewise declared that nothing stated in the *Address* excused the strike which was 'contrary to law and destructive of the very basis of society', and asked whether these 'deluded men' imagined that they could say to their employers '"You shall not increase the value of your property, you shall not adopt inventions or introduce improvements by which your interests may be served and public benefited because we may suffer some inconvenience".'

Some of the above-bridge keelmen were prepared to resume work, but a large body from below 'marched up and overawed them'. Many involved in the disturbance were arrested.[21] On 12 October, to dispel any 'vain hope' about the spouts, the proprietors of seventeen collieries with staithes below the bridge proclaimed that 'no consideration whatever' would induce them to abandon the right to the free and lawful enjoyment of their property. The keelmen had been paid 'liberally' for the work required of them, and it was not intended to reduce their wages, though the price of provisions might seem to justify it.[22] The coal owners had no objection to establishing a general time of hiring before the bonds expired, but beyond this they were not prepared to go. If this was not

---

[19] Press cutting, 11 October 1822, North of England Institute of Mining Engineers, Bell Collection, XIII.

[20] *Tyne Mercury*, 15 October 1822; Maurice Milne, 'Strikes and Strike-Breaking in North-East England, 1815–44: the Attitude of the Local Press', *International Review of Social History*, 22 (1977), pp.226–40.

[21] Press cutting, 11 October 1822, North of England Institute of Mining Engineers, Bell Collection, XIII.

[22] North of England Institute of Mining Engineers, Bell Collection, XIII, 605. The reference to the price of provisions probably relates to the bread-money allowance which had been introduced when the price of corn was high and was originally intended to cease when the price of wheat fell below 48 shillings per quarter, but by 1809 it was regarded as permanent (see above, Chapter 11). A correspondent in the *Newcastle Chronicle* of 2 November 1822 claimed that the strike was caused by fear that this allowance was about to be withdrawn. There is, however, no mention of this in the keelmen's petition or subsequent publications.

accepted they were firmly resolved to petition Parliament to exempt them from the tax which they had imposed on themselves in 1819 for the relief of men who would have shown themselves

> insensible of the benefits conferred upon them, careless of their solemn engagements, willing to exert the most unlawful means for securing to themselves a temporary advantage at the expense of others, and vain and presumptuous enough to imagine that they can with impunity array themselves against the well-known laws of the land.

The owners and fitters of the above-bridge collieries soon published similar resolutions. The fitters who had not already done so would *arle* their keelmen when they returned to work, but 'only such men, and such number of men, as they shall deem proper'. The terms would be the same as for the existing year: £1 per man towards house rent, but no binding-money, except at Stella where an agreement had already been made. If there was not an immediate return to work, they would join the below-bridge proprietors to petition for relief from contributing to the charity, as they felt 'an unqualified abhorrence' at the ingratitude of men who had manifested a total disregard of their duty and the interests of their employers.[23]

Most of the above-bridge keelmen were now prepared to resume work, and a committee of the coal trade proposed an elaborate deployment of civil and military forces to protect them from the assault of those stationed lower down the river.[24] On 16 October, a large number of keels were brought down, but their crews were greatly harassed by stones hurled at them from both shores. One man was seriously injured and the coal owners promptly offered a reward of one hundred guineas for information leading to the arrest and conviction of the stone-thrower and five guineas in respect of everyone participating in the disturbances.[25] Use of the military to protect the keels remained a delicate matter. When asked to arrange such protection on the south side of the river, two County Durham magistrates replied that in the circumstances they did not consider themselves authorized to call for military assistance.[26]

Meanwhile, the keelmen issued a second *Address* in answer to their employers and to statements made in the press.[27] It was headed by the text 'Hear this, O ye that swallow up the needy, even to make the poor of the land to fail' (Amos VIII, 4). They thanked the employers who had renewed agreements with their keelmen on the existing terms, and expressed regret that they were suffering by the strike. The demand for a limit on the use of the spouts might appear to be an unjustifiable interference with rights of private property, but these contraptions gravely damaged the interests of a large body of men and seriously obstructed navigation of the river. No persons, they presumed, ought to be allowed to use

---

[23] 14 October 1822, TWA 394/45.
[24] James Potts, J. Croser and T. Dunn to the Mayor, 15 October 1822, TWA 394/45.
[25] Handbill, 16 October 1822, North of England Institute of Mining Engineers, Bell Collection, XXII; *Tyne Mercury*, 22 October 1822.
[26] Mr Collinson to the Mayor, 21 October 1822, TWA 394/46.
[27] 15 October 1822, North of England Institute of Mining Engineers, Bell Collection XXII.

their property in a manner that injured the community, and, however vain their hopes, they believed that an appeal must lie to the conservators of the river, or to the legislature. By 'oppressing and annihilating' the keelmen, the coal owners would deprive themselves of their chief claim to their monopoly granted especially to encourage a nursery of seamen for national defence. Indeed, the keelmen had provided the navy with some of its best sailors during the late war.[28] They were not seeking increased wages, although as a result of restriction of the vend the price of coal had more than doubled in recent years (a riposte to their employers' assertion that the existing price of provisions could justify a reduction in wages). Despite their employers' denial that they intended to reduce wages, the demand for keel-rent amounting in some instances to a shilling per man each tide, and the abolition of binding-money and other allowances constituted a reduction in their earnings. Above all, they complained of unemployment, chiefly caused by the increasing use of spouts for loading the ships and restriction of the vend, which by maintaining high prices diminished the demand for coal. If the coal owners withdrew their support from the charity, the keelmen, on account of their inadequate means, might do the same, thus throwing heavy additional burdens on the public, including the coal owners themselves. The 'hireling journals' spread 'the most malicious falsehoods' about the keelmen's intentions in order to give 'colourable pretence' for employment of the military against them. They denied that they had 'a kind of committee' for representing their grievances, or, like their masters, a regular organization for management of their interests.

They followed this publication with a letter to Adam Askew, a County Durham magistrate, from whom they evidently hoped for support. The letter incorporated the above *Address* to which was added a list of grievances, several of which concerned the breakdown of the 1819 settlement. They were generally obliged to carry a chaldron overmeasure, which reduced their wages by 2s 6d per tide; the shipmasters did not pay them for the additional labour when they had to cast into vessels with high port-holes; the Corporation had long since ceased to provide work for their unemployed; and buoys positioned in the channel of the river were a 'dangerous nuisance'. Finally, they declared their firm resolution 'that not one man will return to work until every man is liberated who is or may be arrested during the continuance of the stop'.[29] Askew read this to a meeting of the magistrates of the three counties together with representatives of those involved in the coal trade and deputies of the keelmen. There was much discussion about *arling* to which the below-bridge owners were opposed. Eventually, it was agreed by nine votes to four, to *arle* three months before the bonds expired, provided the men immediately returned to their duty. This (which, the proposer believed, could not be regarded as a concession) was the only point that the keelmen gained. The rest of their

---

[28] They did not, of course, mention how they made every effort to avoid service in the navy, see above, Chapter 10.
[29] 18 October 1822, TWA 394/46.

complaints were either rejected or declared to be *ultra vires*. The employers denied that there had been any just complaint of overmeasure since 1819, as the waggons and keels had been strictly weighed and measured under direction of the Board of Customs. They had no control over the shipmasters and could only remind them that extra pay was due when the keelmen had to cast into high port-holes, though in many cases, they claimed, the payment was made. They could not meddle with disposal of the Corporation's funds, and the positioning of buoys in the river was the responsibility of the Conservators of the Tyne and Trinity House. When the keelmen's deputies called for a limitation on the use of the spouts they were referred to the below-bridge owners' declaration of 12 October, and with this absolute rejection of any such restriction the magistrates unanimously concurred. To the demand that those arrested be released, they replied that they could not interfere with administration of the law.[30]

Some of the magistrates believed that a settlement was still within sight, and the Lord Lieutenant, the Duke of Northumberland, convinced that the strike was about to end, ordered that the Northumberland and Newcastle Yeomanry Cavalry be released from duty.[31] After a mass meeting on 21 October the keelmen issued a declaration thanking their employers for the agreement to *arle* and their previous statement about wages. 'All therefore that we would now petition for', they continued, 'is that our binding-money, namely two pounds per keel, and one guinea in lieu of a binding supper, which was formerly allowed, may still be continued to us'. This, however, was not 'all', as they proceeded to beg their employers to consider restricting the amount of coal any vessel might take in from the spouts to 8 keels (64 Newcastle chaldrons), 'by which we presume little loss or inconvenience would be sustained by the proprietors of coals while ... it would give more employment to our body, and long stifle the voice of complaint among us'.[32] Thus, apart from raising the proposed limit of spout loadings from 6 to 8 keels (a difference of 16 Newcastle chaldrons), the men were still seeking a concession to which their employers were adamantly opposed. Also, despite the magistrates' rejection of their former plea, they begged the coal owners and fitters to use their influence to obtain speedy release of those arrested during the strike. They promised to return to work as soon as it appeared that their employers would attend to the prayer of their petition and 'evince a spirit of reconciliation'.

Although the tone was more moderate than that of their previous announcements, it was clear that without concessions they were not prepared to return to work. Michael Green, the staithman at Dunston, who had hoped that the meeting would end the strike, gloomily reported that it was 'quite the contrary' and would remain so until some arrangement was made about the spouts. The strikers, he added, were not without financial resources. 'Mr Piles box, in which many of the keelmen is in, gave out ten shillings a man to enable them

[30] 19 October 1822, minutes of meeting and statement, TWA 394/46.
[31] Duke of Northumberland to Lieutenant-colonel Brandling, 20 October 1822, printed in *Newcastle Chronicle*, 2 November 1822.
[32] Keelmen to the Mayor, 21 October 1822, TWA 394/46.

to live during the stop; also Piscards box on Saturday [19 October] 5 shillings per man, so that they may stand this week very well'.[33] The *Tyne Mercury* of 29 October carried a similar report: 'They have not depended it seems on the precarious pittance they could extort from the hand of charity, but have drawn liberally on certain boxes or private funds belonging to their society'. These clubs were entirely separate from the charity established by the Act of 1788, and it is not surprising that they were being called upon to alleviate members' necessities during the strike. In at least one case there was further involvement in the dispute. At a full meeting of the Hospital Society, three members were deprived of the benefit of an annuity of 10 shillings, 'for going and casting keels during the Keelmen's stop'. The punishment for their part in strike-breaking was later reduced to a fine of 5 shillings.[34] Reports that the keelmen were receiving financial support from their friendly societies led J.J. Wilkinson, a barrister, to suggest that it was 'high time the Legislature should be applied to, to pass an act shutting the Box (as it is termed) during risings except to the sick and aged only'.[35] After receiving a representation on the subject, the Home Secretary, Robert Peel, ordered that the Mayor be asked whether he considered the allegation to be well-founded.[36] The Mayor replied that the magistrates had no grounds to believe that the keelmen obtained assistance from these societies, but he had heard that they had received small subscriptions from other bodies of men employed in the coal trade. They supported themselves chiefly by begging, he added, 'perhaps enforcing their requests by the terror of their numbers'.[37] It is strange that the authorities had no information on a matter that had appeared in the local press and gained wider currency, nor did the Mayor offer to make further inquiry. Perhaps the magistrates preferred to profess ignorance on this delicate subject.

The day after the keelmen's meeting, a committee of the coal trade, believing that most of the above-bridge men would work if they were not intimidated by those lower down the river, recommended that another united effort should be made to open trade. Staithmen and other colliery officials were to be sworn as special constables and together with the military on both sides of the river, and forces embarked in boats, would provide protection for the keels.[38] A notice

---

[33] Michael Green to Mr Watson, 21 October 1822, TWA 394/46.

[34] Minute book of Keelmen's Hospital, 14 December 1822 and 18 October 1823, fols 262,269, TWA, CH.KH. The 10 shillings annuity arose from interest on a bequest of £100 by John Simpson, a former governor of the Hostmen's Company, which was to be distributed to the ten oldest keelmen resident in the hospital, *Account of the Keelmen's Hospital* (Newcastle, 1829), p.23.

[35] James J. Wilkinson (see *DNB*) to Michael Angelo Taylor, MP for Durham, 16 November 1822, National Archives, HO 40/17/393. Such an Act, he added, should be 'judiciously drawn up, otherwise objections will be made to it, and it should apply to all large bodies of workmen'. He asked Taylor to suggest this to the Home Secretary.

[36] Henry Hobhouse, Under-secretary of State, to Robert Bell, 23 November 1822, TWA 394/46.

[37] Bell to Hobhouse, 25 November 1822, National Archives, HO 40/17/398, and TWA 394/46. The *Newcastle Courant* of 7 December 1822 reported that on the previous Saturday night [30 November] numbers of keelmen and their wives were begging and 'received from many thoughtless shopkeepers a premium for their unlawful conduct which was wasted by some of them in public houses on the quay', quoted Milne, 'Strikes and Strike-Breaking in North-East England', p.232.

[38] Printed paper ('private'), 22 October 1822, TWA 394/45.

was issued ordering the keelmen to commence work on 24 October, otherwise their bonds would be immediately cancelled and other workers engaged, or alternative means adopted, to navigate the keels. The magistrates promised ample protection to those who worked, and warned that the law would be enforced not only against rioters but against those who by their presence aided and abetted them.[39]

Accompanied by a civil and military force, the Mayor proceeded upriver on the appointed day, but no keelmen were to be found. During the night all had fled from their homes and dispersed over the countryside. While the Mayor was engaged on this fruitless mission, a mob of sailors from large ships detained at Shields by the keelmen's strike drove the crews out of the small vessels that were able to load at the spouts. The Mayor believed that this was probably done in concert with the keelmen, but the men on the big ships were suffering from the strike and many of their families were said to be reduced to 'actual starvation'. Jealousy at the better fortune of those who could continue to get coal was probably the real motive for their violence. Their action was ill-timed, for the Mayor immediately turned the force assembled to protect the keels against the rioters, and twenty-eight were arrested. Anticipating further trouble, the magistrates urgently begged the Admiralty to send a warship with a strong body of marines.[40] The Duke of Northumberland also feared that a prolonged strike by the keelmen would be 'a severe trial' for the seamen. The employment of substitute workers, he was grieved to admit, had been only partially successful, for besides opposition from the keelmen, 'the windings of the river, the difficulty of access, and a variety of other causes present many impediments to their exertions'. Even so, he again expressed a certain sympathy for the keelmen:

> It is right also to add that the keelmen, however improperly they may have acted upon this occasion, are, generally speaking, a decent body of men; that, misguided as they are, it is by no political delusion, and that their present ill behaviour is mainly to be accounted for by the constant hostility of unenlightened manual labourers to the improvement and facilities of machinery.[41]

There was little sympathy for them elsewhere. The *Tyne Mercury*, noting that they had struck when their services were most in demand, berated them for taking 'ungenerous advantage' of their employers which proved that they did not deserve 'the liberal treatment they demand for [them]selves yet deny others in return'.[42] A correspondent in the *Newcastle Chronicle* was equally severe. Commenting on the keelmen's alleged determination to continue the strike

---

[39] Printed notices, 22 October 1822, TWA 394/45.

[40] *Newcastle Chronicle*, 26 October 1822; Robert Bell to Robert Peel, 25 October 1822, National Archives, HO 40/17/47 and TWA 394/46; copy Nathaniel Clayton to J. Wilson Croker, Secretary of Admiralty, 24 October 1822, TWA 394/45. The seamen were reported to be in a 'truly pitiable' state, chiefly through failure of the Greenland fishery in which 700 or 800 of them had been involved, added to which the strike reduced many of their families to 'actual starvation', *Tyne Mercury*, 29 October 1822.

[41] Northumberland to Peel, 29 October 1822, National Archives, HO 40/17/54.

[42] *Tyne Mercury*, 29 October 1822.

until Christmas unless they gained some concession, he declared that by making it the interest of their employers to dispense with them they had 'taken the
most effectual steps in their power to ruin themselves'. An 'obvious mode' was
to use steam boats to tow keels from the above-bridge staithes. These 'blind
and misguided men' might then be reduced to casting coal aboard ships for 2
or 3 shillings a day instead of the 5 or 6 shillings which they were said to have
averaged over the past eighteen months. Few would pity them or relieve their
necessities, for by their own 'short-sighted folly' they would have 'accelerated
… the march of the steam engine, which has already obliged so many workmen to turn their hands to other employments'. Moreover, for the past month
they had treated the bond that gave them security of employment as waste
paper, and, if he was correctly informed, their employers would soon regard it
likewise. The keelmen could then consider 'the first act of their tragedy' to be
complete.[43]

The keelmen's call for limitation on use of the spouts, 'a demand which
the one party is as resolute in making as the other is in rejecting', remained
the chief obstacle to a settlement.[44] While the coal owners, backed by the
magistrates, continued their attempts to carry on trade with substitute workers, the keelmen's efforts to obstruct them achieved some success. The *Tyne
Mercury*, highly critical of the manner in which the police and military had
been deployed, cited an instance on 31 October when, as a result of mismanagement of the protecting forces, the keelmen had captured four laden keels
at Scotswood.[45] More details of the incident are described in the Home Office
papers. A magistrate with a force of dismounted cavalry and a party of dragoon
guards had proceeded in a barge to Dunston, but, after enabling several keels
to pass safely, he dismissed the barge and left two small police boats to protect
the remaining keels which were stoned from both shores and finally intercepted
by a party of keelmen armed with bludgeons. The sailors who were navigating them escaped in the police boats while the triumphant keelmen seized the
abandoned craft.[46] The military had neither prevented the violence nor protected the navigation, the *Tyne Mercury* commented, but the soldiers were not
to blame: 'the discredit of these unpunished outrages must rest on those under
whose controul they are placed'. A few days later, about forty keels, escorted
by a chain of boats and protected by forces posted at strategic points along the
riverbanks, were successfully brought downriver, but on the return journey
were left to run the gauntlet of the enraged strikers. They almost killed the crew
of one keel, ducked and severely thrashed another crew, and 'most inhumanly'
beat three keelmen who had resumed work.[47] Later, the strikers scuttled fifteen

[43] *Newcastle Chronicle*, 2 November 1822.
[44] *Newcastle Magazine*, 1822, I, pp.607–8.
[45] *Tyne Mercury*, 5 November 1822.
[46] Extract of letter from the Clerk of the Peace to the Duke of Northumberland, 31 October 1822, National Archives, HO 40/17/375–6.
[47] Plan of operations, 4 November 1822, TWA 394/46; *Newcastle Chronicle*, 9 and 16 November 1822; *Tyne Mercury*, 12 and 19 November 1822.

keels near Dunston and seized three boats carrying sailors who were on their way to navigate some keels. The sailors escaped but the boats were 'reduced to chips & thrown into the river'.[48]

Meanwhile, the *Tyne Mercury* was strongly urging cancellation of the keelmen's bonds and accused the coal owners of timidity for failing to adopt this measure and for neglecting to execute warrants against their keelmen. The magistrates, it claimed, had expressed 'the most decided disapprobation of the irresolute conduct of the coal owners'.[49] Disapproval on this account was certainly aired at a general meeting of the magistrates two days later. Revd Charles Thorp questioned whether the coal owners had the 'serious intention' of executing the warrants, and hinted that each owner wished to protect his men (so that they would be available for work as soon as the strike ended). Revd Liddell declared that before he could consent to the use of the military he must be satisfied that the coal owners were determined to execute the warrants 'to a proper extent'. He also called for prosecution of those who engaged the many bound keelmen who had gone to Sunderland, where extra trade on account of the stoppage on the Tyne afforded opportunity of employment.[50] The magistrates themselves did not escape criticism in the press for failing to curb the keelmen's 'excursions to extort charity' which would continue to enable them to maintain the strike unless the magistrates checked 'this vagrancy, so oppressive to the country and so injurious to the most important interests of this town'.[51]

The criticism evidently spurred the coal owners and magistrates into action. On 15 November, the day after the magistrates' meeting, more than twenty Newcastle keelmen working at Sunderland were arrested, fifteen of whom were subsequently committed to the treadmill at Durham. They were escorted there by a detachment of Dragoon Guards who were hooted and pelted as they proceeded through Gateshead.[52] Five keelmen were later arrested at Blaydon at the instance of Revd Charles Thorp, and some, found sleeping rough in Sunderland, were committed to gaol for breach of contract, if they were bound or otherwise for vagrancy. Some arrests were made without warrants, and, although the magistrates discharged those so detained, the *Tyne Mercury* strongly condemned this breach of the freedom of the subject. The special constables, it declared, had shown how unfit they were to exercise the duties of the police.[53]

Unless the keelmen could inflict losses too great for their employers to bear, there was little prospect that they would succeed in wresting concessions from them, but, as they were unable to prevent use of the spouts during the strike,

[48]   Extract of letter from William Cuthbert of South Shields, 18 November 1822, National Archives, HO 40/17/394.
[49]   *Tyne Mercury*, 5 and 12 November 1822.
[50]   Minutes of meeting, 14 November 1822, TWA 394/46. The *Newcastle Chronicle* of 16 November 1822 reported that as a result of the strike many very large vessels had frequented Sunderland and 'materially' increased trade on the Wear. Many Newcastle keelmen had found work casting coal on that river.
[51]   *Tyne Mercury*, 12 November 1822.
[52]   *Newcastle Chronicle*, 23 November 1822.
[53]   *Tyne Mercury*, 19 November 1822.

the vend of the below-bridge collieries, against which it was chiefly directed, actually increased. Their vend of over 59,000 chaldrons for the first month of the strike far exceeded that of all the collieries on the river during the previous month. This 'singular fact', the *Tyne Mercury* commented with evident satisfaction, showed the futility of the keelmen's attempt to injure the below-bridge collieries, 'the greatest gainers in their absence', while it demonstrated as never before the importance of the spouts.[54] Moreover, on 29 October, members of the coal trade agreed to set aside the quotas assigned to these collieries under the regulation of the vend and allowed them to proceed 'at their discretion'.[55] Later, they were permitted to employ pitmen laid off from the above-bridge collieries on account of the strike.[56]

In a handbill offering gratuitous advice to the keelmen, 'A Friend to the Coal Trade' asserted that their only means of limiting use of the spouts was to help the above-bridge owners to increase their trade and consequently their need for keelmen. He attributed the men's demands, 'so inconsistent and so absurd', to 'the wicked designs of some who tamper with your grievances'.[57] This provoked an angry rejoinder from the keelmen. In a third *Address* they denounced the writer as a 'snake in the grass' and advocate for the coal owners, who had refused them even the 'paltry binding money' and countered all their arguments by use of force.

> Many of the keelmen, after being hunted like wild beasts by military and police, have been dragged out of bed at midnight, driven away naked from homes and families, and thrown into dark and unwholesome dungeons, condemned, against all law, to solitary confinement, and deprived of all intercourse with and assistance from their friends.

The coal owners had availed themselves of every advantage derived from their opulence and rank, whether as magistrates or commanders of the local militias, and consequently all the civil and military forces in the district had been arrayed in their support. They had not scrupled to bribe 'the mercenary editors of the public papers' who were continually advocating still more coercive measures against the strikers. The spouts seriously obstructed navigation of the river, and, according to a prominent legal authority, they ought to be indicted as nuisances and the case brought to trial. (This was the first hint that the keelmen had taken soundings as to whether a remedy might be obtained at law.) They acknowledged that the above-bridge proprietors were suffering by the strike, but restriction of the vend, to which they were parties, doubled the price of coal to the consumer and sacrificed the interests of the keelmen, and even greater numbers of other workers, to those of fifty or sixty coal owners. The rent-charge

---

[54] *Tyne Mercury*, 19 November 1822; *Durham County Advertiser*, 23 November 1822.
[55] Northumberland Museum and Archives, Coal Trade Minute Book, VIII, p.53.
[56] An 'immense quantity' of coal had been wrought in the above-bridge collieries while sales were at a standstill. It was therefore decided to stop production, but, as the pitmen were entitled to a certain payment even when they were not at work, it was agreed that they should be employed in collieries below the bridge. *Tyne Mercury*, 12 November 1822.
[57] 12 November 1822, North of England Institute of Mining Engineers, Bell Collection, XXII.

for keels, 'which appeared to bid fair for becoming a general practice', gave the keelmen reason to believe that further encroachments were being meditated against them. They were accused of illegally breaking their engagements, but the bond did not involve mutual obligations and was therefore of questionable legality. Their masters were not compelled to provide sufficient work or suste-nance for them, and they 'could not consider themselves bound by laws either of God or man to starve for their benefit'.[58]

The 'Friend to the Coal Trade' soon repeated that the deluded keelmen had fallen into the power of 'advocates of discontent and enemies of the people', more through inexperience of the views of such men than through any 'mischie-vous design' of their own. The collieries on the Tyne that were still functioning, together with those on the Wear, which had increased their exports, were amply supplying the London market, and he therefore advised the keelmen to return to work and restore prosperity to their 'lamenting families'.[59] The keelmen responded with a fourth *Address* which, as the magistrates banned its public sale, was sold privately at the printing house of the prominent radical John Marshall. Unlike their previous *Addresses*, it forcefully proclaimed some of the radical ideas of the time. The distress of the productive members of the community, 'the bees', arose not from greater use of machinery but from the great increase in the number of 'drones', and their 'ingenuity ... in possessing themselves of the fruits of productive industry', much of which the keelmen generated in the locality. The 'Friend to the Coal Trade', they suspected to be a clergyman, a member of a class 'living in great part on the plunder of the poor, ... constantly arrayed against their interests and ... attached only to the wealthy and insolent oppressors of the land'. The keelmen had in no way been led astray by mischief-makers, as any advice they had received was always contrary to the steps they had spontaneously taken. The spouts impeded navigation of the river, and the question was not whether the coal owners were entitled to use their property to best advantage, but whether the Conservators of the Tyne had the right to permit these obstructions and others connected with them. The keelmen had returned to work in 1819 under an express promise that the Common Council would give every attention to a petition about the spouts, but a deputation sent to amplify the arguments it contained procured neither audience nor answer, and the evils complained of had increased ever since. If the 'Friend to the Coal Trade' were really such, he would seek to persuade the above-bridge coal owners that their interests were inseparably linked to those of the keelmen and the shipowners. All three, as well as the public, were injured by regulation of the vend, and, if these proprietors were to withdraw from the cartel, legal redress for the keelmen's principal grievance would be speedily obtained, under the auspices of both ship and coal owners, whose interests were equally concerned. (The scenario was unrealistic, but the possibility of legal action against the spouts was clearly coming onto the keelmen's agenda.)

---

[58]   14 November 1822, *ibid.*
[59]   19 November 1822, *ibid.*

From coal-owner and clerical magistrates they had suffered great 'cruelty and injustice'. Many of them had been arrested, even without warrants, illegally imprisoned, and treated 'worse than felons under sentence of death'. Such abuses had fostered hostility and prevented conciliation.[60]

The keelmen's prospects of success continued to diminish, as the local newspapers, ever hostile to the strike, were quick to point out. With the aid of steam boats and protection given by marines from several warships that had at last arrived, almost as many keels as normal were being brought down from the above-bridge staithes. This 'must convince these misguided men of the utter hopelessness of the struggle in which they are engaged', declared the *Newcastle Chronicle* of 23 November, and the *Durham County Advertiser* likewise proclaimed the futility of the strike and the 'imbecility, absurdity and folly' of the measures that the keelmen had been 'induced to adopt'.[61] The *Tyne Mercury* predicted that the keelmen's employment, already 'in a great measure superseded', might soon become 'not only not desirable but nugatory'.[62] These constant outpourings of the local press must have seriously damaged the keelmen's efforts to gain the support of public opinion.[63] Still, as the *Durham County Advertiser* admitted, without the keelmen a 'sort of forced trade' was being carried on with 'irksomeness and inconvenience'. Accidents were common, and the keels, dragged by steam boats or navigated by inexperienced crews, sustained 'material injury'. In many keels more than double the usual number of hands had to be employed at higher than normal wages.[64] Besides the difficulties of navigation, there was constant harassment by the keelmen, adept at hurling heavy stones from slings at the passing craft. Eventually a warning was published that the marines had orders to fire on the first man to throw a stone at them, and a glass worker, who had joined the keelmen, was wounded and committed to prison.[65]

Only the 'hot headed, unruly young men', it was believed, were now preventing the 'most sensible part' of the keelmen from submitting.[66] Most of them were certainly prepared to settle for minimum gains. On 28 November at a mass meeting to consider how to bring about 'an amicable reconciliation', it was decided to relinquish the question of the spouts for the time being, in the hope that the coal owners would, 'in the same spirit of conciliation', restore the binding-money and an allowance for a supper.[67] They also requested that keelmen who were at any time out of work might be employed in preference

---

[60] 25 November 1822, *ibid.*
[61] *Durham County Advertiser*, 23 November 1822.
[62] *Tyne Mercury*, 26 November 1822.
[63] On the importance of sympathetic news coverage to strikers, see Milne, 'Strikes and Strike-Breaking in North-East England'. The keelmen's struggle, he argues, was rendered even more one-sided by the radical *Tyne Mercury*'s encouragement of firm action and insistence on the self-defeating nature of the strike.
[64] *Durham County Advertiser*, 23 November 1822; *Tyne Mercury*, 26 November 1822; *Durham Chronicle*, 9 November 1822.
[65] *Tyne Mercury*, 26 November 1822.
[66] *Ibid.*
[67] 28 November 1822, TWA 394/46.

to others as trimmers at the staithes, and they again begged their masters to use their influence to obtain the release of those in custody.

The Mayor hastily summoned a meeting of coal owners and fitters to consider these points, but, determined that the keelmen should gain nothing from the strike, they rejected them almost entirely. Recalling that at the outset they had refused to grant binding-money and the supper allowance, they indignantly declared that they could not be expected to concede these benefits after the keelmen had for many weeks deserted their work, interrupted the trade of the port, and occasioned a most serious loss to many of their employers. However, in a more conciliatory tone, they added that they did not mean to interfere with the discretion of each master to deal with his men as liberally as he thought proper. They had no power concerning those in prison, but, even if they had, they would hardly exercise clemency towards men who by illegal means had injured their interests. They would readily concur if the magistrates considered that leniency was appropriate in some cases, but it was their unanimous opinion that those guilty of violence ought to feel the severity of the law. The men already working as trimmers had generally behaved well and were not to be 'deprived of their bread'.[68]

This largely unyielding response showed that there was little chance of the 'amicable reconciliation' for which the keelmen hoped. Many ships were now laid up for the winter, which reduced the need of some collieries for keelmen, while others were managing well without them. Several keelmen who tried to return to work at Wallsend Colliery were declared redundant, a measure which even the *Tyne Mercury* denounced as 'highly reprehensible' and damaging to the general interests of the port. At the same time it stated that some coal owners had decided not to bind their keelmen or enter into long-term engagements with them.[69] Indeed, two days later, on 5 December, a meeting of the above-bridge employers authorized the fitters to bind or not as they pleased. The terms were to be the same as for the past year, 'and no other' (which precluded any concession being made to the strikers), and no more than three men and a boy were to be engaged for each keel (which obviated a suggestion that a man should be employed instead of a boy). Keelmen who had been legally discharged from their bonds would not be employed during the current year. At a further meeting on 7 December the employers resolved that those imprisoned solely for deserting their work and who had served at least one month of their sentence might be liberated if the committing magistrate approved, but that those charged with assault, riot or obstruction should be prosecuted.[70]

Meanwhile, on 3 December, some of the keelmen employed at Stella attempted to return to work but were intimidated by the violence of several hundred of their brethren. The marines and armed seamen were seriously provoked, but, after Revd Charles Thorp read the proclamation against riots, the

---

[68]   29 November 1822, *ibid.*
[69]   *Tyne Mercury*, 3 December 1822.
[70]   Meeting of above-bridge coal owners and fitters, 5 and 7 December 1822, TWA 394/46.

mob dispersed and bloodshed was averted.[71] This was the keelmen's last concerted effort to maintain the strike. During the next two days the men of Wylam
Colliery resumed work, those of Townley and Walker Collieries followed suit,
and on 6 December the rest of the keelmen submitted.[72] In most previous
strikes they had completely stopped the coal trade, but this time they were
unable to do so. Thanks to the spouts, the exports of the below-bridge collieries
increased, and eventually the more efficient protection provided by the marines
enabled the collieries higher up the river to resume trading. The above-bridge
keelmen started the strike, but it soon became directed against the spouts with
which they had less immediate concern, though they suffered danger and possible loss of tides from the obstruction to navigation which these structures,
and obstacles connected with them, occasioned. Although from time to time
the keelmen's accustomed solidarity showed signs of weakening, intimidation
by the below-bridge men, combined with the desire to gain at least something
from the strike, and resentment at the measures employed against them, kept
the whole body in the struggle. Even so, as their critics were quick to point
out, by continuing the strike they inflicted most harm on the coal owners with
whom their chief prospect of employment lay.

Although magistrates, coal owners and fitters were united in opposition
to the keelmen's demands, their attempts to deal with the strike were at first
somewhat chaotic. The coal owners were reluctant to execute warrants issued
against the keelmen, while the magistrates failed to prevent the extortion
of charity or even to investigate whether the strikers were receiving money
from their friendly societies. The deployment of the armed forces to protect
those attempting to work proved largely ineffective until the marines arrived.
Thereafter, the 'indefatigable exertions' of the naval and military forces, who,
despite great provocation performed their 'harassing duty' with 'temper and
firmness', played an essential role in defeating the strike.[73]

The stoppage lasted almost ten weeks, 'a period unprecedented in its duration and in the extent of the injuries sustained by it'.[74] The keelmen and their
families must have endured great hardship, the above-bridge collieries suffered
considerable loss, and the strike cost the coal trade as a whole almost £2,000.[75]
It was claimed, with much misrepresentation, that the keelmen had won many
important advantages:

> First, they have kept up their wages, which they had reason to apprehend
> were intended to be reduced. In the collieries above bridge, they have

---

[71] *Tyne Mercury*, 10 December 1822.
[72] *Ibid.*
[73] Robert Bell to Duke of Northumberland, 10 December 1822; Duke of Northumberland to Robert Peel,
      13 December 1822, National Archives HO 40/17/ 407–9. Bell expressed appreciation of the assistance
      rendered by the officers, seamen and marines through whose coolness and discretion 'this long struggle
      with a numerous and daring body of men has been unattended with bloodshed', to Peel, 10 December
      1822, TWA 394/46.
[74] Keelmen, *Four Addresses of the Keelmen of the River Tyne* (Newcastle, 1823), p.20.
[75] D. J. Rowe, 'The Decline of the Tyneside Keelmen in the Nineteenth Century', *Northern History* IV
      (1969), p.121.

gained their binding money and other privileges which had been taken from them. By putting one man more into each keel, they got most of their body employed in the regular colliery keels, to the restriction or prevention of the 'led keels' in which a rent charge was paid; and have also engaged not to undertake any 'fit tides' for fitters, a practice very injurious to the interests of the keelmen.[76]

The coal owners denied from the first that they intended to reduce the men's wages, and we have seen how adamant they were in refusing to concede binding-money and other allowances. If some of the above-bridge men received them it must have been as favours granted by individual owners rather than as concessions won for all by the strike. The statement that an extra man was being employed in each keel was particularly misleading, for, like the boy he replaced, he had to be paid by the other members of the crew who would have to contribute a fourth part of their wages instead of the pittance they gave to the youngster. The *Durham Chronicle* seized on the fact that after complaining of low wages the keelmen were now adopting a measure that would effectively reduce their earnings. This it regarded as proof of the 'reprehensibility of their conduct'.[77] On the other hand it was argued that the removal of boys from the keels would cut off the nursery from which the superabundance of keelmen was continually augmented.[78] Above all, it had been demonstrated that the keelmen were not indispensable. The extent to which trade had been carried on without them showed that a strike, certainly a prolonged one, would henceforth be futile. Indeed the keelmen never again employed this weapon. The yearly bond was also brought into question, and in cases where it was replaced by short-term engagements the keelmen's employment was described as an 'uncertain and precarious dependence'.[79] Moreover, the strike stimulated plans for further mechanisation. A model of a steam-powered boat designed to carry eight keel-loads of coal, and requiring a crew of only three or four men, was submitted to the owners of Fawdon Colliery, and, after the strike, a steam boat of 34 horse power was reported to be under construction to facilitate the loading of ships of great burthen without keels.[80]

Despite the virtual failure of the strike and predictions of the imminent demise of their occupation, the keelmen's spirit was by no means broken. Having failed to extort by force a limitation on the use of the spouts, they now began to seek complete removal of these devices and drops from the river by recourse to law.

---

[76] Keelmen, *Four Addresses*, p.20.
[77] *Durham Chronicle*, 14 December 1822.
[78] *Four Addresses*, p.20
[79] Letter to the *Tyne Mercury*, 21 January 1823.
[80] *Tyne Mercury*, 3 and 17 December 1822.

14

The Keelmen Go To Law

As we have seen, the idea that the keelmen should seek a legal remedy against the spouts emerged during the latter part of 'the long stop'. According to the evidence of a keelman, several years later, Thomas Clennell and other magistrates, presumably in an attempt to break the impasse during the strike, encouraged the keelmen to raise money to bring their case against the spouts to trial at law.[1] The Keelmen's *Address* of 14 November 1822 implied that they had taken soundings of legal opinion, and their offer on 28 November to drop the question of the spouts 'for the present' suggests that they had an alternative strategy in view. That the spouts were a major cause of redundancy among the keelmen was not a matter of which the courts would take cognizance, but a prosecution could be instituted on the grounds that the staithes and the spouts and drops erected on them impeded navigation of the river and were therefore a public nuisance. Two weeks after the strike, the keelmen's deputies resolved that a subscription should be raised to try the question and appealed for assistance in a cause in which, they declared, the public was 'materially concerned'. Subscriptions would be received at various inns and at the establishment of John Marshall, the radical printer of their *Addresses* during the strike.[2]

The attack was directed against two staithes erected near Wallsend by Messsrs Russell to load the colliers by means of drops, and in the spring of 1823 the keelmen's attorney, John Lowrey of North Shields, applied for a bill of indictment against these structures as nuisances obstructing navigation of the river. The application failed at Newcastle Sessions, Morpeth Sessions and Newcastle Assizes, even though on the latter occasion twenty-four witnesses gave evidence for the keelmen,[3] but, at the summer Assizes for Northumberland, a 'true bill' was found, and preparations then began for a trial. Since the prosecution alleged a public nuisance, the case was carried on in the name of the crown as *Rex v Russell*. Henry Brougham, a colourful character who at this stage in his career was best known for his defence of Queen Caroline, was briefed for the keelmen, and James Scarlett, KC, for the defence.[4] Brougham obtained a rule to remove the case to York, since a jury in Newcastle or Northumberland was likely to include coal owners or those closely associated with them.

---

[1]   Evidence of William Hume at Carlisle Assizes, *Tyne Mercury*, 19 August 1828; *Durham Chronicle*, 23 August 1828.
[2]   North of England Institute of Mining Engineers, D70, p.81.
[3]   *Durham Chronicle*, 2 August 1823.
[4]   Brougham (1778–1868), created Baron Brougham and Vaux in 1830, was Lord Chancellor 1830–34. Scarlett (1768–1844), later first Baron Abinger, was Attorney General 1827–28 and 1829–30. *DNB*.

3 Drops at Wallsend. The colliery waggon is poised to be lowered over the ship's hold. The staithes project into the river and the ships and their mooring gear further restrict the passage. Note the keel in the foreground. The drops increasingly supplanted keels at Wallsend.

The case was tried before Mr Justice Bayley and a special jury at York Assizes on 11 August 1824.[5] The main thrust of the prosecution was that the defendants, for their private profit, had erected two staithes, 38 feet high and 36 feet wide, which extended into and seriously restricted the navigable channel of the river. At high water one of these structures occupied a ninth part and the other a tenth part of that channel, but at low water they reduced its width by approximately one-fifth. Ships often lay three or four abreast at them, thus further narrowing the channel and increasing the difficulty and danger of navigation, while buoys positioned to indicate moorings presented a further hazard to craft that sought to pass. The ebb tide bore down with great force upon the staithes, and, when the wind was from the south, vessels had sometimes to run aground to avoid being driven against them. Whatever the direction of the wind, navigation could not proceed as formerly, since now only the last quarter of flood tides and the first quarter ebb tides could be utilized. Brougham cited various precedents in which the courts had found restriction of the right of passage to be a nuisance that no compensatory factors could make

---

[5] John Bayley (1763–1841) was appointed judge of King's Bench in 1808 and of the Exchequer 1830–34. *DNB*. The following account of the trial is based on reports in the *Tyne Mercury*, 17 August 1824, and *Durham Chronicle*, 14 August 1824.

lawful.[6] The staithes, he argued, were of great benefit to the coal owners, but none to the public. As the difficulty experienced in initiating the present action showed, powerful vested interests, including the Corporation of Newcastle, had obstructed measures against these obstacles, and, anticipating what the defence would contend, he asserted that the motives behind the prosecution were not relevant, the question at issue being solely whether or not the staithes constituted a public nuisance. He called seventeen witnesses including John Bell, a prominent local surveyor, and pilots with experience of the river who testified about the difficulties of navigation and accidents that had occurred.

For the defence Scarlett admitted that the staithes restricted the navigable channel, but contended that since they promoted the trade of Newcastle and the County of Northumberland the restriction was not a nuisance in point of law. Trade would be seriously damaged by a verdict for the prosecution which had been brought in order that the number of keels might be greatly increased. The keelmen could then make what terms they pleased, close collieries, shut up the London market, and 'exercize a power which by such a set of men had never before been exercized in the world'. He granted that a tier of ships moored at the staithes obstructed navigation, but this promoted commerce and was therefore not a nuisance. The Thames was obstructed by vessels to a far greater extent than the Tyne, but no one thought of instituting a prosecution there. A public port existed to facilitate the loading and unloading of ships and the more this was increased the more the public benefited. The question was whether the public gained more than was lost by restriction of the navigation. Witnesses for the prosecution had admitted that the trade of Newcastle had doubled in the last twenty years. He denied the relevance of the precedents cited by Brougham and quoted another in which a prosecution against quays and projections in Gosport and Portsmouth Harbour failed since the court held that they were advantageous to the commerce of the Port and had been erected for that purpose.[7] The evidence of obstruction given by Brougham's witnesses ought to have been much more striking than the dozen instances stated to have occurred over a period of two decades. Only one shipowner had been called and he had admitted the superior quality of the coal for the London market when loaded from the staithes instead of keels. His ship had been impeded not by the staithes but by other vessels waiting to be loaded. No other shipowner had been called, a tacit proof that those particularly concerned in navigation of the river considered that the staithes were advantageous. The evidence that had not been presented, he asserted, was of equal importance to that brought before the court. The Corporation of Newcastle with an interest in a flourishing coal trade

---

[6] The principal case cited by Brougham was 'Rex v. Lord Grosvenor and others' for causing an obstruction in the Thames by means of a wharf. The court ruled that although the wharf provided some benefit it occasioned much harm, and the conservators of the river were bound to preserve it from nuisances.

[7] Scarlett, who had been involved in the above case, denied its relevance as the wharf had not been built for commerce and there was no advantage to the public to compensate for the obstruction it caused in the Thames. He also quoted Lord Hale's dictum that not every building below high or low water mark was *ipso facto* a nuisance in law, otherwise every quay in the country would be destroyed.

had allowed these structures, nor had any objection against them been raised by the County of Northumberland. Returning to his opening theme, he invited the jury to consider 'to what London would be reduced if the trade of the Tyne were placed in the hands of the keelmen'. The staithes, he concluded, greatly contributed to the prosperity of Newcastle and the absence of complaint from those most deeply concerned with navigation of the river was decisive proof of the injustice of the prosecution. He delivered this speech 'with extraordinary force and animation' and called no witnesses.

In summing up Mr Justice Bayley laid great emphasis on the possible public benefits as opposed to private profit that might arise from restriction of the right of passage on a navigable river :

> my opinion is that the use of a public water is not for passage only, but for many other purposes, and that many of those purposes are entitled to super-sede the right of passage and to narrow the right of passage to those parts which may not be requisite for greater and more beneficial purposes.[8]

Thus, part of the water over and above what was sufficient for navigation might be most usefully applied to the purposes of commerce, and a great public benefit resulting from abridgment of the right of passage rendered that restriction proper. If, therefore, the jury found that in this case what had been taken from the opportunity of passage was for public purposes and benefit, and that enough was left for ordinary and reasonable purposes of passage, he would recommend a verdict for the defendant; but if they considered that reasonable space was not left for passage, and that no public benefit resulted, they should find for the Crown. It had been suggested, he added, that the staithes were for private purposes only, but, besides the benefit to the proprietor, 'both the man who receives the coals at the staithe, and the man who buys his coals at London coming from that staithe, are benefited if they are either got by those means cheaper, or … better than they otherwise would be'. He directed the jury to consider whether the staithes were in a reasonable place and applied to purposes of public benefit; whether reasonable space was left for the purpose of navigation; and whether the public benefit resulting from the staithes offset the prejudice which individuals might sustain by restriction of their rights of passage. This, he believed, was the ground on which their verdict should be founded. He was about to recapitulate the evidence but the jury indicated that this was unnecessary. The proceedings had lasted twelve hours, but in about three minutes the jury returned a verdict for the defendant.

Brougham immediately indicated that he would apply to the Court of King's Bench to set aside the verdict and enter it for the Crown on grounds of mis-direction by the judge. Accordingly, in Michaelmas term 1824, he obtained a rule for entering a verdict against the defendant or for a new trial. The case came before the judges of the Court in Hilary term 1826.[9] The point at issue was the judge's emphasis on the public benefit arising from the staithes,

---

[8] *English Reports*, 108, pp.568–9.
[9] For detailed report of the proceedings see *ibid.*, pp.560–73.

especially his statement that by their means coal was supplied more cheaply and in better condition than otherwise. Brougham and his colleagues argued that the notion of justifying obstruction of a public right by showing that a collateral benefit resulted was entirely unprecedented. It was fully established that a public right could not be infringed, even if an equivalent were given, without royal licence, and if compensation were admissible, it must be in the nature of a public right. In this case the injured parties were those navigating the river, but the alleged compensation was to consumers of coal in London or elsewhere, besides which it was not a public right but only a benefit that could be withdrawn. The only matter for the jury to decide in this and like cases was whether or not the accused had occasioned the alleged obstruction, and neither collateral advantages to other persons nor considerations of public policy were legitimate grounds for decision. If a question of fact was put to the jury with a wrong direction in point of law the verdict ought not to stand.

Scarlett and three other counsel showed cause against the rule. It was clear, they argued, both from authorities and precedents, that a building in a port or navigable river was not to be deemed a nuisance simply because it obstructed the water-way. Whether or not it constituted a nuisance was a question not of law but of fact to be determined by a jury. The judge's charge to the jury conformed to these principles and the authorities cited in support of them, and he was entitled to point out the advantages that the staithes rendered to commerce, compensation being the only justification that could be advanced for an encroachment. His further remark that the consumers also benefited, even if incorrect, was an illustration, not a direction in law, and this observation was very properly put to the jury in answer to the assertion that the staithes were for private benefit only, as the cheapness of the coal resulted directly from their effect upon the navigation. Various Acts of Parliament for regulation of the coal trade recognized the existence of such structures and by implication encouraged their use.

The case stood over until 26 May 1827 when the judges gave their opinions separately. Mr Justice Holroyd[10] pointed out that there were many public rights on navigable rivers, the exercise of any of which might obstruct the others. Whether such obstruction was a nuisance depended upon the circumstances and was a question of fact to be determined by a jury. The statutes that regulated the loading of ships in turn at the staithes clothed them with public rights and showed that they were not *per se* to be regarded as nuisances. The restriction of the opportunity of passage was thus for the exercise of rights deemed by the statutes to be beneficial. The judge's observations in answer to the prosecution's unfounded suggestion that the staithes were for private benefit only was perfectly proper, but they did not form part of his direction to the jury. That direction was in substance correct and there were no grounds on which the verdict should be set aside.

---

[10] Sir George Sowley Holroyd (1758–1831), judge of King's Bench 1816–28. *DNB*.

Mr Justice Bayley, who had tried the case, declared that, having fully considered the matter he could not, in justice to the defendants, give up his original opinion concerning the relevance of benefit to the public. The motive of private profit could give rise to public benefit, and in this case the consumer had more than 100,000 chaldrons of prime coal in an unbroken state from the two staithes instead of inferior keel coal, and if supplied at a lower price this constituted a public benefit to the London buyers. He believed that the probable effect on the price and the improved condition of the coal were circumstances proper for consideration of the jury and would be so if the case were to be tried again.

The Lord Chief Justice, Lord Tenterden,[11] dissented from the above opinions. Though he was not prepared to say that the verdict should be entered for the crown, he declared that he would be more satisfied if the case were tried by another jury. He pointed to circumstances that considerably qualified the alleged public benefit of the staithes. They had been erected for the private convenience of certain colliery owners and, though the coal arrived at market less broken than if subjected to shipment in keels, it was doubtful whether it came at a cheaper rate. Coal in the best state would fetch the highest price and the advantage would be to the colliery owners, not to the public. In any case, he did not think that possible advantages to the public in respect of price and quality of the coal were relevant to the question whether the staithes injured the navigation. He believed that the verdict had been materially influenced by remarks concerning public benefit that, in his opinion, ought not to have affected it. He would therefore be more content if the matter were tried again, but, as his brethren considered that the verdict should stand, the rule for setting it aside and entering one for the crown had to be discharged.

The keelmen had lost the battle and had to pay the costs of suit, but they were not ready to accept defeat. Although the verdict at the trial had gone against them, it had been proved by their witnesses and admitted by the defence that the staithes obstructed the navigation and the question therefore rested on whether the obstruction was sufficient to constitute a nuisance in law. On this point another jury might come to a different conclusion, and in view of this and the Lord Chief Justice's opinion that the verdict might have been unduly influenced by the judge's remarks on public benefit, counsel advised the keelmen to go to the expense of a new trial. Thus at the Newcastle Assizes in March 1828 their lawyers again applied for a bill of indictment against Messrs Russell. The judge, once again Mr Justice Bayley, observed that the Grand Jury were doubtless aware that the question had previously been before the courts and that the judges had disagreed, though only on minor points (a statement from which eminent lawyers in the future would dissent). However, when so large a body of men as the keelmen felt aggrieved, it was important that they should have their case fully considered in the highest court of the kingdom. If the jury considered that the staithe in question constituted an obstruction or hindrance to the navigation, or if they thought it was improperly positioned, they ought

11 Charles Abbott, first Baron Tenterden (1762–1832), Lord Chief Justice from 1818. *DNB*.

to find a true bill.[12] This they did, and in August 1828 the case was brought to trial at Carlisle Assizes (having been removed by writ from Newcastle) before Baron Hullock[13] and a special jury. Brougham and Scarlett again led on opposite sides.

Brougham employed most of the arguments he had used in the previous trial but with some additional points.[14] If docks were constructed, staithes could be erected in them without obstructing navigation of the river, but, rather than going to that expense, the coal owners preferred to injure the public. They had built these structures in the very place where they caused the greatest impediment to navigation. Although ships could be towed by steam boats past the staithes, the staithe owners did not pay the cost. He called numerous witnesses, several of whom had given evidence in the former trial, to testify to the obstruction and accidents that had occurred. However, on cross examination, some of them were forced to admit that loading by keels also caused obstruction and took longer than at the staithes.

Scarlett repeated most of his previous arguments, and, ignoring the long-standing complaints of the keelmen against the spouts, asserted that the staithes had received 'universal acquiescence' as benefiting the Port of Newcastle, and that no public or private attempt had been made against them prior to 1821 when the use of steam boats began seriously to threaten the keelmen's employment. He stressed that the question concerned not only a navigable river but a port where structures for the purpose of loading and unloading ships inevitably caused obstructions that were in no way nuisances. Keels had to be loaded at staithes which, though they did not extend as far into the river as those under attack, still caused obstruction. Some of the few accidents described by witnesses had been caused by buoys that had been removed by the conservators of the river six years previously, and others could have been caused by lack of skill or the vagaries of wind and tide rather than by the staithes which in fact reduced the possibility of accidents as ships were loaded there quickly, thus preventing their detention in the river. Despite the alleged obstruction, twenty vessels now came up the river compared with one formerly. The prosecution was brought not to preserve the navigation but to increase demand for a particular sort of craft and to place the Port of Newcastle under control of the keelmen. The question was whether the staithes provided a better mode of loading ships than keels, and this he believed was proved by a great increase in trade, and by testimony in their favour by the Corporation of Newcastle, the great body of ship owners, and the legislature. He spoke for almost two and three-quarter hours and called for a verdict on every principle of law, justice and reason. As in the first trial he summoned no witnesses, thus depriving Brougham of an opportunity to reply.

---

[12] *Tyne Mercury*, 11 March 1828.
[13] Sir John Hullock (1767–1829), Baron of the Exchequer 1823–9. *DNB*.
[14] The proceedings are reported in the *Tyne Mercury*, 19 August 1828, and *Durham Chronicle*, 23 August 1828.

Baron Hullock's summing up differed widely from that of Mr Justice Bayley, particularly on benefit to the public that might arise from the staithes. He did not concur in Scarlett's statement of the law that if considerable advantage resulted from their use they could not be removed under the indictment. His own opinion was that if they constituted a substantial impediment to the navigation they were nuisances in point of law, notwithstanding the collateral effects they might produce. The owners of the staithes did not erect them for the public good, or to serve the Port of Newcastle, but for their private advantage. The question was not, as had been represented, whether removal of these staithes would occasion another nuisance. He dismissed several other points on which Scarlett had placed great emphasis. He made it clear that the motives behind the prosecution were of no concern to the jury, and, although the existence of the staithes had been recognized in Acts of Parliament, these statutes had been passed to serve the ship owner, not the proprietor of the structures; nor did he consider the acquiescence of the Corporation of Newcastle, or failure of the river jury to present them as nuisances, to be of much significance. On the other hand, he attached little importance to the accidents that had occurred, and in effect endorsed Scarlett's argument about the importance of the evidence that had not been brought. If the staithes were indeed a nuisance, he would have expected the plaintiffs to have been the ship owners of Newcastle, who must have been the greatest sufferers, yet only three or four of that great body had been called to give evidence. Moreover, it appeared that until recently no complaint had been made against the staithes, and he asked the jury whether this acquiescence did not infer that they were not regarded as a serious obstruction. In the absence of the sort of evidence that he thought would have been most proper, it was for the jury to determine whether the staithes were so prejudicial to the navigation as to constitute a nuisance. If this was their opinion they must find for the crown, even though this might cause the defendants inconvenience and financial loss.

After four hours, the jury returned a written verdict: 'We find that part of the navigable channel of the river Tyne opposite to Wallsend has been straitened, narrowed, lessened and obstructed, as described in the indictment, but that the trade of the town and port of Newcastle has notwithstanding increased'. Counsel on both sides agreed that the words 'by the gears erected by the defendants' should be added after 'obstructed', but there was then 'considerable squabbling' among them over the verdict. Counsel for the prosecution argued that unless it was 'in form' it was no verdict at all, while counsel for the defendants objected to a general verdict, but eventually agreed to take it in the jury's words. The Judge did not think himself competent to alter the written verdict and said to the jury: 'You mean this as a special verdict and leave it to the court above to decide whether it is a finding guilty or an acquittal under the indictment'. To this they assented, whereupon he accepted the verdict as it was. It was generally believed that the verdict was in the keelmen's favour, but whether they had at last gained their objective depended on the decision of the Court of King's Bench.

On 24 May 1830 the case was argued by counsel before Lord Chief Justice Tenterden.[15] The matter had by this time become further complicated by the death of Baron Hullock. Brougham and his colleague, Mr Cresswell,[16] contended that the verdict could be settled from Hullock's notes, while Scarlett, now Attorney General, argued that it would be 'wild and visionary' to settle the verdict from this very imperfect source. He declared that the judge had summed up for the defendant, but the jury on the specific facts had thought fit to find no verdict, one way or the other. He did not know how the matter could be settled unless counsel for the crown would agree to the introduction of certain material facts which should be considered as having been found by the jury for the defendant but which were not included in the judge's notes. To this Brougham strongly objected while Scarlett continued to insist on it. Lord Tenterden agreed that it would be 'utterly impossible' to settle the matter from the notes and favoured a new trial. Brougham, concerned at the 'enormous' expense already incurred, said that rather than more delay and expense he would be satisfied if the facts in dispute were to be ascertained by a gentleman of the bar, but Scarlett was not prepared to accept this without authority from his client. He asserted that the judge had made some erroneous statements and declared that he would move for a new trial if it were held that the prosecution was entitled to a verdict on those grounds. Finally it was agreed that an attempt should be made to settle out of court and, on Brougham's suggestion, the papers were given to Mr Justice Bayley who was already well acquainted with the case.

On 8 June counsel met at his chambers when, after hearing arguments on both sides, he declared that Mr Cresswell for the crown had gone 'a great deal too far', and Mr Ingham for the defence 'still further'. They must take the verdict as written and each might use what emphasis he liked in reading it. He then read aloud part of the shorthand writer's notes of remarks by the foreman of the jury, that there was no count in the indictment in which the trade and navigation were separated. It seemed that the intention the jury meant to express was simply that the navigation was injured by the gears but that the trade had improved. He thought that the jury in the first trial might have expressed their verdict in similar terms. Thus he settled the matter by declaring the verdict to be consonant with that returned on the first trial.[17]

After more than eight years of battle in the courts the keelmen had failed to gain the victory they considered so vital for their future prospects of employment, though there can be no doubt that had they succeeded, the coal owners and their lawyers would have spared no effort or expense to overturn the verdict.

---

[15] *Proceedings at Law in the Case of the King versus Russell and others relative to the Coal Staiths erected at Wallsend on the River Tyne* (Newcastle, 1830). Published by John Marshall, the radical printer of the keelmen's Addresses in 1822. Copy in the Central Library, Newcastle, in Bell, 'Collections relative to the Tyne, its Trade and Conservancy', III, 64–67.

[16] Sir Cresswell Cresswell (1794–1863), a leader of the northern circuit. Later King's Counsel and Judge. *DNB*.

[17] *Proceedings at Law.*

One approach they might have adopted is indicated by John Buddle, secretary to the coal trade and manager of Wallsend Colliery. In evidence before a parliamentary select committee, he declared that the trial was not about the right to load coal by spout, 'but merely as to whether the extension of a spout was a nuisance or not; whether it extended too far into the river or not; it was for an abatement, not for an abolition of the nuisance'.[18] That was certainly not the keelmen's aim, and the legal wrangling would undoubtedly have continued. Moreover, it would probably have been contended that the verdict applied only to the structures against which the prosecution had been directed, not to the other staithes and spouts on the river, and the keelmen would then have been faced with the prospect of many more lawsuits, the cost of which would have been far beyond their means.

Aside from such speculation, the best that could be said on the keelmen's behalf was that the settlement prevented the necessity of a new trial, thus saving 'a very considerable expense to their body, who have already suffered so severely by the Law's delay'.[19] They had suffered, too, in other ways. As the Lord Chief Justice suggested, the verdict in the first trial may have been unduly influenced by comments of the judge which ought not to have affected it, and indeed the law as then stated was not upheld in future cases of a similar nature.[20] In both trials, especially the second, Scarlett made incorrect statements about the strike of 1822 and the allegedly previous 'universal acquiescence' in the existence of the staithes, which, in the latter case, the judge accepted as particularly important when summing up. The choice of Mr Justice Bayley to settle the verdict, although suggested by Brougham, was perhaps not in the keelmen's best interests, for although he knew more than any other judge about the matter, he might have found it difficult, in view of his own opinions, to be entirely impartial.

The settlement did not constitute a definitive judicial decision. Several years later, Mr Cresswell observed that on account of the judge's death 'difficulties had arisen in settling the verdict, and the case had not proceeded', one reason being 'that the question had been rendered less important by the general use of steam boats for towing'.[21] This was true so far as ship owners were concerned, but the increasing use of steam-powered boats to tow large colliers to and from the staithes was one of a number of developments that contributed to the decline of the keelmen, and to this subject we must now turn.

---

[18]   *Minutes of Evidence before the Select Committee on the State of the Coal Trade* (1830), p.308.
[19]   *Proceedings at Law.*
[20]   In 1836 Lord Chief Justice Denman declared that the authority of 'Rex v. Russell' was 'much doubted', 'Rex v. Ward', *English Reports*, 111, p.838. It was held overruled in 'Jolliffe v. Wallasey Local Board', 1873, and disapproved in 'Attorney-General v. Terry', 1873–4, *English Reports*, 108, p.560.
[21]   *English Reports*, 111, p.834n.

15

The Decline of the Keelmen

During the eight years of the legal proceedings following 'the long stop' the use of spouts and drops continued to erode the employment of the below-bridge keelmen. At Wallsend staithes, for example, where 60 keelmen had once been employed, the number had fallen to 24 by 1828, and scarcely any keels were being used there by 1842.[1] The increasing use of steam-powered tugs to tow large ships to and from the below-bridge staithes made the menace of redundancy ever greater for the keelmen. Between 1814 and 1822 fifteen such tugs had been introduced on the Tyne and numerous others were produced from each prototype.[2] As Mr Cresswell observed in 1836, towing by steam power had by that time become general,[3] and by 1863 more than 250 tugs were employed on the river.[4] Statistics of coal shipped from Heaton Staithe between 1837 and 1849 show the small proportion transported by keels and the particularly sharp decrease in their use after 1843.[5]

	By Spout	By Keels
1837	24,158 chaldrons	2,324 chaldrons
1838	24,963	2,792
1839	23,816	3,796
1840	22,944	2,280
1841	23,916	2,024
1842	21,502	2,248
1843	20,692	2,120
1844	15,984	1,968
1845	24,088	1,552

[1] Evidence of William Hume, keelman, at Carlisle Assizes, *Tyne Mercury*, 19 August 1828. The keelmen's contribution per tide worked from that staithe during the year fell from £32 in 1828 to £1 10s 8d in 1842, the most rapid reduction being between 1828 and 1834. North of England Institute of Mining Engineers, WAT/1/20.

[2] *The Industrial Resources of the Tyne, Wear, and Tees, including the Reports on the local Manufactures, read before the British Association, in 1863* (London and Newcastle, 1864), p.268.

[3] *English Reports*, 111, p.834n.

[4] *Industrial Resources of the Tyne ...*, p.256.

[5] Evidence of William Jameson, staithman at Heaton Staithe, at the Admiralty Inquiry on the Tyne Navigation Bill, *Newcastle Guardian*, 23 February 1850, cutting in Bell, 'Collections relative to the Tyne its Trade and Conservancy', VI.

(cont.)	By Spout	By Keels
1846	20,182	1,656
1847	17,936	608
1848	15,488	264
1849	16,288	276

Eight keels were once employed at that staithe but by 1850 only one remained and that was little used. A similar pattern can be seen at the neighbouring Gosforth and Coxlodge Staithe:[6]

	By Spout	By Keels
1841	40,044 chaldrons	3,987 chaldrons
1842	34,404	4,408
1843	35,473	1,950
1848	35,006	946
1849	31,004	648

The staithman declared that an increasing number of large ships were coming to his staithe, and vessels that formerly took in only part of their load there were now filled to their capacity. The largest vessels which could not be towed to the staithes had still to be loaded from keels, but obviously fewer keelmen were needed for these purposes, and the number of occasions on which their services were required continued to decrease.

Developments on the River Wear were likewise threatening the employment of the keelmen and their fellow labourers whose numbers had progressively increased each year during the last decade of the eighteenth century. In 1790 there were 412 keels each navigated by a man and a boy and by 1799 the number had grown to 520. Ten years later there were said to be 570 coal keels, 13 ballast keels, 13 'crimp keels' supplying coal to the townspeople and 8 keels engaged in carrying stone or timber. It was estimated that 750 keelmen and 507 casters, trimmers and associated labourers were then employed on the river.[7] The first spout-staithes were erected in 1812, much later than on the Tyne. The coal was conveyed by waggonway over a timber bridge spanning a deep ravine known as Galley's Gill, at the side of which was a large depot

---

[6] Evidence of John Banks, staithman at Gosforth and Coxlodge Staithes, *ibid.*
[7] *Report on the State of the Coal Trade* (1800), Appendix 53, p.631; Taylor Potts, *Sunderland: A History of the Town and Port, Trade and Commerce* (Sunderland, 1892), p.132; Robert Surtees, *History and Antiquities of the County Palatine of Durham,* (London, 1816), I, p.266. Another estimate puts the number of keelmen at 1,100 or 1,200, but this may take account of the boys not included in the 750 men mentioned in the text above, Martin Douglas, *The Life and Adventures of Martin Douglas, Sunderland Keelman and Celebrated Life Saver* (Stockton on Tees, 1848), p.43. There is a good account of the keelmen of the Wear in Stuart Miller, 'The Progressive Improvement of Sunderland Harbour and the River Wear 1717–1859', University of Newcastle, MA thesis (1978), C81, Appendix A, pp.344–9.

and machinery for lowering the waggons down an inclined plane to the spouts. In 1815, on hearing that this method of loading was likely to be more widely adopted, a mob of about 1,200 keelmen and others demolished the bridge and set fire to the depot, causing damage estimated at £6,000. A party of dragoons from Newcastle restored order on land but the keelmen proceeded to blockade the river. An association of the inhabitants of Sunderland circulated an address to the keelmen which, according to a newspaper report, 'contributed much to open the eyes of the deluded multitude', and, combined with the efforts of the fitters and magistrates, persuaded the keelmen to return to work.[8] The following year, in petitions to Lady Frances Vane Tempest and J.G. Lambton, the keelmen pointed out the great distress to which they and their families would be reduced if the principal coal owners carried out their reported intention of transporting their coal overland to Sunderland and loading the ships by spouts.[9] John Buddle, Lord Londonderry's agent, certainly proposed to do this, thereby saving the wages of the keelmen, 'by far the best paid men in the coal trade'; but, he told Londonderry, it would be 'the height of imprudence to attempt it until we are able to fight them with the sure means of victory in our power – the spouts at Sunderland'. The plan was shelved, but in 1831 the opening of Seaham Harbour, linked by railways to the collieries, diverted much of Londonderry's coal from the Wear. Later, despite 'special means of access' to the river and harbour, the Marchioness of Londonderry and the Earl of Durham took advantage of 'cheap railway transit' to ship much of their coal from the Tyne.[10] The spouts attacked in 1815 soon became fully operational again, and by 1818, out of a total of 405,504 chaldrons shipped from the Wear, 41,200 were loaded from them. In 1820 the corresponding figures were 43,264 out of 421,061½ chaldrons. Drops were then substituted for the spouts, and by the early 1840s eleven drops on the site were capable of shipping 150 keel-loads per day.[11] Meanwhile, in 1818, Lambton's agent introduced tubs, each containing a chaldron of coal, which could be hoisted from the keels by crane and

[8] T.H. Hair, *Sketches of the Coal Mines in Northumberland and Durham with Descriptive Sketches and a Preliminary Essay on Coal and the Coal Trade by M. Ross* (London, 1844), p.41; Sykes, *Local Records of Remarkable Events*, II, p.89; Potts, *Sunderland*, pp.132–9; *Durham County Advertiser*, 25 March and 1 April 1815; Douglas, *Life and Adventures,* pp.31–8. Douglas, who at the time was working as a running fitter, warned his skippers that Mr Nesham was going to convey his coals overland and urged them to demonstrate against this by blocking navigation of the river. When a skipper objected that one railway would never do them any harm, Douglas told them that 'it would be the means of bringing more Railways down – when your children's children will feel the effects of it for ages to come – then it will be too late for you to pull the Railways up'. That was not what Douglas intended – he strongly disapproved of the riot that started at the door of his house – but he may have inadvertently provoked it.

[9] Press cutting, 3 May 1816, in North of England Institute of Mining Engineers, Bell Collection XI, p.75.

[10] Buddle to Londonderry, 5 January 1823, quoted in J.A. Jaffe, 'Competition and Size of Firms in the North-East Coal Trade, 1800–1850', *Northern History*, XXV (1989), pp.235–55, citation p.239; Christine E. Hiskey, 'John Buddle, 1773–1843, Agent and Entrepreneur in the North-East Coal Trade', University of Durham M.Litt. Thesis (1978), pp.123–4; Potts, *Sunderland*, p.154; T.Y. Hall, 'The Rivers, Ports and Harbours of the Great Northern Coal-field', *Transactions of the North of England Institute of Mining Engineers*, 10 (1861), p.52.

[11] Potts, *Sunderland*, pp.146–7; Hair, *Sketches of the Coal Mines*, p.42.

emptied into the colliers by release of a hasp. Londonderry began to adopt this method in or about 1822 and he and Lambton became its largest users during the next twelve to fourteen years, thus preserving the need for keelmen but dispensing with casters except for ships that had to finish loading in the roads.[12] The erection of more spouts and drops on the river further reduced the keelmen's employment, as did the North Dock equipped with four drops, which began to ship coal in 1840. The South Dock, opened in 1850 and extended during the next five years, rapidly assumed greater importance, and by 1858 was dealing with more than 42% of total coal exports from the river. By 1862 the use of keels for the export of coal from the Wear had ceased, though some keels were still used for other purposes.[13]

Meanwhile, some keelmen on the Tyne were evidently being forced to accept unfavourable terms. In 1833, several of the Marquess of Bute's men complained of very peculiar hardships, 'not having the same indulgence as their brother keelmen on the Tyne'. For the past four years they had been obliged to pay £225 per annum for their craft, 'more than any of the other keelmen' on the river.[14] The Marquess' agent explained that the coal owners provided fifteen keels, but, in the case of a further six, the men paid 'some certain rent per tide to the persons who find the keel, which may probably amount to the above sum stated of £225 p.a.'[15] The petitioners implied that other keelmen paid rent for their craft, though at a lower rate. It is not known how widespread this system had become, but the strike of 1822, which had been fuelled by fears of such a practice, had clearly failed to eradicate it.

Payment in drink for certain tasks also persisted, despite repeated attempts against it. In a petition of 1849, the inhabitants of Stella Parish alleged that keelmen employed by the Stella Coal Company were being deprived of £250 per annum through payments in liquor and tobacco, while habits of intoxication and improvidence, often resulting from this system, impoverished their families and drove them ultimately to dependence on the poor rate. The petitioners prayed that the provisions of the 1831 Truck Act should be extended to include this class of workers.[16] The *Newcastle Journal* attacked 'such gross oppression and injustice ... a striking instance of the evil of the truck system – that ever reprobated device of the sordid and avaricious task master',[17] but a correspondent in the *Gateshead Observer* denied that these customary payments in liquor, which were still made at some other staithes, were oppressive or the cause of the alleged evils.[18] However, such payments in kind, which in

---

[12]   Jaffe, 'Competition and Size of Firms', p.238; Hiskey, 'John Buddle', pp.124–5; Potts, *Sunderland*, p.153; Miller, 'Progressive Improvement of Sunderland Harbour', appendix A.

[13]   Taylor Potts, pp.140, 154–5, 295–6; Miller, 'Progressive Improvement of Sunderland Harbour', p.314.

[14]   Petition to the Marquess of Bute, 10 April 1833, reproduced by permission of Durham County Record Office, D/CG6/1260.

[15]   Note by Mr Grey, *ibid.*

[16]   Letter, dated 24 April, in *Gateshead Observer*, 28 April 1849.

[17]   *Newcastle Journal*, 7 April 1849.

[18]   *Gateshead Observer*, 28 April 1849.

the past had often provoked complaints by the keelmen themselves, were especially likely to occasion hardship at a time when the keelmen's employment was being eroded.

As prospects of employment in the coal trade decreased, many keelmen sought alternative work, some on other river craft such as wherries or even on the hated steam boats, while others took to keels which transported materials and goods to and from the various manufactories situated alongside the river. In 1850 it was estimated that about 150 craft of various sorts, mainly keels and wherries, were engaged in such work above Newcastle bridge.[19] Some men were said to earn in this manner as much as they used to do in the coal trade. Certainly, the terms of a bond of 1857 under which keelmen were employed to carry bricks, sand, and other materials compare well with those obtaining in the transport of coal.[20]

There are no precise figures to show the number of keelmen at any given time and to monitor their decline we have to rely on scraps of information culled from various sources and statements made by persons in a position to be well informed. It was estimated that there were about 900 keelmen in 1822, and 735 appear to have been in work in 1827,[21] which shows some, but not a drastic, decline. A good indication of the extent to which the keelmen were employed is provided by the accounts of the keelmen's charity which state the amounts deducted from their wages for the fund each tide they worked. In 1826 £1,640 was raised in this manner, but the total fell to £1,037 in 1829 and to £1,020 in 1832.[22] The quantity of coal shipped by all methods in these years was fairly constant, and it appears therefore that there was some reduction in the keelmen's employment betweeen 1826 and 1829, though scarcely any between 1829 and 1832. Since even a reduced number of keelmen raised more than £1,000 in the course of their work in the latter year, it is clear that their importance to the coal trade continued during the decade following their great strike, and their contributions to the charity during the rest of 1830s which, with one exception, varied roughly between £800 and £1,000, show that their role remained significant. This was mainly because the above-bridge collieries, which in 1824 were said to provide about one-third of the coal shipped from the Tyne,[23] still used keels, but during the next four decades the keel was largely supplanted by alternative means of transport.

The rapid development of railways after 1825, most of them initially constructed for the carriage of coal in waggons drawn by locomotives, stationary

19 'Mr Cowen on the Tyne above bridge', *Gateshead Observer*, 9 March 1850.
20 Mr Cowen's terms with his keelmen, 14 January 1857, reproduced by permission of Durham County Record Office, NCB I/Sc/560.
21 Minutes, 4 October 1822, TWA 394/46; calculation from keelmen's muster rolls, 1827, TWA 394/50.
22 Mackenzie, *Descriptive and Historical Account of Newcastle*, II, p.552; accounts of the charity, 1827–42, North of England Institute of Mining Engineers D/70 and WAT/1/20. The total contributions per tide given here are calculated by adding the sums returned from the fitters' offices to the sums collected for bye-tides which are stated separately.
23 Rowe, 'The Decline of the Tyneside Keelmen in the Nineteenth Century', citation p.125.

engines, horses, or a combination of all three, was a severe blow to the keel-men. In 1830 John Buddle declared that 'from the continual diminution of employment by the increase of spouts, and loading by railways direct from the mines, the employment of the watermen [i.e. the keelmen] is constantly diminishing'.[24] Six years later he stated that the number of keelmen was much reduced and their occupation 'almost gone', as keels were to a great extent being superseded by spouts and railroads.[25] He was probably speaking of the situation below-bridge, especially of Wallsend Colliery where he was man-ager, and where 'almost gone' was an accurate description, but new methods of transport and loading were certainly accelerating the keelmen's decline else-where. The accounts of the keelmen's charity reflect a sharp reduction in the use of keels from 1840 onwards. In that year contributions by tides worked dropped from the previous year's total of £855 to £620 and fell to £512 in 1841. Although there were some slight rises subsequently (£540 in 1842 and £571 in 1845), only £360 was contributed in 1849 and £281 in 1852,[26] a year in which stewards of the keelmen's hospital, which received nothing from this fund, remarked on the 'decay in the keelmen's trade'.[27] In a book published that year, Matthias Dunn, a prominent figure in the industry, stated that the number of keels had become 'quite inconsiderable, since so large a proportion of the coal is delivered into the vessels by public railways'.[28] Two years later, a House of Commons committee was informed that for the same reason the keel-men were 'very considerably decreased, and are still decreasing'.[29] (All this contradicts a view, based on misinterpretation of an account wrongly attributed to the keelmen's charity, that the quantity of coal transported by keels and the weekly average number of journeys made by them in the late 1840s was potentially 'far above' that achieved twenty years earlier.)[30]

---

[24] *Minutes of Evidence before the Select Committee on the State of the Coal Trade* (1830), p.307.

[25] *Report from the Select Committee on the State of the Coal Trade together with the Minutes of Evidence* (1836), p.115.

[26] Accounts of the charity, 1827–42, North of England Institute of Mining Engineers, WAT/1/20; for 1845 and 1849, D/70. The account for 1852 is printed in the *Gateshead Observer*, 18 March 1854.

[27] Petition, Stewards of the hospital to the Mayor and Aldermen, 1 September 1852, TWA 394/49.

[28] Matthias Dunn, *A Treatise on the Winning and Working of Collieries* (Newcastle and London, 1852), p.130.

[29] *Gateshead Observer*, 1 April 1854, reporting proceedings of the committee on bill to amend the Acts relating to the skippers and keelmen employed on the Tyne.

[30] Rowe, 'Decline of the Keelmen', p.129. In arguing for the continued importance of the keelmen 'well into the nineteenth century', Rowe, who evidently did not see these accounts, overstates his case on the basis of another account which he mistook for one relating to the keelmen's fund. 'In 1848, according to the official account of the treasurer of money received as the keelmen's contribution to their charitable fund from their wages, 156,462 keels of coals were loaded in the Tyne. For 300 keels this would have provided an average of ten journeys a week, far above what was being achieved in the "twenties"'. The 1848 account did not concern the keelmen's charity but was produced under an Act to Regulate the Loading of Ships with Coals in the Port of Newcastle upon Tyne (8 & 9 Victoria c. 73, 1845), which imposed the charge of a penny 'for every keel of coals put on board every ship or vessel loading coals upon the River Tyne', the monies raised being for payment of the expenses of obtaining the Act, the maintenance of a night office, and other associated purposes. The term 'keel' was commonly used to describe a load of eight Newcastle chaldrons, and the '156,462 keels' here represents the quantity of coal loaded onto vessels by spouts and drops as well as by keels and is therefore not evidence for 'the continuance of the keelmen as a sizeable body', or the use of keels 'far above' that of the 1820s. In 1863

However, several large collieries continued to use keels, despite the proliferation of railways across the coalfield,[31] and, up to the 1860s, the keel continued to be 'an important auxiliary of the Tyne coal trade'.[32] In some cases the comparative costs favoured transport by water. In 1840, Buddle advised the owners of Walbottle Colliery against construction of a railway to enable direct loading at the staithes and quoted the case of West Townley Colliery, where carriage by rail had proved to be uneconomic.[33] The owners of the collieries in west and central Durham, who used the Pontop and South Shields Railway to transport their coal to the Tyne, had to pay heavy carriage rates and at times suffered from delays arising from the inclined plane system and single line traffic for part of the way.[34] In 1854 it was estimated that keels were employed for about one-seventh of the coal exported from the Tyne,[35] which, although a vast reduction in the proportion once so carried, still represents a large amount, especially as output from the collieries was ever increasing. The agent to the Marquess of Bute stated in 1850 that all his employer's coal and coke, 70–80,000 tons per annum, was conveyed in keels from Derwenthaugh Staithe,[36] and, ten years later, keels were still carrying all or part of the coal from collieries at Walbottle, Benwell, Elswick, Garesfield, Chopwell, Wylam and from those owned by the Stella Coal Company.[37] Walbottle Colliery, which despatched all its coal by keels, employed 50 keelmen at this time,[38] but the Stella Company, which transported part of its coal by railway, had gradually reduced its use of keels during the previous decade. In 1849 it had 14 keels and 42 keelmen; in 1852, only 13 keels with 39 men and 6 boys; and in 1857, 10 keels and 30 men. Further reductions were evidently being contemplated at that time as it was stipulated in the bond that the Company might discharge four or more of the keels at the expiration of the first six months of the year.[39] Alternative means of transport was certainly on the Company's agenda. 'It has recently occurred to me', Robert Simpson wrote, 26 January 1857, 'that if a small screw vessel to carry 200 tons of coal could be constructed so as to be able to go up the Tyne to our Stella staith, and after being loaden proceed direct to London, it might be of great service to us'. Messrs Mitchell & Co. replied that such a vessel could

---

measure by the keel-load was abolished by the leading firms in Newcastle as a source of trouble and inconvenience. Robert Galloway, *Annals of Coal Mining and the Coal Trade* (reprinted, Newton Abbot, 1971), I, p.461.

[31] Rowe, 'Decline of the Keelmen', p.130.

[32] Fordyce, *A History of Coal, Coke, Coal Fields ... and Iron, its Oars and Processes of Manufacture*, p.60; Johnson, *The Making of the Tyne*, p.8.

[33] Rowe, 'Decline of the Keelmen', pp.128–9.

[34] Johnson, *The Making of the Tyne*, p.199.

[35] *Gateshead Observer*, 1 April 1854.

[36] Report on Admiralty Inquiry into the Tyne Navigation Bill, *Newcastle Courant*, 1 March 1850.

[37] Fordyce, *A History of Coal, Coke, Coal Fields ... and Iron, its Oars and Processes of Manufacture*, pp.63–100.

[38] *Ibid.*, pp.88–9.

[39] Copy bonds 1852 and 1857, reproduced by permission of Durham County Record Office, NCB I/Sc/548, 550.

be supplied at a cost of £4,800.[40] It is not known whether the Company pursued the matter, but for a considerable time it had practised cost-cutting at the keelmen's expense. In 1842 it reduced the keelmen's pay for a journey between certain staithes by two shillings per tide and halved the binding money of £9. By 1857 it had further reduced the binding money to £3.[41]

Developments following the Tyne Improvement Act of 1852 posed further threats to the keelmen. The commodious Northumberland Dock opened in 1857, the first project undertaken by the newly established Tyne Commissioners, facilitated direct loading of the colliers on the North side of the river. Two years later, the Tyne Dock, sponsored by the North Eastern Railway Company, was opened on the South side, and though smaller than Northumberland Dock, 'surpassed it in its equipment and facilities for the rapid loading of coal'. With their 'exceptional coal-shipping facilities' the two docks provided despatch that was 'the marvel of the day'. The equivalent of a keel-load of coal could be discharged into a steamer in a couple of minutes, and a thousand tons in less than two and a half hours.[42] Obviously this was extremely detrimental to the keelmen, but R.W. Johnson in his otherwise valuable work *The Making of the Tyne* (1895) gives a misleading impression of the impact of this development when he states that up to the opening of these docks 'the great bulk of the coal exported from the Tyne found its way to the ship in keels'.[43] As we have seen, the use of keels had been greatly reduced before the docks were created.

Ironically, the numerous sandbanks, shoals and narrows of the river which prevented large ships proceeding to the staithes had to some extent safeguarded the keelmen's employment, but once these obstacles were removed the keelmen's occupation was virtually doomed. J.F. Ure, appointed engineer to the Tyne Improvement Commissioners in 1858, proposed

> to deepen, widen and straighten the river from its mouth to Ryton, a distance of some 20 miles, thus making a channel easily navigable for the largest vessels, between the sea and Shields harbour, the docks there, and Newcastle; and for such a class of vessels in the upper part of the river as can be passed under the High Level Bridge at Newcastle, a sufficient depth of water to be carried up to the river walls for the purpose of traders having establishments on the banks.[44]

In 1861 parliament approved his plans, and another engineer, T.Y. Hall, described the anticipated results when the project was fully implemented:

> Ships and steamers of 2,000 or 3,000 tons will be able to come into these docks, whilst ships of 600 tons and steam vessels of 1,200 tons will be able

40 Robert Simpson to Messrs Mitchell & Co., 26 January 1857; Mitchell & Co. to Simpson, 3 February, reproduced by permission of Durham County Record Office, NCB/I/Sc/631 (73–74).
41 Notebook containing 'keelmen's tides' and agreements, 1841–42, reproduced by permission of Durham County Record Office, NCB/ I/RS/4; copy bonds 1852 and 1857, NCB/I/SC/548, 550.
42 Johnson, *The Making of the Tyne*, pp.80, 82, 298; J. Guthrie, *The River Tyne, its History and Resources*, (Newcastle, 1880), p.114.
43 Johnson, *The Making of the Tyne*, pp.17–18.
44 *Industrial Resources of the Tyne, Wear, and Tees*, p.293.

4 Bill Reach. This drawing by J.W. Carmichael, 1800–68 (see *DNB*), shows part of the Tyne before it was deepened, widened and straightened in accordance with J.F. Ure's plan. The cliff known as Bill Point had to be removed. Note the keel in mid-stream.

to ascend with ease and economy 4 or 5 miles above the High Level Bridge into the very centre of the western portion of the district ... Coal owners will no longer have to carry their coals by railway or in keels, for long distances, to the ships moored in the Tyne, and so the prosperity of the Town and trade of Newcastle, as well as that of the whole of the Tyne, will be immensily increased.[45]

Clearly the keelmen would have no share in this expected prosperity. By 1863 Ure reported that part of his plan had been carried out and estimated that in about four years the improvements would have been completed up to Newcastle and in a further four up to Ryton.[46] This proved to be too optimistic, for millions of tons of sand, silt and rock had to be dredged from the river bed and obstacles, especially the cliff known as Bill Point, which projected into the river, had to be removed; but, though the work took longer than expected, the effect on the keelmen was inevitable. In 1868, J. Nanson, writing from the Townley, Stella and Whitefield Coal and Coke Office, noted 'the rapid manner in which the shipment of coals by keels is falling off'.[47] By 1876 only 63 keelmen were still

[45] Hall, 'The Rivers, Ports and Harbours of the Great Northern Coal Field', pp.41–82.
[46] *Industrial Resources of the Tyne Wear and Tees*, as in n.2, p.295.
[47] Nanson to R. Simpson, 9 April 1868, reroduced by permission of Durham County Record Office, NCB/I/Sc/631 (74).

contributing to the charity by the tide, while 89 others, evidently former keel-men, retained membership by paying sixpence per week.[48]

The old Tyne bridge at Newcastle that had prevented ships passing under its low arches was demolished and replaced by the swing bridge in 1876. This and the extension of improvements to the higher reaches of the river eventually sealed the fate of the remaining keelmen. An observer noted in 1889 that when keels were needed 'steamboats now do the work; keels are towed to and from the ships'. Keelmen still had to cast the coal, but, he added, 'it seems to me that the time is not far distant when keelmen will be numbered with the things of the past'.[49] They no longer formed a distinct community in Newcastle. One side of Sandgate had been demolished and the other filled with 'poor Irish and their families'.[50] Few 'genuine old caulker-built eight chaldron keels' now remained, another writer lamented. He did not regard the 'strings of goods laden and coal carrying craft towed up and down the river' as true Tyne keels. Soon, he wrote, 'the advisability may have to be considered of arranging space in our largest museum of antiquities for the reception of an undoubted speci-men of the old Tyne keel'.[51] Unfortunately such action was not taken and not a single specimen of these craft has survived.

Steam power both on land and water played a large part in the demise of the keelmen. 'It's them steamers that's brust up the keelmen', declared the last keelman remaining in the hospital in 1897. 'It's a bonny bad job, but it can-not be helped'.[52] Like many workers before and after them, the keelmen were forced to yield to technical innovation, and thus faded away the colourful body of men who gave 'a distinctive character to the river population'[53] and who for long had been 'the very sinews of the coal trade'.[54]

[48] Press cuttings citing report by T.Y. Strachan on the Society of Keelmen, 1876, in W. Brockie, 'The Keelmen of the Tyne', copy in the Central Library, Newcastle.
[49] John McKay, 'Keels and Keelmen', *Newcastle Weekly Chronicle Supplement*, 9 November 1889.
[50] Middlebrook, *Newcastle upon Tyne*, p.262.
[51] J.I. Nicholson, 'Keels and Keelmen', *Newcastle Weekly Chronicle Supplement*, 9 November 1889.
[52] Eric Forster, *The Keelmen* (Newcastle, 1970), p.29.
[53] Johnson, *The Making of the Tyne*, p.18.
[54] *Tyne Mercury*, 31 May 1803.

16

The Magistrates and the Keelmen

The keelmen were undoubtedly the most turbulent section of the workforce on Tyneside and since many of them lived, often in a 'necessitous and rude condition', in Sandgate, just outside the walls of Newcastle, the preservation of public order was a constantly recurring problem for the City's magistrates, the Mayor, Recorder and Aldermen. It seems worthwhile, therefore, to review their efforts to deal with this large body of robust men ever liable 'to rise and become tumultuous upon the least pretence'.

As the Duke of Northumberland once remarked, 'any interruption of the coal trade must be attended with great inconvenience not only to the neighbourhood of Newcastle but to the nation in general', and disturbances that cut off coal supplies to the metropolis were apt to attract the attention of the central government, which was not always welcome to the local authorities.[1] Secretary of State Sir John Coke clearly thought that they had failed to take sufficiently vigorous action to suppress a serious outbreak of disorder among the populace in the Spring of 1633. 'If you had set a better guard on them [those arrested who had been rescued]', he wrote to the Mayor, 25 March, 'and terrified the rest by proclamation and by raising the trained bands, your service had been greater and the tumult sooner settled'.[2] The magistrates' reply reveals their inherent weakness when faced with a popular uprising. They had made the proclamation in sundry places, evidently with little effect, but 'doubted their power' to call out the trained bands of townsmen, besides which, they had found 'not such forwardness as they expected in them to assist the Mayor', and feared 'thereby to add more strength to the rioters'. In an earlier report to the Council they alleged that the burgesses had secretly sided with those creating the tumult. Secretary Coke believed that the real cause of the disorder was not, as had been represented, the construction of a lime kiln on the local drying ground, but the desire of the inhabitants for a change in their government.[3]

When the keelmen struck in March 1659/60 the magistrates were anxious 'lest some misinformation or causless complainte may become before the Counsell of State agt us in some things pertaineing to the Coale Trade',[4] and

[1] SP 16/408 f.96; Duke of Northumberland to M. Ridley, 29 June 1771, Northumberland Museum and Archives, ZRI 25/6; Cuthbert Smith, Mayor, to Duke of Newcastle, 21 April 1746, SP Domestic, Geo. II, 83.

[2] Secretary of State Sir John Coke to the Mayor, 25 March 1633, *Calendar of State Papers, Domestic, Charles I, Addenda 1625–49*, p.453.

[3] Mayor and others to Coke, 26 March 1633, *Calendar of State Papers, Domestic, Charles I, 1631–33*, p.585; Report, 11 March 1633, *ibid.*, p.567.

[4] Robert Shafto and others to unnamed person, 24 March 1659/60, TWA 394/1.

in 1671, although the King professed not to doubt the magistrates' 'prudent care and circumspection' in dealing with the striking keelmen, he put the Earl of Ogle and Lord Widdrington in charge of suppressing the disorder by means of the trained bands of the City and the County of Northumberland.[5] The following year, in view of the 'accidents and attempts' to which Newcastle might be subjected during the war against the Dutch, he made further arrangements for the safety of the Town and security of the coal trade, again by-passing the magistrates.[6]

Although the magistrates might not welcome interference by the central government, they were usually quick to call on it for military aid when the keelmen enforced a strike. Indeed, Secretary at War 2nd Viscount Barrington once rebuked them for what he regarded as too frequent applications for such assistance which had an inherent tendency towards the evils of military goverment.[7] In 1710 the Mayor pointed out that the City's 'raw and undisciplined' militia was no match for the keelmen, and that if an attempt to free navigation of the river was made and repulsed it would be 'of very ill consequence'.[8] Even a regiment of regular troops failed to re-open trade, and the strike was ended not by force but by negotiation in which the military officers took part.[9] As we have seen in Chapter 5, the prolonged interruption of coal supply to London resulted in an inquiry by the Privy Council into combinations in the trade, and the Act of 1711 made cartels such as that of the Newcastle coal owners illegal, though the law was frequently evaded.

In 1719 the magistrates repeated that the keelmen were 'too numerous for our townsmen to suppress',[10] but, when troops were sent, their commanding officer lacked authority to act in the separate jurisdictions of Northumberland and Durham whither many of the principal offenders escaped. The officers evidently had other doubts about their authority to assist the magistrates in executing the laws since the Secretary at War was ordered to write to them 'that they may have no scruple in this respect'. The strike was ended by negotiation involving some hard bargaining, though the threat that some of the arrested keelmen, including two of the ringleaders, would be impressed into the navy was a determining factor. In 1738, when the magistrates again called for troops against the keelmen, they stressed that the commander must have authority to act in the neighbouring counties, otherwise 'the end of their march may be fruitless as happened about 20 years ago'.[11]

During the disturbances of 1740 the magistrates' worst fear was that the keelmen would join the pitmen, thus making 'a most formidible body not to be restrained by any civil authority'.[12] There were inevitably delays before an

5 Secretary of State Arlington to William Earl of Ogle, 4 June 1671, SP 44/31/72.
6 Arlington to Mayor of Newcastle, 2 April 1672, SP 44/31/87.
7 Morgan and Rushton, *Rogues, Thieves and the Rule of Law*, p.202.
8 Nicholas Ridley (Deputy Mayor) to Secretary of State, 23 June 1710, SP 34/12/101.
9 Jonathan Roddam (Mayor) to same, 11 and 21 July, SP 34/12/126 and 144.
10 Magistrates to Secretary Craggs, 16 May 1719, State Papers, Domestic, Regencies, SP 43/57.
11 Magistrates to Secretary of State, 6 May 1738, SP 44/130/343–4.
12 Cuthbert Fenwick to Secretary of State, 20 June 1740, SP 36/51/127–9.

appeal to the government for troops could receive a response, and even when that was favourable a cumbersome administrative process had usually to be completed before forces could be despatched. Thus, before the Mayor's urgent appeal was answered, the keelmen marched into the city. A better disciplined force than the hastily armed band of local gentry might not have been panicked into firing on the crowd which provoked the sacking of the Guildhall. The troops who arrived and restored order were fortuitously on their way from Berwick to Stockton. However, when the Mayor begged for additional troops immediately after the riot, the Lords Justices of the Regency sent orders by express for three more companies of General Howard's regiment to proceed to Newcastle and two further companies were ordered to follow.[13] The magistrates were grateful for this support against 'the threats and outrages of a numerous people in our neighbourhood too ready on any occasion to join in an insurrection', but news that the commanding officer had orders to withdraw the forces from the city during the assizes occasioned 'no small uneasiness' to the inhabitants because of threats by the keelmen and others to release their brethren from gaol. The magistrates therefore requested that some of the troops should be quartered in Gateshead and the rest in parts of Newcastle where they would not impede the assizes, as otherwise the city could not be sufficiently protected.[14] In the event no rescue attempt was made, but as a precaution the magistrates authorized repulsion of force with force, despite any qualms that the recent Porteous case might have aroused.[15]

During the strike of 1750, the magistrates, fearing a 'great disturbance', again called for troops,[16] and the Secretary at War, acting on information from Sir Walter Blackett that there was 'some uneasiness brewing amongst the keelmen', directed six companies of Lord Ancram's regiment to proceed to Newcastle.[17] Three companies arrived from Berwick on 30 March, eleven days after the strike began, and by 30 April a further three companies had joined them by a forced march, perhaps, as the keelmen claimed, on account of a 'false aspersion' against them.[18] Even when sixteen skippers were committed to prison, the keelmen remained quiescent, contrary to expectations that a riot and rescue attempt by the 'rabble part' would provide grounds for the magistrates to employ the military to force the strikers to resume work.[19] The military eventually broke the strike by protecting substitute workers. A direct attack, even at the cost of bloodshed, would almost certainly have failed in its purpose.

In 1794 the magistrates called for military aid after the keelmen destroyed several spouts and forcibly stopped work in some of the pits. A party of the

[13] TWA 394/10.
[14] Draft letters to Duke of Newcastle and Secretary at War, 19 July 1740, TWA 394/10.
[15] 11 July 1740, TWA 394/10. About Porteous see above, Chapter 6.
[16] William Brown to C. Spedding, 30 April 1750, North of England Institute of Mining Engineers, Brown /1.
[17] R.N. Aldworth and R. Leveson Gower to Mr Stone, 4 May 1750, SP 44/318/12–14.
[18] *Newcastle Courant*, 31 March 1750; R. Sorsbie to Duke of Bedford, 30 April, SP 36/112/331; petition of keelmen, TWA 394/19.
[19] Brown to Spedding, 30 April 1750, as in n. 16.

Earl of Darlington's Durham Rangers was brought into Newcastle to aid the North and West York militia, and two troops of the Lancashire Light Dragoons arrived by 'an uncommonly rapid' march from Derby. More than one hundred special constables, gentlemen of the 'first respectability', were enrolled at this 'peculiar crisis'. Some of the most refractory keelmen were arrested and sent under a strong escort of dragoons to Durham gaol.[20] The keelmen remonstrated against the tactics of the horse and foot forces who, without regard to guilt or innocence, terrified women and children. Had the expenditure on the military been used to relieve their distressed families, the keelmen claimed, the commotion, to which many of them were opposed, might have ended sooner.[21]

When the keelmen struck in 1809, the magistrates, instead of appealing to the government, took it upon themselves to call on the military for assistance in executing warrants and protecting substitute workers. They also persuaded Captain Charleton, the officer in charge of impressment, to provide boats and men.[22] It seems extraordinary that Charleton should have deployed his forces against the keelmen without orders from the Lords of Admiralty, who, judging by their reluctance to aid the civil power against the seamen a few years later, might not have given their approval. He may have had misgivings, since in the first instance his support lasted for only two days, and subsequently the Mayor had again to solicit his assistance.[23] The Mayor also begged Sir Edmund Nagle, the commander at Leith, to send a warship, though he promised to inform the Admiralty of the request.[24] All this was done without reference to the Home Office until a demand for a report arrived from that department.[25] The elaborate operations against the keelmen achieved little, and concessions rather than force ended the strike.

Probably mindful of the implied rebuke from the Home Office in 1809, the Mayor immediately informed the Home Secretary when the keelmen enforced a strike in 1819. He emphasized the inadequacy of the forces then in the locality.[26] 'Shields harbour never should be without a ship of war', Nicholas Fairles, a county Durham magistrate, wrote two days later. The presence of such a ship, he thought, might have prevented the strike.[27] A sloop of war was promptly sent to the Tyne and another arrived somewhat later. The generally disturbed state of the region, the growth of reform societies, and the prospect of a huge meeting to protest at the recent 'Peterloo massacre' increased the authorities' alarm and added weight to their pleas for armed assistance. Without a strong

20   *Newcastle Courant*, 19 and 26 July 1794.
21   'Address to the Public', *Newcastle Courant*, 16 August 1794.
22   G. Knowsley to Charleton, 31 October 1809, J. Bell, 'Collections relative to the Tyne', II, fol.90.
23   I. Cookson to Charleton, 3 November 1809, *ibid.*, fols 96–7; Norman McCord, 'The Seamen's Strike of 1815 in North-East England', *The Economic History Review*, new series, 21 (1968), pp.127–43. The Lords of Admiralty at first refused to employ a military force in a case that appeared to belong to the civil power, pp.130–1.
24   Cookson to Nagle, 3 November 1809; Nagle to Cookson, 4 November 1809, TWA 394/37.
25   Cookson to Home Secretary, 11 November 1809, replying to letter from the Home Office, National Archives, HO 42/99/593–5.
26   Joseph Forster to Lord Sidmouth, 28 September 1819, National Archives, HO 42/195.
27   M. Fairless to Sidmouth, 30 September 1819, National Archives, HO 42/195.

naval force it was 'utterly out of our power to protect the port and shipping', the Mayor declared, as continuance of the keelmen's strike raised fears that pitmen and sailors thereby laid idle would also become insubordinate.[28] He begged major-general Sir John Byng, commander of the Northern District, to supply at least four companies of infantry, and, a week later, after riot at North Shields, he wrote to him again, stressing the 'absolute necessity' that the military force should be forthwith increased. Meanwhile he had requested the officer in command at Sunderland to supply as many infantrymen as he could spare.[29] The officer sent 230 men, evidently without his superior's approval, for a few days later Byng called for their return to Sunderland, at which the Mayor protested that a diminution of the force at Newcastle would probably have 'the most fatal results'.[30] He had again reminded the Home Secretary that an adequate force of warships and marines as well as an increased land force should be supplied urgently. He also supported the plea of the County Durham magistrates to the Earl of Darlington, commander of the South Tyne Yeomanry Cavalry, for assistance. Darlington complied with the request, but with evident misgivings lest there should be another Peterloo. He strongly advised the magistrates against ordering the military to act, unless the civil power was 'overcome or incompetent'; compulsion was 'not the way to ameliorate the state of the country'.[31] However, according to John Buddle, who had witnessed many strikes in the area, the keelmen and pitmen generally regarded the local yeomanry as a 'laughing stock', a view that was evidently shared by the seamen who enforced a prolonged stoppage of trade in 1815. 'A painted staff with G.R. upon it is more awful in the hand of a Special Constable than a sabre in the hand of the same individual as a yeomanry man', Buddle declared.[32] As usual, the strike was ended by negotiation, but the magistrates were grateful to the military for guarding the collieries and the spouts, the more so as an attempt to raise a volunteer corps in Newcastle had little success. Only 150 men enrolled instead of the thousand or more that had been expected. As in 1633, the inhabitants proved 'very tardy' in offering their services.[33]

At the beginning of the strike of 1822 the Duke of Northumberland urged the Mayor to 'take every step towards conciliation which may be compatible with magisterial firmness and with the just interests of individuals ... and

---

[28] Archibald Reed to Sidmouth, 6 October 1819, National Archives, HO 42/196, and TWA 394/42.

[29] Reed to Sidmouth, 6 October 1819; Reed to major-general Sir John Byng, 14 October 1819, TWA 394/42.

[30] *Newcastle Chronicle*, 16 October 1819; Reed to Sidmouth, 20 October 1819, National Archives, HO 42/197.

[31] Darlington to Sidmouth, 15 October 1819, National Archives, HO 42/196/413–4; 21 October 1819, HO 42/197/577–8.

[32] Buddle to Lord Londonderry, 11 December 1830, quoted in Robert Colls, *The Pitmen of the Northern Coalfield, Work, Culture and Protest, 1790–1850* (Manchester, 1987), p.241. John Cartwright to Lord Sidmouth, 14 October 1815, quoted in McCord, 'The Seamen's Strike', p.137. The yeomanry cavalry, Cartwright declared, 'are *really the derision* of these old sailors, who have faced death in all its terrors'.

[33] Reed to Sidmouth, 30 October 1819, National Archives, HO 42/197/708–9; Mayor and others to Coke, 26 March 1633, *Calendar of State Papers, Domestic, Charles,I, 1631–33*, p.585.

dispense with military interference till the last extremity',[34] but, despite this advice, the Mayor called on the commander at Sunderland for two companies of infantry. The troops were sent, but the magistrates were shocked when major-general Byng, who had not been consulted, withdrew the force without reference to them. They suspected that he was motivated by pique, but he explained that the paucity of his force necessitated his tight personal control of deployments. When the magistrates complained to the Home Office, it was made clear that they could not assume that the regular armed forces were at their beck and call.[35] Much annoyed, they were obliged to rely on local forces such as the Northumberland and Newcastle Volunteer Cavalry whose period of duty was increased from eight to thirty days. When, on 20 October, the Duke of Northumberland, believing in error that the strike was about to end, authorized disbandment of this force, its commander, lieutenant-colonel Brandling, protested that if it were withdrawn an attack would be immediately made upon the spouts.[36] During the early part of the strike military operations against the keelmen were largely ineffective. The *Tyne Mercury* blamed the magistrates for failing to use the forces under their control to best advantage, and later strongly criticized the conduct of the special constables.[37]

Strike-breaking was not a task for which commanders of the regular armed forces in the area showed any enthusiasm,[38] and, although protection of black-legs and work-related property made important contributions to ending strikes, attempts to round up large numbers of strikers often proved fruitless as they simply disappeared into the neighbouring countryside. When confrontations that could easily have resulted in tragic loss of life did occur, the military, despite great provocation, generally exercised commendable restraint. No evidence has been found to support the keelmen's claim in 1770 that during strikes before that date the military had killed or wounded 'several' of their number, but even if well founded the allegation does not indicate extensive bloodshed.[39] When the armed forces opened fire in 1819 and 1822, neither of the two casualties was a keelman.[40]

In view of the importance of the coal trade to Newcastle, it is not surprising that there were always some magistrates directly involved in it, while most magistrates were members of the Hostmen's Company and so associated with the 'trading brethren' of that fraternity. The close connexion of the magistracy

---

[34] Northumberland to the Mayor, 7 October 1822, TWA 394/46.
[35] Correspondence concerning withdrawal of infantry from Newcastle, 9–17 October 1822, TWA 394/46.
[36] *Tyne Mercury*, 15 October 1822; Northumberland to Brandling, 20 October 1822, printed in *Newcastle Chronicle*, 2 November 1822; Brandling to Northumberland, 31 October 1822, National Archives, HO 40/17/373–4.
[37] *Tyne Mercury*, 5 and 19 November 1822.
[38] Norman McCord, 'The Government of Tyneside 1800–1850', *Transactions of the Royal Historical Society*, 5th series, XX, pp.5–30. McCord found no instance of an army or naval officer serving in the North East in that period showing any eagerness to employ his forces for repressive purposes.
[39] Keelmen's resolutions, 5 January 1770, TWA 394/29.
[40] An innocent bystander who had only joined the throng a few minutes earlier was shot and killed in 1819 during the riot in North Shields, and the stone-thrower wounded in 1822 was a glass-worker.

with the trade was particularly well established in the period around 1770 when nine of the twelve magistrates were either coal owners or fitters. Although at times of strikes they must have found difficulty in distinguishing between their own interests and their legal responsibilities, they had to act as mediators between the strikers and the rest of the employers. The keelmen had no option but to recognize that role, however much they might distrust those who were directly or indirectly their masters.[41] Magistrates who employed keelmen must have been well aware that the men's complaints, especially those concerning over-loaded keels, were justified. They must also have known some of the men, particularly the skippers, personally. These factors may have had a moderating influence in disputes. In attempting to persuade his keelmen to end the strike of 1768, the Mayor, himself a fitter, used the familiar terms 'My lads go to work and will endeavour to have no more than King's measure', though in another context he described the keelmen as 'a set of men by no means to be trusted'.[42]

The magistrates' initial efforts to settle disputes seldom had success. During the strike of 1710 they desired advice and assistance from the Judges of Assize, and military officers participated in the negotiations that finally ended the stoppage.[43] In 1719 the keelmen's persistence in a demand for a large increase in wages left the magistrates 'at a loss what to do'.[44] A century later, the Mayor, Archibald Reed, tried to end the 1819 strike by addressing a full meeting of the keelmen, and Thomas Clennell, chairman of the Northumberland quarter sessions, also spoke to a large gathering of the strikers. These efforts to persuade the men to return to work proved unsuccessful, but Clennell later managed to broker a settlement. Reed and Clennell had difficulty with a few employers who at first refused to accept the terms, and, later, when some breached the agreement, Reed sent a strong protest to the secretary of the coal trade, evidently with good effect.[45] Thus the part played by the magistrates on these occasions must not be viewed in an entirely negative light, however quick they were to call for military aid and make alarmist predictions in support of their pleas.

Although several keelmen's strikes occurred in close proximity to periods of political unrest, their actions were not politically motivated, a fact that was generally acknowledged by the authorities, despite fears that were occasionally raised. The government's anxiety lest the keelmen should espouse the Jacobite cause in 1715 was proved to be groundless when seven hundred of them volunteered to defend Newcastle against the insurgents. William Cotesworth, who had been a government agent in the area on that occasion and could speak with

---

[41] *Journals of the House of Commons*, 32, p.778; Morgan and Rushton, *Rogues, Thieves and the Rule of Law*, p.200.

[42] Evidence of George Purvis, former keelman, to Commons committee, 1770 (not reported in *Journals of the House of Commons*), TWA 394/29, p.39.

[43] Jonathan Roddam to Secretary of State, 11 July 1710, SP 34/12/126.

[44] Magistrates to Secretary of State, 30 May 1719, State Papers, Domestic, Regencies, SP 43/57.

[45] See above, Chapter 12.

authority, deprecated the description of the keelmen's strike of 1719 as a rebellion, and urged that their consistent loyalty to the king and government should be made known to the central authorities.[46] Indeed, after the strike, the Lords Justices of the Regency were reported to be 'tender of these poor people ... the only well affected mob in England', and anxious that their complaints should be investigated and justice done.[47] In 1750, however, the proclamation of the Pretender, which was probably no more than a prank by a few individuals who had had too much to drink, caused a flurry of over-reaction by the central authorities, still nervous in the aftermath of the rising of 1745, when questions about the keelmen's loyalty had again been raised. The Mayor expressly stated that the strikers were not doing 'any mischief', and there was nothing in his report to justify the conclusion that the support they received from the lawyer Mungo Herdman was equivalent to stirring them up 'to sedition', or to apply the terms 'riots and treasonable practices' and 'insurrection' to the strike.[48] Although the petition, which Herdman dictated, included the expressions 'our opponents made formidable by the sweat of our brows', and 'such as spend their lives and labours to enrich those that oppress us', these sentiments do not indicate a desire to overturn the existing order as the prayer of the petition was that the magistrates would deal justly with the keelmen's complaints. The other petition, which appears to have been composed by the keelmen themselves, ends with the aspiration 'that the coal trade may be carried on with quietness and expedition to accomplish which our laborious endeavours shall never be wanting'.[49] The keelmen seldom used other than deferential language in their petitions. However, in 1738, the coal owners were denounced in particularly robust terms, but this petition, drawn up by one skipper, did not represent the views of his fellows, some of whom, both at the time and later, expressed their disapproval.[50]

In 1794, when events in France were raising fears of revolution in England, the keelmen protested that during their strike against the spouts the military had been deployed against them as if they intended 'to turn the world upside down', whereas all they wanted was work to support themselves and their

[46]   William Cotesworth to Sir Henry Liddell, 24 May 1719, Cotesworth Papers, CJ3/8–12; Leo Gooch, *The Desperate Faction?*, pp.43–4; Richardson, *The Local Historian's Table Book*, Historical Division, I, p.349.

[47]   Delafaye to magistrates, 9 June 1719, State Papers, Domestic, Regencies, 43/61; Delafaye to Hedworth and Ettrich, 16 June 1719, SP 44/281/62–3.

[48]   Robert Sorsbie to Duke of Bedford, 30 April 1750; R.N. Aldworth to Sorsbie, 3 May 1750; Aldworth and R. Leveson Gower to Andrew Stone, 4 May 1750, SP 36/112/331; SP 44/318/11–14. As in 1715, queries as to the loyalty of the keelmen were raised in 1745. General Wade claimed that he was reluctant to move his forces out of Newcastle 'because he could not trust the keelmen', but there were certainly not 20,000 of them. Gooch, *The Desperate Faction?*, p.161. See also, Sir Edward Blackett to the Mayor of Newcastle, 11 April 1746, stating that he had information that disaffected persons were planning to seize Newcastle and expected many keelmen to assist them, S.P., Domestic, George II, 83. The rebels did not attack Newcastle, but, although there was alarm in the City, the Whig Mayor, Matthew Ridley, brought the citizens united through the crisis. W. A. Speck, 'Northumberland Elections in the Eighteenth Century', *Northern History*, 28 (1992), pp.164–77.

[49]   Petitions of the keelmen, 1750, TWA 394/19.

[50]   Petition, 9 May 1738; affidavit of skippers, TWA 394/9.

families.[51] Again, in 1819, when the authorities were particularly fearful of radical reformers, the Mayor stated at the outset of the keelmen's strike that it was not politically motivated, and, although 'seditious' pamphlets were said to be circulated among them, the keelmen were reported to have taken little interest in the great political meeting held in Newcastle during the stoppage.[52] The only direct evidence that radical ideas may have gained ground among them appears in the last of their *Addresses* issued during the strike of 1822. One writer considers that the sentiments therein expressed indicate that the keelmen were 'slowly imbibing the radical economic doctrine of the period', but the appearance of such ideas may owe more to the fact that the *Address* was printed and sold at the premises of the prominent radical John Marshall than to the opinions of the keelmen at large. The Duke of Northumberland was certainly correct in stating that the keelmen were not acting through 'political delusion'.[53] The absence of demands of a political nature was indeed characteristic of strikes enforced by other groups of workers in the north east during the eighteenth century and first quarter of the nineteenth century, and to a large extent helps to explain the leniency with which the authorities tended to treat those involved in these outbreaks.[54]

Sentences on keelmen even guilty of assaults or violence during strikes were remarkably lenient compared with those passed on thieves or perpetrators of other common offences in the locality, as a glance through the newspapers of the time will show. In 1719, the magistrates both of Newcastle and County Durham were anxious that the keelmen arrested during the strike should be released without punishment. As John Hedworth remarked, 'nothing can conduce more to keep the rest in quietness at their work than an entire discharge of them'. The employers, too, were probably wary of alienating the workforce by seeking severe penalties. In 1822 they showed reluctance even to execute warrants issued against their bound men for breach of contract. No doubt they wanted their men to be available for work as soon as the strike ended, besides which they probably realized that imprisonment of the offenders would not serve much purpose. As long ago as 1765, during a great strike by the miners,

---

[51] 'Address to the Public', *Newcastle Courant*, 16 August 1794. Typical of the fears at the time are the remarks by Thomas Powditch, a shipowner, who in a letter to the Prime Minister, 3 November 1792, declared that Tyneside was 'covered with thousands of Pittmen, Keelmen, Waggonmen and other labouring men, hardy fellows strongly impressed with the new doctrine of equality, and at present composed of such combustible matter that the least spark will set them ablaze' (quoted in H.T. Dickinson, *Radical Politics in the North-East of England in the Later Eighteenth Century*, Durham County Local History Society, 1979), p.16. The *Newcastle Advertiser*, 23 August 1794, reported that Robert Lister was transported for life for using treasonable and seditious language. Dickinson, *ibid.*, p.16, identifies him as a keelman involved in the recent strike, but this is not stated in the *Advertiser*, although it lists separately several keelmen punished for riot. The *Newcastle Courant*, 23 August 1794, states that Lister was transported for horse-stealing, while the *Newcastle Chronicle* of the same date states that another person was charged with uttering seditious language but indicates that no bill was found against him.

[52] Joseph Forster to Sidmouth, 28 September 1819, National Archives, HO 42/195; Nicholas Fairless to Sidmouth, 12 October 1819, Earl of Darlington to Sidmouth, 15 October 1819, HO 42/196.

[53] Rowe, 'The Decline of the Tyneside Keelmen in the Nineteenth Century', p.117; Duke of Northumberland to Peel, 29 October 1822, National Archives, HO 40/17/54.

[54] McCord, 'The Seamen's Strike', especially p.142.

it had been pointed out that punishment of relatively few men by a month's imprisonment did not carry 'the least appearance of terror so as to induce the remaining part to submit', but would merely create martyrs to be brought home in triumph at the end of their confinement.[55] Even so, on several occasions the keelmen tried to bargain for the release of prisoners, especially in 1719, after the arrest of two keelmen 'whose example and authority did very much influence the rest'. This was probably the only time that arrests (though in this instance combined with the threat that the prisoners would be impressed into the navy) contributed significantly towards ending a strike.

As the Mayor declared in 1819, the magistrates had 'the most formidable set of men to contend with', sailors, keelmen, pitmen and radical reformers.[56] Of these groups, the keelmen, 'a mutinous race', for long characterized by 'ferocity and savage roughness' and living in close proximity to Newcastle, were the most troublesome to the authorities.[57] Often they used violence against substitute workers and any of their own number who attempted to work during a strike, but they did not attack their employers, nor, apart from the exceptional case of 1740, embark on a rampage of looting. Even so, the inhabitants of Newcastle must often have been apprehensive when bands of these robust men roamed the streets and surrounding districts to solicit charity. The city militia was virtually powerless against them, and, when strikes occurred, the magistrates almost invariably called for the assistance of the regular armed forces. The importance of the coal trade to London and the nation in general added weight to their pleas, but, although the government generally complied with their request, it was occasionally made clear to them that they did not have, as they tended to assume, an automatic right to such aid. However prolonged or vigorous the strike, bloodshed was remarkably rare and, in most cases, settlements were eventually achieved by negotiation. Although dealing with the keelmen was often a problem for both their masters and the authorities, all concerned had to recognize that they were essential to the coal trade, and this remained the case until they were gradually superseded by mechanical methods of loading and new means of transport.

---

[55] J.B. Ridley to the Earl of Northumberland, 13 September 1765, *Calendar of Home Office Papers, Geo. III*, I, 1760–65, p.599.
[56] Archibald Reed to Sidmouth, 20 October 1819, National Archives, HO 42/197/671–4.
[57] Thomas Pennant, *A Tour in Scotland* (London, 1790), I, 39; Baillie, *An Impartial History of Newcastle upon Tyne*, p.143.

17

The Keelmen and Trade Unionism

The foregoing account of the many instances of collective action by this body of proletarians from the mid-seventeenth century onwards raises the question whether they have a place in the history of trade unionism. Information about combinations of such labourers for increased wages or redress of grievances in the seventeenth and early eighteenth centuries is not plentiful, but the activities of the keelmen are unusually well documented. In their classic *History of Trade Unionism* (1894) Sidney and Beatrice Webb defined a trade union as 'a continuous association of wage-earners for the purpose of maintaining or improving the conditions of their employment', but by insisting on continuity they excluded manifestations of united action that lacked evidence of permanence. The earliest trade unions they found among skilled craft-workers such as tailors and woolcombers who possessed sufficient independence of character to resist, when necessary, the will of their employers and form enduring, as opposed to ephemeral, associations.[1] Modern historians, however, have abandoned insistence on continuous association, and, as John Rule puts it, have 're-incorporated into trade union history' the innumerable instances of collective action that the Webbs dismissed as 'episodic and spontaneous labour reactions':[2]

> It is not useful to think of a polarisation of organised trade union activity at one pole and sporadic 'one-off' actions at the other. Instead there was a spectrum of responses with *recurrent* forms linking the ephemeral with the continuous. By recurrent is understood a situation in which groups of workers although not necessarily keeping an organisation for trade-protecting purposes in permanent being, nevertheless preserved in experience and tradition a sufficient knowledge of possible forms of action.[3]

The keelmen, congregated in Sandgate and linked by ties of family through intermarriage as well as, in many cases, by Scottish origin, and employed on the one waterway in work often involving danger and demanding mutual assistance, acquired from these constant patterns of association a habit of solidarity, 'the foundation of effective trade unionism'.[4] This appeared earlier than among other labourers such as the miners, also noted for their solidarity, but

---

[1]   Sidney Webb and Beatrice Webb, *History of Trade Unionism* (London, 1894), pp.1, 24–6, 37–8. In the 1920 edition of their work the Webbs noted the keelmen's 'fierce strikes' in the eighteenth century, but, without particulars of their association, concluded that they were 'probably ephemeral', p.44n.

[2]   John Rule, 'The Formative Years of British Trade Unionism: An Overview', in *British Trade Unionism 1750–1850*, edited by Rule (London, 1988), pp.1–2.

[3]   John Rule, *The Experience of Labour in Eighteenth-Century Industry* (London, 1981), p.151.

[4]   E.J. Hobsbawm, *Labouring Men, Studies in the History of Labour* (London, 1968), p.9.

who in the seventeenth century worked in independent groups in dispersed locations which lessened their opportunity to take effective united action.[5] Professor E.R. Turner was the first to suggest that the keelmen might provide an example of trade union activity earlier and different from those cited by the Webbs. The keelmen, he believed, were organised in a by-trade subordinate to the Hostmen's Company, but by using this body to seek improved terms of employment they tended to transform it into 'something like a trade union, representing, perhaps, a phase of transition from old to new':

> Always a body of wage-earners, during the latter part of the seventeenth and in the early part of the eighteenth century it strove for better conditions and sought increased wages for its members, and not only pursued the same objects but adopted some of the methods of the tailors and woolcombers, among whom trade-unionism in England is acknowledged to have had its origin.[6]

Unfortunately this theory as it stands cannot be sustained, since by the dawn of the seventeenth century the ancient company of keelmen had disappeared and attempts to revive it in some form had no lasting success.[7] This also seems to have escaped notice by John Hatcher who states in his *History of the British Coal Industry* (1993) p.468 that the keelmen and their employers provide 'an interesting chapter in early industrial relations', as both sides were 'collectively organized', the keelmen in their fellowship, first mentioned in 1516, and the Hostmen in their Company chartered in 1600. Although the keelmen's ancient guild did not survive, their charity, founded at the dawn of the eighteenth century and funded by contributions deducted from the men's earnings, was a potential basis for a trade union, especially when disputes over the collection and use of the money arose. Indeed the Webbs state that friendly societies composed of members of the same trade 'almost inevitably' developed into trade unions.[8] The struggle between the keelmen and their masters for control of the charity was often closely associated with strikes for increased wages and remedy of grievances, as in 1707, when the men formalised their combination by 'a writing or obligation under a penalty', and in the prolonged strike of 1710.[9] Part of the charity money, once out of the Hostmen's direct control, was dissipated in 'idle drinking', but there was probably truth in the allegation that the funds were also employed to promote mutinies and support those imprisoned

---

[5] Levine and Wrightson, *The Making of an Industrial Society – Whickham 1560–1765*, p.392. Throughout the eighteenth and early nineteenth centuries the miners demonstrated 'a real flair for extemporary organization as occasion demanded', an ability largely assisted by the nature of their living and working environments and the discipline demanded by the dangers of their occupation, Michael Flinn, *The History of the British Coal Industry, 1700–1830: The Industrial Revolution* (Oxford, 1984), pp.410–11.

[6] Turner, 'The Keelmen of Newcastle', pp.542–5.

[7] See above, Introduction.

[8] Webb and Webb, *History of Trade Unionism*, p.23n.

[9] See above, Chapter 2.

for their part in them.[10] Thus the Hostmen and magistrates vigorously opposed the keelmen's bid for a charter of incorporation that would give them a permanent legal status and independent control of the fund. In his *Rise of the British Coal Industry*, J.U. Nef concludes that the keelmen were seeking to gain recognition, under the only form that seemed open to them, for what was in effect a trade union, and in this early attempt by a body of wage-earners to better their conditions he sees a 'new step in the direction of modern industrial organization'.[11] The bid for incorporation, however, was probably suggested and certainly encouraged by Daniel Defoe who, although sympathetic to the keelmen, was pursuing his own agenda of opposition to monopoly in the coal trade. The bitter attacks on the Hostmen and magistrates in the various publications that then appeared may well have expressed the sentiments of many keelmen, but it should be remembered that the author was Defoe.

Defoe apparently severed his connexion with the keelmen after their bid for incorporation failed, but their desire to obtain independence in this manner via the charity revived for a time in 1719, again arousing the Hostmen's apprehensions of 'entire ruin not only to this Company but to the Corporation and trade in general'.[12] Whatever the moves that provoked these fears, they were evidently unconnected with the Society of the Tyne and Wear Keelmen formed later that year under articles of combination drawn up by the Sunderland schoolmaster Richard Flower. In its short-lived existence the combination manifested many characteristics of a trade union, having both aggressive and defensive aims; aggressive in the demand for a big increase in wages, defensive in seeking restoration of lost benefits and remedy of grievances. Although some concessions were granted on the Tyne and possibly also on the Wear, the strikers failed to extort an increase in wages. The combination collapsed and Flower found himself in danger of severe punishment.[13]

The Wear men were not involved in the strike of 1744, when the Newcastle keelmen obtained a new wages settlement which purported to remedy the grievance of overmeasure, nor in their long-lasting strike of 1750, resulting to a large extent from non-observance of that agreement; but in 1768, under the auspices of the attorney Thomas Harvey, an attempt was made to unite both bodies of workers in a new and sophisticated phase of what was in essence trade union action. The society into which he organized the keelmen had both charitable and industrial aims. Fines, backed by threats of legal action, were imposed on keelmen who navigated over-loaded craft, and a contribution was levied on each crew to fund an application to Parliament both to establish the Newcastle charity and obtain a statutory provision against overmeasure. Officers of the society sought support for the bid against overmeasure from the keelmen at Sunderland, but Harvey could not substantiate his claim that the Newcastle petition also represented the views of more than four hundred skippers and

---

[10] *Ibid.*
[11] Nef, *The Rise of the British Coal Industry*, pp.177, 180.
[12] 5 March 1718/19, Dendy, *Records of the Hostmen's Company of Newcastle upon Tyne*, p.186.
[13] See above, Chapter 5.

casters on the River Wear who were afraid to sign their names. A counter petition from the Wear men dissociating themselves from the Newcastle charity
ended the attempt at co-operation and no future efforts in this direction seem to
have been made. The society collapsed after Harvey abandoned his proposed
bill in order to support Rose Fuller's concerning overmeasure, which, however,
did not proceed beyond the second reading.[14]

Sixteen years later, when an 'acting committee' proposed the establishment
of a permanent charity for the keelmen, a statutory provision against overmeasure formed an essential part of the scheme. Other suggestions concerning beer
allowances and payment for work at the staithes were dropped,[15] but the draft
rules of the proposed society indicate that it was intended that it should have a
role in industrial disputes :

> As it sometimes happens that causes of complaint are given to the keelmen,
> and they being separated from one another, have not an opportunity of know-
> ing each others' sentiments, by which means matters are often carried too
> far to the manifest disadvantage of all concerned. But by this Association
> all these disagreeable circumstances will be avoided, as the opinion of the
> whole body of keelmen will be easily got, laid before the magistrates, and
> immediately decided.[16]

Although their long history of united action indicates that the keelmen had less
difficulty in learning each others' sentiments than suggested above, there were
certainly potential divergencies of interest between the men of different employers. When the keelmen struck in 1750 they admitted that some of the fitters had
not imposed hardship on them,[17] and again the issue of the spouts threatened
to divide those employed above-bridge from those stationed below. However,
despite such circumstances, the keelmen maintained their solidarity.

Soon after the Act of 1788 had established the charity, the keelmen expected
its Guardians to take cognizance of work-related matters,[18] but these expectations were disappointed. However, the keelmen's stewards, elected under the
Act to represent the whole body, tended to become involved in industrial matters. In 1794 they petitioned the coal owners on the 'many evils' arising from
the spouts, but when a strike began they withdrew from the action, and other
delegates had to be chosen to negotiate with the employers and magistrates.
When the strike continued, the stewards were brought back into the negotiations and helped to persuade their fellows to return to work. The keelmen
were well organized on this occasion. They held at least three general meetings to which their delegates or the stewards reported, and subsequently 'the
Committee of Delegates for the whole body of Keelmen' issued an 'Address to

---

[14] See above, Chapter 3.
[15] Preliminary proposals concerning the society, TWA 394/57.
[16] Abstract of rules, TWA 394/57.
[17] Petition of keelmen, 1750, TWA 394/19.
[18] See above, Chapter 4.

the Public' to explain their grievances and conduct.[19] Again, at the beginning of the strike of 1822, the stewards, who claimed that they had tried to prevent the stoppage, represented the keelmen's complaints to the coal owners and magistrates.[20] At other times the skippers, the natural leaders of the keelmen, took a prominent part in struggles for improved conditions. The procedure generally conformed to a well-established pattern.[21] Following a petition from the keelmen, the Mayor would convoke a meeting of the employers, magistrates and representatives of the men, usually a skipper from each work, who would explain their grievances and report the outcome, often, as in 1794, to a mass meeting, when it would be decided whether to accept terms or continue the strike. Leadership of the keelmen during strikes involved risk, as in 1719 when warrants were issued for the arrest of four ringleaders, two of whom were later captured, and in 1750 when sixteen skippers were sent to gaol. Non-keelmen who assisted them during strikes were liable to severe punishment as was the schoolmaster Richard Flower in 1719 and Mungo Herdman in 1750.

The magistrates, often themselves involved in the coal trade, were generally quick to promise redress of grievances but slow to grant a wage increase. The basic scale of keel-dues established in 1654 and, with some modifications, set down on parchment in 1710, was not further altered until 1809, though various small adjustments were made to the owners' wages element of the men's pay in the intervening period. Promises of redress, especially regarding overmeasure, were frequently broken, thus inspiring deep distrust among the keelmen. That they were unable permanently to curb the abuse of overmeasure, and win some restriction on the use of the spouts, were major defeats, but in other respects they usually gained something from their strikes, at least in the short term, except in 1822 when their employers absolutely refused any concession.

Intimidation always played a part in maintaining the keelmen's solidarity during strikes, and since all keels had to pass down the one waterway it was relatively easy for a band of determined strikers to enforce a complete stoppage. Keelmen who broke ranks received rough treatment, sometimes even life-threatening, besides which they would have to endure resentment that was bound to persist in their closely-knit community long after the strike ended. Substitute workers always needed military protection, but if they enabled trade to continue, however inefficiently, the strike would sooner or later collapse. Occasionally strikers scuttled keels and, more often, jettisoned or smashed their equipment to prevent use by strike-breakers. In 1794 parties of strikers destroyed several spouts, but in claiming that the majority of the keelmen were

[19] 'Address to the Public by order of the Committee of Delegates for the whole body of Keelmen', *Newcastle Courant*, 16 August 1794. Their statement that 'the stewards of the Fund were ordered to wait on the gentlemen who accordingly attended', does not make it clear whether the order was issued by the magistrates or by the general meeting of the keelmen, but the fact that the employers, too, were evidently summoned, suggests that the magistrates convoked the meeting.

[20] Minutes, 4 October 1822, TWA 394/46.

[21] On conscious organization indicated by such procedures, see Robert W. Malcolmson, 'Workers' Combinations in Eighteenth-Century England', in Margaret and James Jacob, eds, *The Origins of Anglo-American Radicalism* (London, 1984), pp.149–61.

opposed to disorder, a view endorsed by one of the Newcastle newspapers, their delegates implicitly apologized for this.[22] In 1822 the keelmen explicitly apologized for the 'irregularities' committed by some of their number.[23] Violence during strikes was generally limited to attacks on blacklegs and, despite occasional threats made by some of the keelmen, and fears oft expressed by the municipal authorities when calling for military assistance, never extended to the persons or homes of their employers as sometimes happened in other areas. 'Collective bargaining by riot', in the sense of using violence and destruction of property unconnected with their work to wring concessions from their employers, was never part of the keelmen's tactics.[24] The destruction in the riot of 1740 did not arise from an industrial dispute, so far as the keelmen were concerned, and even on that occasion the magistrates, though terrified, were not harmed.

The keelmen were a robust race well accustomed to coping with hardship and this helps to account for their remarkable endurance during prolonged strikes. In 'the long stop' of 1822 begging was a main source of their support, as it probably was during earlier stoppages.[25] Some keelmen and their families may have survived on credit, or resorted to what they could gather legitimately or otherwise from the surrounding countryside. Casual labouring work was another source of support, but those who employed keelmen during the term of their bonds risked prosecution.[26] Strikers could not draw on the charitable fund established by the Act of 1788, but this did not necessarily apply to the keelmen's friendly societies or box clubs. Apart from the Hospital Society little is known about these bodies. They were mentioned in connexion with charitable relief in 1758, and by 1800 they were said to exercise a beneficial discipline over the keelmen.[27] Partly for that reason, such clubs could foster trade union activity, and although the evidence is slight, it seems that at least in 1822 they actively did so. The Hospital Society punished three of its members for working during that stoppage, and, despite the magistrates' professed ignorance on the subject, there is no doubt that other box clubs provided financial support to

---

[22] 'Address to the Public'. The *Newcastle Courant*, 19 July 1794, attributed the destruction to a part of the keelmen 'more turbulent than the rest'.

[23] First *Address*, 9 October 1822.

[24] For wrecking as a technique of trade unionism before and during the early phases of the industrial revolution, see Hobsbawm, *Labouring Men*, pp.7–9, but C.R. Dobson claims that the emphasis on violence does not do justice to the level of organization achieved by the early trade unions, *Masters and Journeymen, a Prehistory of Industrial Relations, 1717–1800* (London, 1980), pp.16–17.

[25] Robert Bell to Henry Hobhouse, 25 November 1822, National Archives, HO 40/17/398..

[26] In 1750 the fitters issued a list of about 800 bound keelmen and threatened prosecution against anyone who employed them in 'any work or service whatsoever', Bell, 'Collections relative to the Tyne, its Trade and Conservancy', I. In 1822 one of the magistrates, Revd Liddell, urged that prosecutions be commenced against those who employed bound Newcastle keelmen at Sunderland, Minutes, 14 November 1822, TWA 394/46. During the strike of 1771 some of the keelmen found work at Sunderland, Matthew Ridley to George Ward, 28 June and 5 July 1771, letter book 1767–77, p.113, Northumberland Museum and Archives, ZRI 38/2

[27] Dendy, *Records of the Hostmen's Company*, p.205 ; J. Baillie, *An Impartial History of Newcastle upon Tyne* (Newcastle, 1801), p.143. About box clubs and their connexion with trade unionism see Dobson, *Masters and Journeymen*, pp.38–9, 45.

the strikers that year.[28] Even so, such *ad hoc* relief must be distinguished from the deliberate accumulation of a strike fund, for which there is no evidence.

The keelmen showed themselves to be particularly well organized in the strikes of 1819 and 1822. When the owners of one colliery refused to accept the terms of the settlement arranged after the initial strike of 1819, the whole body of keelmen, in true trade union fashion, turned out again. In 1822 they denied that they had a committee for representing grievances or any regular organization like their employers,[29] which was not surprising in view of the Combination Laws, then still in force, but they nevertheless maintained a united front during the ten weeks of the strike, negotiated through delegates who reported to mass meetings, published a series of *Addresses*, and raised a public subscription to try a case against the spouts. Without some form of organization they could not have pursued the matter through the courts at 'enormous expense' for eight years, but there is no evidence of continued united action thereafter, though this does not prove than it did not exist. Although the Combination Laws posed a threat to workers during the first quarter of the nineteenth century, they were never invoked against the keelmen in their strikes of 1809, 1819 and 1822, probably because breach of the covenants of the bond provided sufficient grounds for prosecution without involving difficulties that an action under the Combination Laws might have entailed. Combinations of masters to lower wages or increase work were also prohibited, and awkward questions might have been raised about the coal owners' cartel to restrict the vend, which reduced the keelmen's earning power, while the overloading of the keels increased the men's work without a corresponding rise in pay thereby lowering their wages. Moreover, as many of the Newcastle magistrates were the keelmen's employers, they would have been disqualified from dealing with cases brought under these laws.[30] Other laws, such as those against conspiracy, carried far harsher penalties but were never actually invoked against the keelmen. During the strike of 1809 a draft notice urged the men to return to work to avoid the 'dreadful consequences of the law', but the final notice merely threatened prosecution for desertion of service which incurred only a short term of imprisonment.[31]

Although it cannot be claimed that the keelmen ever formed a permanent organization dedicated to safeguarding and improving the conditions of their employment, this body of life-long wage-earners, rough and largely unlettered as they were, exhibited from an early date a tradition of solidarity and a persistent tendency towards collective action, 'the essence of trade unionism'.[32] From time to time their efforts to obtain higher wages or remove grievances

[28] See above, Chapter 13.

[29] Second *Address*, 15 October 1822.

[30] 39 & 40 George III, 1800, cap.106, sections 16–17. E.P. Thompson states several other possible reasons why prosecutions were not instituted under the Combination Acts, *The Making of the English Working Class* (1968 edn), pp.551–4.

[31] Heads of proposed handbill, and printed version, 5 November 1809, TWA 394/37.

[32] Rule, *The Experience of Labour in Eighteenth-Century Industry*, p.150 (quoting H.A. Turner, *Trade Union Growth, Structure and Policy*).

were associated with attempts to gain an independent status, ostensibly to govern the charity, which, as their employers feared, would almost certainly have become a cloak for a fully fledged trade union. A close parallel is provided by the merchant seamen, who although not in a permanent association, enforced remarkably well organized strikes on the Tyne and Wear in the 1790s and in 1815, and later, under the guise of a friendly society, pursued trade union activities.[33] Even before the keelmen's charity was founded, the circumstances in which they lived and worked helped them to combine earlier than other workers who subsequently became noted for their solidarity. The keelmen certainly deserve a place in the history of trade unionism.

---

[33] McCord, 'The Seamen's Strike of 1815 in North-East England'; D.J. Rowe, 'A Trade Union of the North-East Coast Seamen in 1825', *Economic History Review*, 25 (1972), pp.81–98.

Bibliography

Primary Sources

Durham Cathedral Library
Additional Manuscript 97.

Durham County Record Office
Clayton and Gibson Papers.
National Coal Board Records.
Strathmore Papers.

Durham University Archives and Special Collections
Durham Probate Records.
Earl Grey Papers: 2nd Earl, and Miscellaneous books, V No.6.
Shafto Papers.

House of Lords Record Office
Manuscript Bill concerning the Keelmen's Charity, 1712, petitions against it, and associated papers.

National Archives (Public Record Office)
Admiralty Records.
Home Office Papers.
Privy Council Registers.
State Papers.

Newcastle Upon Tyne Central Library
Bell, J., 'Collections Relative to the Tyne, its Trade and Conservancy', 6 volumes of manuscript and printed material.
Booklet by William Brockie, 'The Keelmen of the Tyne'.
Montague family letter book (microfilm).

North of England Institute of Mining and Mechanical Engineers
Bell Collection for a History of Coal Mining: 22 volumes of manuscripts, press cuttings and other printed material.
William Brown's Letter Book.
Easton Papers.
Watson Collection.

Northumberland Museum and Archives

'Annals and Historical Events, Newcastle' vol. II (among the Newcastle Society of Antiquaries' papers).
Carr-Ellison Papers.
Coal Trade Minute Books.
Ridley Papers.

Tyne and Wear Archives

Accession 394: a large collection of manuscripts concerning the keelmen including petitions, letters and legal papers.
Cotesworth Papers.
Ellison Papers.
Minute books of the Hostmen's Company.
Records of Newcastle Corporation: Letter Book, 1771; Estate and Property sub-Committee Minute Book, 1790–99; Calendars of minute books of the Common Council and of petitions to the Common Council.

Newspapers and Magazines

Black Dwarf.
Durham Chronicle.
Durham County Advertiser.
Gateshead Intelligencer.
Gateshead Observer.
Gentleman's Magazine.
Mercurius Politicus (London, 1654).
Newcastle Advertiser.
Newcastle Chronicle.
Newcastle Courant.
Newcastle Guardian.
Newcastle Journal.
Newcastle Magazine.
Newcastle Weekly Chronicle Supplement.
Review of the State of the English Nation.
Tyne Mercury.
Westminster Journal.

Secondary Sources

Archer, David, ed., *Tyne and Tide. A Celebration of the River Tyne* (Daryan Press, Ovingham, 2003).
Armstrong, Sir W.G., Bell, I. Lothian *et al.*, eds, *The Industrial Resources of the Tyne, Wear and Tees, including the Reports on the local Manufactures, read before the British Association in 1863* (London and Newcastle, 1864).
Ashton, T.S. and Sykes, J., *The Coal Industry of the Eighteenth Century* (Manchester, 1929).
Aspinall, A., *The Early English Trade Unions* (London, 1949).
Baillie, J., *An Impartial History of Newcastle upon Tyne* (Newcastle, 1801).
Bell, John (junior), *Rhymes of the Northern Bards* (Newcastle, 1812).

Blake, J.B., 'The Medieval Coal Trade of North East England. Some Fourteenth Century Evidence', *Northern History*, II (1967), pp.1–26.

Bohstedt, John, *Riots and Community Politics in England and Wales 1790–1810* (Cambridge, MA and London, 1983).

Bohstedt, John, 'The Pragmatic Economy, the Politics of Provision and the "Invention" of the Food Riot Tradition in 1740', in Randall, Adrian, and Charlesworth, Andrew, eds, *Moral Economy and Popular Protest: Crowds, Conflict and Authority* (London, 2000), pp.55–92.

Brand, J., *History and Antiquities of the Town and County of Newcastle upon Tyne*, 2 volumes (London, 1789).

Brewer, E. Cobham, *Dictionary of Phrase and Fable* (New York, 1978).

Chandler, Edward, *A Charge Delivered to the Grand Jury at the Quarter Sessions held at Durham ... 16 July 1740 concerning the Engrossing of Corn and Grain and the Riots that have been Occasioned Thereby* (Durham, 1740).

Charleton, R.J., *A History of Newcastle on Tyne from the Earliest Records to its Formation as a City* (Newcastle, 1885).

Colls, Robert, *The Pitmen of the Northern Coalfield: Work, Culture and Protest, 1790–1850* (Manchester, 1987).

Cromer, P., 'The Coal Industry on Tyneside, 1715–1750', *Northern History*, XIV (1978), pp.193–207.

Cruickshanks, E., Handley, S., and Hayton, D.W., eds, *History of Parliament 1690–1715*, 5 volumes (Cambridge, 2002).

Curnock, Nehemiah, ed., *Journal of the Reverend John Wesley* (London, 1909–16).

Dendy, F.W., ed., *Extracts from the Records of the Hostmen's Company of Newcastle upon Tyne* (Surtees Society, CV, 1901).

Dickinson, H.T., ed., *The Correspondence of James Clavering* (Surtees Society, CLXXVIII, 1967).

Dickinson, H.T., *Radical Politics in the North-East of England in the later Eighteenth Century* (Durham County Local History Society, 1979).

Dietz, B. 'The North-East Coal Trade, 1550–1750: Measures, Markets and the Metropolis', *Northern History*, XXII (1986), pp.280–94.

Dobson, C.R., *Masters and Journeymen, a Prehistory of Industrial Relations, 1717–1800* (London, 1980).

Douglas, Martin, *The Life and Adventures of Martin Douglas, Sunderland Keelman and Celebrated Life Saver* (Stockton on Tees, 1848).

Dunn, Matthias, *A Treatise on the Winning and Working of Collieries* (London and Newcastle, 1852).

Ellis, Joyce M., 'A Study of the Business Fortunes of William Cotesworth c.1668–1726' (unpublished D.Phil thesis, Oxford, 1976).

Ellis, Joyce M., 'Urban Conflict and Popular Violence, the Guildhall Riots of 1740 in Newcastle upon Tyne', *International Review of Social History*, XXV (1980), pp.332–49.

Ellis, Joyce M., ed., *The Letters of Henry Liddell to William Cotesworth* (Surtees Society, CXCVII, 1987).

Fewster, Joseph M., 'The Keelmen of Tyneside in the Eighteenth Century', *Durham University Journal*, new series, XIX (1957–58), pp.24–33, 66–75, 111–23.

Fewster, Joseph M., 'The last Struggles of the Tyneside Keelmen', *Durham University Journal*, new series, XXIV (1962–63), pp.5–15.

Finch, Roger, *Coals from Newcastle – The Story of the North East Coal Trade in the Days of Sail* (Lavenham, Suffolk, 1973).

Flinn, Michael, *The History of the British Coal Industry, 1700–1830: The Industrial Revolution* (Oxford, 1984).

Fordyce, T., *Local Records or Historical Register of Remarkable Events which have occurred in Northumberland and Durham, Newcastle upon Tyne, and Berwick-upon-Tweed, 1833–1866* (Newcastle, 1876).

Fordyce, W., *A History of Coal, Coke, Coal Fields ... and Iron* (London, 1860).

Forster, Eric, *The Keelmen* (Newcastle, 1970).

Galloway, Robert, *Annals of Coal Mining and the Coal Trade*, 2 volumes (reprinted, Newton Abbot, 1971).

Garbutt, George, *Historical and Descriptive View of the Parishes of Monkwearmouth and Bishopwearmouth and the Port and Borough of Sunderland* (Sunderland, 1819).

Gardiner, Ralph, *England's Grievance Discovered in Relation to the Coal Trade* (1655, reprinted Newcastle, 1796).

Gooch, Leo, *The Desperate Faction? The Jacobites of North-East England 1688–1745* (Hull, 1995).

Gray, William, *Chorographia, or a Survey of Newcastle upon Tyne* (Newcastle, 1649, reprinted 1818).

Guthrie, J., *The River Tyne, its History and Resources* (Newcastle, 1880).

Hair, P.E.H., 'The Binding of the Pitmen in the North-East 1800–1809', *Durham University Journal*, new series XXVII (1965–66), pp.1–13.

Hair, T.H., *Sketches of the Coal Mines in Northumberland and Durham, with Descriptive Sketches and a Preliminary Essay on Coal and the Coal Trade by M. Ross* (London, 1844).

Hall T.Y., 'The Rivers, Ports and Harbours of the Great Northern Coal Field', *Transactions of the North of England Institute of Mining Engineers*, X (1861), pp.41–82.

Hatcher, John, *The History of the British Coal Industry, Before 1700: Towards the Age of Coal* (Oxford, 1993).

Healey, George Harris, ed., *The Letters of Daniel Defoe* (Oxford, 1955).

Heslop, R. Oliver, 'Keels and Keelmen', manuscript in the North of England Institute of Mining Engineers, D/71.

Hiskey, Christine E., 'John Buddle, 1773–1843, Agent and Entrepreneur in the North-East Coal Trade', University of Durham M.Litt thesis (1978).

Historical Manuscripts Commission: *The Manuscripts of the Earl of Carlisle preserved at Castle Howard* (London, 1897); *The Manuscripts of the Duke of Portland preserved at Welbeck Abbey*, VI (*Manuscripts of the Harley Family*) (London, 1901); *The Manuscripts of the House of Lords*, series 17, new series IX 1710–12 (London, 1947–8); *Manuscripts of S.H.Le Fleming of Rydal Hall* (London, 1890).

Hobsbawm, E.J., *Labouring Men: Studies in the History of Labour* (London, 1968)

Home Office, *Calendar of Home Office Papers, George III, 1760–65* (London, 1878).

Hostmen, *The Case of Charles Atkinson, John Johnson, John Simpson, and great Numbers of the Trading Hoast-men, commonly called Fitters, of the Town and County of Newcastle upon Tyne* (1712) Lincolns Inn Tracts, M.P., 102.

Howell, Roger, junior, *Newcastle upon Tyne and the Puritan Revolution* (Oxford, 1967).

Hughes, Edward, *North Country Life in the Eighteenth Century; the North-East, 1700–1750* (London, 1952).

Hughes, Edward, ed., 'Some Clavering Correspondence', *Archaeologia Aeliana*, 4th series, XXXIV (1956), pp.14–26.

Hughes, Edward, ed., *The Diaries and Correspondence of James Losh, 1811–1823*, 2 volumes, Surtees Society, CLXXI (1962), CLXXIV (1963).

Jaffe, J.A., 'Competition and Size of Firms in the North-East Coal Trade, 1800–1850', *Northern History*, XXV (1989), pp.235–55.

Johnson, Alastair, ed., *Diary of Thomas Giordani Wright, Newcastle Doctor, 1826–29*, Surtees Society, CCVI (2001).

Johnson, R.W., *The Making of the Tyne, A Record of Fifty Years' Progress* (Newcastle, 1895).

Journal of Imperial and Commonwealth History, XII (London, 1983–84).

Keelmen, *The Case of the Poor Skippers and Keelmen of Newcastle Truly Stated; with some Remarks on a Printed Paper, called and pretended to be their Case* (London, 1712).

Keelmen, *Articles of the Keelmen's Hospital and Society* (Newcastle, 1781).

Keelmen, *Four Addresses of the Keelmen of the River Tyne* (Newcastle, 1823).

Keelmen, *Articles of the Keelmen's Hospital and Society with Rules for the Hospital, to which is added an Account of the Hospital and Society* (Newcastle, 1829).

Kenwood, A.G., *Capital Formation in North East England 1803–1913* (New York and London, 1985).

Law Reports, *The English Reports, King's Bench Division*, vols 102, 108, 111 (Edinburgh, 1910).

Levine, David and Wrightson, Keith, *The Making of an Industrial Society – Whickham 1560–1765* (Oxford, 1991).

Linsley, Stafford, 'The Port of Tyne', in David Archer, ed., *Tyne and Tide*.

Locke, John, *Two Treatises of Government ... Essay concerning the true Original, Extent and End of Civil Government* (London, 1690).

McCord, Norman, 'Tyneside Discontents and Peterloo', *Northern History*, II (1967), pp.91–111.

McCord, Norman, 'The Seamen's Strike of 1815 in North-East England', *The Economic History Review*, new series, 21 (1968), pp. 127–43.

McCord, Norman, 'The Impress Service in North-East England During the Napoleonic War', *The Mariner's Mirror*, LIV (1968), pp.163–80.

McCord, Norman, 'The Government of Tyneside 1800–1850', *Transactions of the Royal Historical Society*, 5th series, XX (1970), pp.5–30.

McCord, Norman, *North-East England, The Region's Development 1760–1960* (London, 1979).

McCord, Norman and Brewster, D.E., 'Some Labour Troubles of the 1790's in North East England', *International Review of Social History*, XIII (1968), pp.366–83.

McKay, John, 'Keels and Keelmen', *Newcastle Weekly Chronicle Supplement*, 9 November 1889.

Mackenzie, E., *A Descriptive and Historical Account of the Town and County of Newcastle upon Tyne*, 2 volumes (Newcastle, 1827).

Malcolmson, Robert W., 'Workers' Combinations in Eighteenth-Century England' in *The Origins of Anglo-American Radicalism*, Margaret and James Jacob,eds (London, 1984), pp.149–61.

Manders, Francis, 'The Tyneside Keelmen's Strike of 1710: Some Unpublished Documents', *Gateshead and District Local History Society Bulletin*, No.1 (1969).

[Marshall, John] ed., *Proceedings at Law in the Case of the King versus Russell and others relative to the Coal Staiths erected at Wallsend on the River Tyne* (Newcastle, 1830).

Middlebrook, S., *Newcastle upon Tyne, its Growth and Achievement* (Newcastle, 1950).

Miller, Stuart, 'The Progressive Improvement of Sunderland Harbour and the River Wear 1717–1859', unpublished MA thesis, Newcastle University (1978).

Milne, Maurice, 'Strikes and Strike-Breaking in North-East England, 1815–44: the Attitude of the Local Press', *International Review of Social History*, 22 (1977), pp.226–40.

Mitcalfe, W.S., 'The History of the Keelmen and their Strike in 1822', *Archaeologia Aeliana*, 4th series, XIV (1937), pp.1–16.

Mitchell, Andrew, *Address to the Society of Keelmen of the River Tyne with a Correct Statement of the Dues of the River* (Newcastle, 1792).

Moore, John Robert, *A Checklist of the Writings of Daniel Defoe* (Bloomington, IN, 1960).

Morgan, Gwenda and Rushton, Peter, *Rogues, Thieves and the Rule of Law, the Problem of Law Enforcement in North-East England 1718–1800* (London, 1998).

Mott, R.A., 'The London and Newcastle Chaldrons for Measuring Coal', *Archaeologia Aeliana*, 4th series XL (1962), pp. 227–39.

Murray, Alexander, *An Address to Young Keelmen* (Newcastle, 1781).

Namier, Sir Lewis B., *The Structure of Politics at the Accession of George III*, 2nd edn (London, 1957).

Namier, Sir Lewis B. and Brooke, John, eds, *The History of Parliament, The House of Commons 1754–1790*, 3 volumes (London, 1964).

Nef, J.U., *The Rise of the British Coal Industry*, 2 volumes, 2nd edn (London, 1966).

Nicholson, J.I., 'Keels and Keelmen', *Newcastle Weekly Chronicle Supplement*, 9 November 1889.

Parliament, House of Commons, *Journals of the House of Commons*, XV (1705–8), XVI (1708–11), XVII (1711–14), XXXII (1768–1770), LXXV (1819–20), CIX (1854).

Parliament, House of Lords, *Journals of the House of Lords*, XIX (1709–14).

Parliament, Reports from Committees: *Report on the State of the Coal Trade* (1800); *Minutes of Evidence before the Select Committee on the State of the Coal Trade* (1830); *Report from the Select Committee on the State of the Coal Trade together with the Minutes of Evidence* (1836).

Patent Rolls, *Calendar of Patent Rolls, Richard II, 1381–85* (London, 1897); *Henry V, 1416–22* (London, 1911).

Pennant, Thomas, *A Tour in Scotland* (London, 1790).

Potts, Taylor, *Sunderland: A History of the Town and Port, Trade and Commerce* (Sunderland, 1892).

Randall, Adrian and Charlesworth, Andrew, *Moral Economy and Popular Protest: Crowds, Conflict and Authority* (London, 2000).

Richardson, M.A., *The Local Historian's Table Book of Remarkable Occurrences chiefly illustrative of the History of the Northern Counties*, Historical Division, 4 volumes (Newcastle, 1841–44).

Richardson, M.A., *Reprints of Rare Tracts and Imprints of Ancient Manuscripts chiefly illustrative of the History of the Northern Counties*, 7 volumes (Newcastle, 1847–49).

Richardson, William, *History of the Parish of Wallsend* (Newcastle, 1923).

Richmond, T., *Local Records of Stockton and Neighbourhood* (Stockton, 1868).

Robinson, John, *The Delaval Papers, How they were Discovered, with Numerous Family Letters and others of National and General Interest* (Newcastle, n.d.).

Rogers, Nicholas, *Crowds, Culture and Politics in Georgian Britain* (Oxford, 1998).

Rogers, Nicholas, *The Press Gang: Naval Impressment and its Opponents in Georgian Britain* (London and New York, 2007).

Rowe, D.J., 'The Strikes of the Tyneside Keelmen in 1809 and 1819', *International Review of Social History*, XIII (1968), pp.58–75.

Rowe, D.J., 'The Decline of the Tyneside Keelmen in the Nineteenth Century', *Northern History*, IV (1969), pp.111–31.

Rowe, D.J., 'A Trade Union of the North-East Coast Seamen in 1825', *The Economic History Review*, new series, 25 (1972), pp.81–98.

Rule, John, *The Experience of Labour in Eighteenth-Century Industry* (London, 1981).

Rule, John, ed., *British Trade Unionism* (London, 1988).

Runciman, Sir Walter, *Collier Brigs and their Sailors* (London, 1926 and 1971).

Smith, Raymond, *Sea Coal for London: History of the Coal Factors in the London Market* (London, 1961).

Speck, W.A., 'Northumberland Elections in the Eighteenth Century', *Northern History*, XXVIII (1992), pp.164–77.

State Papers: *Calendar of State Papers of the Reign of Charles I, Domestic Series, V, 1631–33* (reprint, Liechtenstein, 1967); *Addenda, 1625–49* (London, 1897); *Calendar of State Papers, Domestic Series, Commonwealth, 1652–53* (reprint, 1965); *Calendar of State Papers, Domestic Series, 1659–60* (London, 1886).

Statutes: *Statutes at Large*, III, 1685–1711 (London, 1758), V, 1734–1750 (London, 1758), XII, 1760–1767 (London, 1811), XVII, 1788–92 (London, 1811), XX, 1798–1800 (London, 1811); *Statutes of the United Kingdom of Great Britain and Ireland, 55 George III, 1815* (London 1815), *Statutes of the United Kingdom ... 24–25 Victoria, 1861* (London, 1861).

Surtees, Robert, *History and Antiquities of the County Palatine of Durham*, 4 volumes (London, 1816–40).

Sutherland, C.H.V., *English Coinage 600–1900* (London, 1982).

Sweezy, Paul M., *Monopoly and Competition in the English Coal Trade 1550–1850* (Cambridge, MA, 1938).

Sykes, J., *Local Records of Remarkable Events*, 2 volumes (Newcastle, 1833).

Thompson, E.P., *The Making of the English Working Class* (London, 1968).

Thompson, E.P., 'The Moral Economy of the English Crowd in the Eighteenth Century', *Past and Present*, 50 (1971), pp.76–136.

Thompson, E.P., *Customs in Common* (London, 1991).

Turner, E.R., 'The Keelmen of Newcastle', *American Historical Review*, XXI (1915–16), pp.542–5.

Turner, E.R., 'The English Coal Industry in the Seventeenth and Eighteenth Centuries', *American Historical Review*, XXVII (1921–22), pp.1–23.

Viall, H.R., 'Tyne Keels', *The Mariner's Mirror*, XXVIII (1942), pp.160–2.

Webb, Sidney and Beatrice, *History of Trade Unionism* (London, 1894 and 1920).

Welford, Richard, *Men of Mark 'Twixt Tyne and Tweed*, 3 volumes (London and Newcastle, 1895).

Welford, Richard, 'Early Newcastle Typography 1639–1800', *Archaeologia Aeliana*, 3rd series, III (1907), pp.1–134.

Wesley, John, *Journal of the Rev. John Wesley*, 4 volumes, Everyman's Library (London, 1930).

Whitelocke, Bulstrode, *Memorials of the English Affairs* (London, 1682).

Wilson, Kathleen, *The Sense of the People: Politics, Culture and Imperialism in England, 1715–1785* (Cambridge, 1995).

Index